A History of Chocolate in York

For Anne, Rachael, Michael and Rebecca

A History of Chocolate in York

Paul Chrystal

With a contribution by Joe Dickinson and
photography by Mark Sunderland

First published in Great Britain in 2012 by
REMEMBER WHEN
An imprint of
Pen & Sword Books Ltd
47 Church Street
Barnsley
South Yorkshire
S70 2AS

ISBN 978-1-84468-123-5

A CIP catalogue record for this book is available from the British Library

Typeset by Mac Style, Beverley, East Yorkshire
Printed and bound by CPI Group (UK) Ltd., Croydon, CR0 4YY

Pen & Sword Books Ltd incorporates the Imprints of Pen & Sword Aviation, Pen & Sword Family History, Pen & Sword Maritime, Pen & Sword Military, Pen & Sword Discovery, Wharncliffe Local History, Wharncliffe True Crime, Wharncliffe Transport, Pen & Sword Select, Pen & Sword Military Classics, Leo Cooper, The Praetorian Press, Remember When, Seaforth Publishing and Frontline Publishing.

For a complete list of Pen & Sword titles please contact
PEN & SWORD BOOKS LIMITED
47 Church Street, Barnsley, South Yorkshire, S70 2AS, England
E-mail: enquiries@pen-and-sword.co.uk
Website: www.pen-and-sword.co.uk

Contents

Acknowledgements

Thanks go to the following for their help and support in the research for this book and in the provision of images; without them the book would be much diminished: Alex Hutchinson, Nestlé Heritage, York; Dr Amanda Jones and colleagues, Borthwick Institute, University of York; Sarah Brown, Brand Manager, Tangerine Confectionery; Robert Cunningham-Brown, Caley of Norwich Ltd; Sarah Foden, Cadbury UK; Sarah McKee, Bettys & Taylors of Harrogate; Beth Hurrell, Joseph Rowntree Foundation; Colin Carr; Jackie Logan, York Museums Trust; Maggie Wright, Joseph Rowntree School; Chris Headley, New Earswick Folk Hall; Brian Harton for the loan of his 'Trip to York' game; Melvyn Browne; Peter Stanhope for the information on, and photographs of, Thomas Thompson; Jo Sharper for her collection of *Cocoa Works Magazines*; Keith Chapman for sharing his memories of the 'music room'; Sue Smith, Haxby Library; Staff of the Archives and Local History section, York Explore Centre; David Hulme for the photographs on pages 203 and 206; Sophie Jewett at *Little Pretty Things*; Monk Bar Chocolatiers; Juliana Delaney, Continuum Group and the *Sweet History of York* visitor attraction; and to *York Press* for permission to use the photograph on page 211. I have consulted numerous publications whilst researching this book, all of which are listed in Further Reading on page 216. However, two books have been particularly useful and informative: they are Robert Fitzgerald's *Rowntree and the Marketing Revolution* and Van Wilson's *The Story of Terry's* – a fascinating oral history of the firm with numerous anecdotes and interviews with the people who worked there over the years.

Other Books by Paul Chrystal

Knaresborough Through Time

North York Moors Through Time

Villages around York Through Time

Northallerton Through Time

Richmond & Swaledale Through Time

Tadcaster Through Time

Hartlepool Through Time

Redcar, Marske & Saltburn Through Time

Pocklington and Surrounding Villages Through Time

Harrogate Through Time

York: Places of Learning Through Time

York Past & Present

York: Business & Industry Through Time

Chocolate: A History of the British Chocolate Industry

A Children's History of Harrogate & Knaresborough

A–Z of Knaresborough History

Forthcoming 2012

Cadbury & Fry – An Illustrated History

Confectionery in Yorkshire – An Illustrated History

Introduction

WHEN YOU think of York you think of the Minster, the city walls, railways – and chocolate. York has been a centre of chocolate and confectionery manufacturing since July 1862 when Henry Isaac Rowntree bought the Tukes' business, a shop specializing in the sale of coffee, chicory and drinking chocolate, and began to produce Tukes's Superior Cocoa, later to become Rowntree's Prize Medal Rock Cocoa. Henry relocated the business to Tanner's Moat in 1864.

In 1823 another Joseph, apothecary Joseph Terry, married Harriet Atkinson, a relative of Robert Berry who ran a small confectionery business with William Bayldon near Bootham Bar. Terry gave up being a chemist and druggist and joined Berry in St Helen's Square. George Berry succeeded his father to form the musical sounding Terry & Berry but George left in 1826 leaving Joseph Terry to develop what then was essentially a confectionery business. By 1840 Terry's product was being delivered to seventy-five towns

Mary Tuke's shop in Walmgate, 1860s.

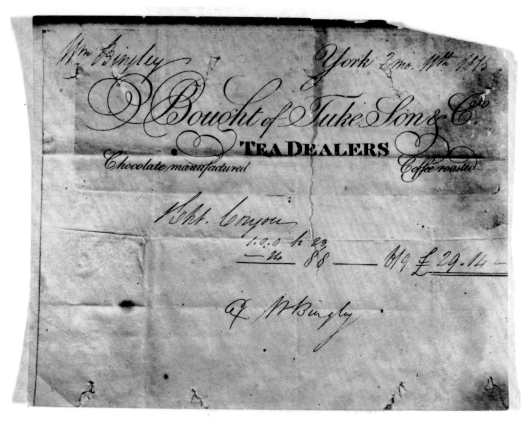

An early invoice from Tuke's, 1815.

all over England. Chocolate production began around 1867 with thirteen chocolate products (including chocolate creams and batons) adding to his other 380 or so confectionery lines.

In 1843 Thomas Craven is described in the *York Courant* as starting out as a purveyor of 'confectionery, teas, coffees & c'. On 30 April 1851 he married Mary Ann Hick, a union which paved the way for the establishment of M.A. Craven, confectioners, in Coppergate.

This book is a history of chocolate and confectionery production in York. It provides a fascinating 150-year story which takes in the origins and development of Rowntree, Terry and Craven from the reigns of Victoria, Edward VII and George V, through two world wars, the intervening Depression, and revolutions

Mary Ann Craven.

in industry and corporate marketing, right up to their respective takeovers by Nestlé, Kraft and Tangerine.

The early chapters will provide some context: firstly, a brief look at how chocolate came to England via Central and South America and Spain and its role and reception in Eighteenth and Nineteenth Century English society; secondly, a survey of York around the same time to discover the sort of city Rowntree, Terry and Craven were setting up in, from an industrial and commercial viewpoint. We will then examine the role Quakerism played in Rowntree and Terry, and the influence this had on company ethos, particularly with respect to philanthropy and industrial welfare and in the provision of housing, social and recreational amenities and education. Other chocolate companies, in particular Fry and Cadbury, are then considered, as these two firms pioneered much of what was to follow with Rowntree and Terry. We then look at smaller chocolate and confectionery businesses such as Needler's, Thornton's and Packer, as well as the foreign competition from Toblerone, Mars and Nestlé.

In our chapters on Rowntree we pause to examine two important aspects of the company's development. First, the *Cocoa Works Magazine* and the vital role it played as a tool of communication and mouthpiece for executives and workers alike. At the same time *CWM* often gives a fascinating insight into aspects of factory life and of society at large. New Earswick, the model village Joseph Rowntree built to accommodate, educate and entertain not just his workers but other York folk too, is also described in a separate chapter.

New Earswick gala outside the Folk Hall, 1907.

OVER

An 1890s advertisement for Rowntree's Rock Cocoa showing cocoa beans.

We then cover the chocolate industry and the role of chocolate in times of war, particularly the First World War, before moving on to the golden age of Rowntree and Terry in the thirties when such iconic brands as KitKat, Aero, Black Magic, Fruit Pastilles and Polo, All Gold and Chocolate Orange were launched and became established amongst the chocolate eating public, albeit temporarily, due to the onset of another war.

What the chocolate companies did in the Second World War, and what the war did to, and with their chocolate, is described next; this is followed by a survey of the boom years after the lifting of rationing in the early fifties. The age of corporate takeovers and mergers began in 1969 with the Rowntree merger with Mackintosh. Chapters follow on the history of Caley and Mackintosh (Caley had been bought by Mackintosh in the 1930s). They and their products now become inextricably linked with Rowntree.

Joe Dickinson's chapter on *Collecting Rowntrees* provides a unique and fascinating description of the fifty years he has spent accumulating what is probably the world's biggest collection of Rowntree artefacts, photographs and memorabilia. His chapter is shot through with the joy – and heartache – involved in building up and conserving such a marvellous repository.

The years up to the takeover of Rowntree PLC by Nestlé in 1988 round off the Rowntree coverage. Our description of Terry's history is punctuated by two chapters on the shop, restaurant, outside catering and ballroom in St Helen's Square, and a chapter on Terry in World War Two. We then chart the rise and development of M.A. Craven. This is followed by a separate chapter on the all-important business of marketing chocolate – with special reference to Rowntree and Terry. Promoting chocolate to the consumer was, from the earliest days, absolutely crucial to the success of individual products and to their companies. This chapter charts the role of advertising and other forms of promotion in the industry and places the efforts and contributions of Rowntree and Terry into context.

Our final chapter looks at Rowntree, Terry and Craven as they exist in the York of the Twenty-First Century. They are all now components, but important components for all that, of larger multi-national organisations; respectively Nestlé, Kraft and Tangerine. Rowntrees and Craven are still in York in name and in spirit, but Terry is a memory only. Nestlé, Kraft and Tangerine now promote and sell our brands on dynamic, interactive websites, on social network sites, and through augmented reality. In the case of Nestlé, raw materials are sourced and brands are produced with what one hopes will continue as a genuine and effective growing sense of responsibility and conscience through Fairtrade.

Paul Chrystal, December 2011

Early Days for the Food of the Gods

CHOCOLATE (or *theobroma cacao* – 'food of the gods' – to give it its botanical name) is derived from cocoa powder from the beans of the cacao tree. A temperamental plant, it grows mainly in Central America and eastern South America, West Africa and Indonesia – but only within 20 degrees of the Equator, below 1,000 feet and where temperatures above 16C are normal.

It was the Mayans who probably first cultivated chocolate from about AD600. They called it *xocoatle* and drank it unsweetened and spiced with vanilla or chilli. Cocoa beans were valuable and were used as currency. For example, a rabbit cost eight beans, a prostitute around ten (depending on the service required), and a slave 100 beans.

A 1930s advert in the Strand Magazine *showing cocoa being harvested and the Five Boys bar.*

The Aztecs from around 1500 AD also enjoyed and valued chocolate; they called it *cacahuatl*. Montezuma II established a bean bank, accepted cacao beans as tribute and regularly traded with beans. It was around this time that chocolate's alleged medicinal and aphrodisiac qualities originated. Montezuma himself reputedly drank fifty cups a day in the belief that it was an aphrodisiac, and Bernal Diaz, the conquistador, noted that the Aztecs 'took it for success with women.' The successful wooing of women is a theme we will see time and time again in the advertising and marketing of chocolate products. Hernan Cortes and the Conquistadores had come looking for El Dorado – but they also found chocolate. It was Cortes, the Jesuits, and missionary Dominican monks, who between them were responsible for introducing chocolate to Europe via the Spanish court around 1528, during the reigns of Charles V and Philip III.

One of the first recorded associations with England came in 1648 when Thomas Gage, the English traveller, observed in his *New Survey of the West Indies* that 'all, rich and poor, loved to drink plain chocolate without sugar or other ingredients.'

In Europe, chocolate's reputation with the medical and the erotic continued to grow. For the socialite and letter-writing gossip Marquise de Sévigné, chocolate had an important role to play in embryology. One of her missives in 1671 tells us that 'The Marquise de Coëtlogon took so much chocolate during her pregnancy last year that she produced a small boy as black as the devil, who died,' thus neatly, if not outrageously, combining sexual and diabolical associations. She probably epitomised French society generally, blowing hot and cold over chocolate. One day in 1671 she saw it as an ideal soporific, two months' later, 'it is cursed.....the source of vapours and palpitations... suddenly lights a continuous fever in you that leads to death.' Louis XV's mistresses, Mesdames du Barry and Pompadour played their parts in sexing up chocolate. Du Barry was scurrilously accused of using chocolate to excite her lovers in order to satisfy her own lust. Pompadour, on the other hand, was frigid apparently and, according to Stanley Loomis, used hot chocolate along with 'aphrodisiacs, truffle and celery soup to stir a sensuality that was at best sluggish.'

Voltaire's Candide learns that the transmission of syphilis to Europe by Columbus's explorers was a fair price to pay in return for the simultaneous introduction of chocolate and cochineal to the old world. The works of the Marquis de Sade have frequent references to chocolate, consumed before and after sex, and it features regularly in his orgies. His petulant letters from prison to Mme de Sade (Rénee de Montreuil) demonstrate a genuine personal craving. This from 16 May 1779: 'The sponge cake is not at all what I asked for. 1st, I wanted it iced all over; 2nd I wanted it to have chocolate inside as black as the devil's arse is black from smoke, and there isn't even the least trace of chocolate. I beg you to have it sent to me at the first opportunity. The cakes must smell of it, as if you're biting into a bar of chocolate.' De Sade's greatest chocolate moment, possibly fabricated – certainly exaggerated – is told by Louis Petit de Bachaumont in his *Mémoires secrets pour servir à l'histoire de la République des Lettres en France depuis 1762 jusqu'à nos jours*. At a ball given by de Sade the host laced chocolate pastilles with Spanish fly, an aphrodisiac. 'It proved to be so potent that those who ate the pastilles began to burn with unchaste ardour and to carry on as if in the grip of the most amorous frenzy. Even the most respectable of women were unable to resist the uterine rage that stirred within them. And so it was that M. de Sade enjoyed the favours of his sister-in-law, several persons died of their frightful priapic excesses, and others are still quite sick.' To Giacomo Casanova it was as good an icebreaker as champagne and, like Samuel Pepys, he enjoyed a morning draft to set the day off.

A Cadbury magazine advertisement showing cultivation of cocoa beans.

Chocolate Reaches England

BY THE mid Seventeenth Century chocolate houses had begun to emerge throughout Europe alongside the already well-established coffee houses. But where chocolate was concerned, England had got off to an inauspicious start. Thomas Gage records in 1579 how, 'When we have taken a good prize, a ship laden with cocoa, in anger and wrath we have hurled overboard this good commodity not regarding the worth and ·goodness of it, but calling it in bad Spanish *cagarutta de carnero* or "sheep dung" in good English.' José de Acosta in his 1590 *Natural and Moral History* tells how an English corsair burnt 100,000 loads of cacao in Huatulco, New Spain, the equivalent of 2.4 billion beans. Its arrival in England was nevertheless hastened by our capture of Jamaica from Spain in 1655 where cacao walks, or plantations, were already well established.

It took a Parisian shopkeeper to open the first English chocolate shop in London, in June 1657. The 23 June 1659 edition of Needham's *Mercurius Politicus* ran the following advertisement: 'An excellent West India drink called chocolate, in Bishopsgate Street, in Queen's Head Alley, at a Frenchman's house being the first man who did sell it in England. Ready at any time, and also unmade at reasonable rates, it cures and preserves the body of many diseases.' M. Sury's chocolate house pamphlet in Oxford in 1660 describes chocolate as a marvellous cure-all. 'By this pleasing drink health is preserved, sickness diverted. It cures consumptions and Coughs of the Lungs; it expels poison, cleanseth the teeth, and sweetneth the Breath; provoketh Urine; cureth the stone and strangury, maketh Fatt and Corpulent, faire and aimeable.' He also claims fertility benefits. 'Nor need the Women longer grieve, Who spend their oyle yet not Conceive, For 'tis a Help Immediate, If such but Lick of Chocolate.'

For the British these medical benefits were complemented by apparent aphrodisiacal qualities. Dr Henry Stubbs notes, 'The great Use of Chocolate in Venery, and for supplying the Testicles with a Balsam, or a Sap is well known' and 'if Rachel had known [about chocolate] she would not have purchased Mandrakes for Jacob. If the amorous and martial Turk should ever taste it, he would despise his Opium. If the Grecians and Arabians had ever tried it, they would have thrown away their Wake-robins and Cuckow pintles; and I do not doubt that you London Gentlemen, do value it above your Cullises and Jellies; your Anchovies, Bononia Sausages, Soys, your Ketchups and Caveares, your Cantharides [Spanish fly] and your Whites of Eggs.' James Wadsworth adds to the 'evidence' in his *Curious History of the Nature and Quality of Chocolate*. 'Twill make Old Women Young and Fresh, Create New Motion of the Flesh, And cause them Long for you know what, If they but taste of Chocolate.'

Samuel Pepys' diary entries clearly demonstrate that 'Jocolatte' was very much part of his life and society, thus elevating chocolate to one of the drinks of choice among men of influence and affluence. He received an anonymous gift of chocolate in 1660 and on the morning of 24 April 1661, used it as a cure for a hangover and 'imbecility of the stomach' after a night out celebrating Charles II's Coronation, waking up, 'with my head in a sad taking through last night's drink which I am sorry for. So rose and went out with Mr Creede to drink our morning draft, which he did give me, chocolate to settle my stomach.' In October 1662 he and Mr Creede drank it with Captain Ferrers in Westminster Hall. The day of 3 May 1664 dawns to find Pepys 'Up, and being ready went by agreement to Mr Blands and then drank my morning draft in good Chocolatte, and slabbering my band, sent home for another.' Likewise, on 24 November 1664, he tells us, 'Up and to the office, where all the morning busy answering of people. About noon out with Commissioner Pett, and he and I to a coffee house to drink Jocolatte, very good.'

But Pepys was not alone. Hester Thrale Piozzi records how Samuel Johnson used chocolate as a substitute for alcohol. 'He took his chocolate liberally, pouring in large quantities of cream, or even melted butter.' And over the years chocolate begins to feature more in literary circles. Cecilia, in Frances Burney's eponymous novel, is presented with chocolate as a sign of prosperity. Jane Austen's affluent General Tilney is a chocolate-drinker in *Northanger Abbey*. Arthur Parker, a sham invalid in *Sanditon*, is nearly found out through his love of it, and Caroline Austen, Jane's niece, tells us how chocolate competed for glory with the wedding cake at her stepsister Anna Austen's wedding in 1814. In his 1859 *A Tale of Two Cities*, Dickens describes Monseigneur's prodigious morning chocolate consumption which took four men and the cook to

Plantation workers sorting cocoa on a Rowntree plantation in Trinidad in the early Twentieth Century.

administer. From the Eighteenth Century chocolate appears in the cookery books of the day. *The Accomplished Female Instructor* of 1704 shows how to make the best chocolate. Chocolate puffs are included in Mary Kettilby's 1719 pithily-titled *A Collection of Above Three Hundred Receipts in Cookery, Physic and Surgery; For the Use of all Good Wives, Tender Mothers and Careful Nurses.*

London chocolate houses were mostly concentrated around Covent Garden, Pall Mall and St James's. Lorenzo Magolotti, a London resident from 1668 to 1688, tells us they competed with the ubiquitous and established coffee houses as somewhere else to eat, play cards and dice, gamble, drink cider, sherbet (a drink then), tea and cock ale (beer with bits of fowl floating in it), and to converse and discuss the burning issues of the day.

White's opened at 4 Chesterfield Street in 1693 under the management of the Italian Francis White (Francesco Bianco) who called it 'Mrs. White's Chocolate House'. At this time, chocolate was still of course, a luxury beverage for the wealthy.

By 1709 White's had built up such a reputation for fashionability that Richard Steele wrote his pieces for *The Tatler* there. 'All accounts of Gallantry, Pleasure and Entertainment shall be under the article of White's Chocolate House. Poetry under that of….' In Alexander Pope's *Dunciad* it was where you went to 'teach oaths to youngsters and to nobles wit.' In 1733 it was still the place to be and to be seen at when William Hogarth set his gambling scene there in *The Rake's Progress* just before it was destroyed by

William Hogarth's gambling scene in White's as the fire takes grip, from The Rake's Progress.

fire. By the mid 1700s White's had moved to St James's Street and had become, in effect, a gentleman's club taking its notoriety for gambling with it.

But not everybody was convinced. To some, chocolate was 'the invention of the Evil One' and in 1624 Johan Franciscus Rauch, an Austrian professor, wrote a thesis in an attempt to ban chocolate from monasteries and urged monks not to drink chocolate as he said it 'inflamed passions'. The lawyer Roger North, writing at the dawn of the Eighteenth Century, was somewhat guarded when he said that the emerging chocolate houses were 'rooks and rullies of quality, where gaming is added to all the rest and where plots against the state were hatched by idle fellows.' Jonathan Swift was less than impressed, describing White's Chocolate House as a place to be 'fleeced and corrupted by fashionable gamblers and profligates.'

Swift preferred the other famous chocolate house, The Cocoa Tree, which opened around 1698 in Pall Mall before moving to St James's Street. It also enjoyed Steele's patronage; this time with Joseph Addison who wrote articles for *The Spectator* from there when it was launched in 1711. Addison ranked chocolate alongside 'romances' and 'novels' as one of life's great 'inflamers'. Gibbon, Sheridan and Byron were members. The Cocoa Tree had other functions, not least as a useful ticket agency for such events as animal baiting in Marylebone Fields, as reported in the *Daily Post* one day in June 1721: '… will be baited a large panther to fight several bull and bear dogs for 200 guineas … likewise is a green bull to be baited to death and a large bear.' The Cocoa Tree was not without its casualties too, as Captain Lloyd of Sackville Street was to discover. '… as he was drinking a dish of chocolate at the Cocoa Tree [he] fell down and died.' A Mrs Pilkington confirms the tradition for sedition when reporting the words of some young man: 'I dress and at about 12 o'clock go to the Cocoa Tree where I talk treason.'

The Scottish spy, James Macky, who exposed James II's intended invasion of England in 1692, on his journey through England in 1722, noted that Pall Mall was the natural habitat of strangers, partly on account of coffee and chocolate houses concentrated there 'where the best company frequent … at twelve o'clock the Beau Monde assembles in several coffee and chocolate houses, the best of which are the Cocoa Tree, White's Chocolate House, St James's, the Smyrna and the British Coffee House, and all these are so near to one another that in less than an hour you can see the company of them all.' The generalization of Charles-Lewis, Baron de Pollnitz, formed after his 1745 visit to London, is interesting, echoing as it does Mrs Pilkington, 'The average Englishman starts his day with a walk in the park, afterwards he saunters to some coffee or chocolate house frequented by persons he would see where they talk business or news, read the newspapers and often look at each other without opening their mouths.'

Other chocolate houses included Saunders's at 85 St James's Street, and Ozinda's on the north side of St James's Palace.

Chocolate, as we have seen, became politically charged. Charles II tried to close down the chocolate houses in 1675 in an attempt to quell the sedition and radical sentiments they nurtured. The Cocoa Tree was known as the 'Tory Cocoa Tree Club' and by the Battle of Culloden in 1746, it was the chocolate house of choice for Jacobites and their Parliamentary headquarters. From 1783 White's acted as the headquarters of the Tory party. Ozinda's was another Tory stronghold. In his diary William Byrd of Virginia tells us that drinking chocolate, betting and reading the newspapers were the main attractions there. Jonathan Swift records that one of the meetings of his dining club was held at Ozinda's, and that the meal was brought in from the Palace. 'Dinner was dressed in the

Queen's kitchen and was mighty fine. We eat it at Ozinda's Chocolate-house, just by St. James's. We were never merrier, nor better company, and did not part till after eleven.'

By now chocolate house owners were starting to realise the wider opportunities their establishments offered; so they rewrote their business plans to convert them into proprietary clubs for the rich, the privileged and the male and, in doing so, created the English gentleman's club.

This was the situation in England which saw the dawn of the chocolate-manufacturing industry, when in 1728, Walter Churchman opened a successful drinking chocolate shop in Bristol and was granted Letters Patent in 1729 by George II, allowing him to produce and sell chocolate. This was the shop which the Quaker and chemist Joseph Fry bought in 1761. Churchman was one of many 'cottage industry' manufacturers supplying chocolate to meet growing local markets up and down the country. Another pioneering couple were Messrs Berry and Bayldon who established their business in York in 1767 and eventually joined up with Joseph Terry, another chemist. In 1824 John Cadbury opened his tea, coffee and cocoa shop in Bull Street, Birmingham, while in 1862 Henry Rowntree acquired William Tuke and Son, a chocolate and cocoa business run by the Quaker Mary Tuke in York. The same year in another part of the city, Mary Craven took on the family confectionery business.

An indication of the increasing acceptance of cocoa and chocolate came in 1780 when Fry was commissioned to supply the Royal Navy with a ration of chocolate in cocoa slab form to replace rum and to provide sailors with something a little more nutritious to go with their ship's biscuit.

The English were at the forefront of efforts to make chocolate more palatable and purer. When the beans are ground the resulting essence produces about fifty-five per cent cocoa butter. Various attempts were made to counteract the viscosity and greasiness of the liquid. The English tried arrowroot, potato starch, sago flour and powdered seashells, and to darken the colour they added iron rust or brick dust. This was, thankfully, made illegal under the Food and Drugs Act 1860 and the Adulteration of Food Act 1872 after a *Lancet* study in 1850 by Dr Arthur Hassall in which over half of all chocolate sampled was found to contain brick dust. Chocolate products which were exposed by this research also included oatmeal chocolate, acorn chocolate, Icelandic moss and barley chocolate. The purity issue was to become a key issue in the manufacturing and advertising of the early pioneers of English chocolate.

It was Coenraad van Houten, a Dutch chemist and confectioner, who made the real breakthrough.

In 1828 he invented a hydraulic press which squeezed out most of the cocoa butter from the liquor, thus reducing the cocoa butter content from over fifty-five per cent to twenty-seven per cent, and leaving chocolate powder or, as we know it, cocoa. Then, by adding alkalis such as potassium or sodium carbonate in to the liquor (known as Dutching), van Houten was able to render his cocoa darker, mellower, more mixable and softer and, with added sugar, sweeter. Much to the dismay of his English competitors at the time, van Houten's new soluble cocoa was winning the approval of eminent scientists at such august institutions as the Pharmaceutical Society of Great Britain and the Society of Public Analysts.

This revolution led the way to the mass production of cheaper chocolate in powder and solid form. Along with the squalid deployment of tens of thousands of slaves, mechanisation soon began to help increase production and foster commercialisation. It was Joseph Fry who had led the way in 1761 when he bought a water mill and warehouse, and set up a sales agency network in fifty-three English towns. In 1795 he industrialised chocolate production in England when he used a James Watt steam engine to grind his beans. Reductions made by Gladstone in the oppressive chocolate duty in 1852 from 2s to 1d per pound also had an elevating effect on consumer affordability and demand. This demand was met not just by grocers and confectioners, but also by apothecaries, for the medicinal properties attributed to chocolate led to a clamour for chocolate-coated pills and lozenges, or confections.

The discarded cocoa butter amounted to thirty per cent wastage and something productive had to be done with it. The solution was to make it into *eating* chocolate. Joseph Fry & Sons were again the pioneers. They had been making drinking chocolate since 1728, and in 1847 they manufactured bars of eating chocolate by returning some of the cocoa butter to the mix, producing a thinner paste much easier to mould.

The Fry launch took place at a Birmingham trade show in 1849, and two years later the new moulded chocolate was on the market, branded as 'Chocolat Delicieux a Manger'. The French name was no accident or whim; it was intended to exploit the cachet associated with fashionable French-sounding food and to dent the popularity of French imports. Cadbury followed. George Cadbury visited van Houten in Holland and returned home with one of the machines. He started producing Cocoa Essence from 1866. Sales of chocolate in 1852 were nine tons; in 1904 they were 12,000 tons.

Henry Mayhew's 1851 *London Labour and the London Poor* gives us some idea of the relative size of the confectionery market in mid Nineteenth Century London. It stood at £10,000 per annum compared with £31,200 for tea and coffee, £19,448 for hot eels, £14,000 for baked potatoes, £11,400 for fried fish, £6,000 for muffins and crumpets and £3,000 for pies. There were 230 sweet sellers in the capital. In Manchester in 1772 there were two confectioner's shops, increasing to 308 in 1872 (by comparison there were 804 butchers and 374 bakers). Confectionery schools opened; the most famous being the Ladies' Confiserie Company and the Piping and Ornamentation School on London's Tottenham Court Road.

The next crucial development was the development of milk chocolate in 1879 by Swiss manufacturer Daniel Peter. He combined powdered milk – which had recently been launched by Henri Nestlé as an infant food – with chocolate and cocoa butter to produce a solid that was easy to mould and shape. Soon after, Rodolphe Lindt introduced 'conching' – a process which resulted in a smoother, more pleasant flavour which we now know as fondant chocolate. Thus, the milk chocolate bar and the chocolate-coated sweet were born. With improving mechanisation, the chocolate industry was totally transformed in England and in the rest of Europe. Chocolate was now being eaten as well as drunk, although it would not be until the early Twentieth Century that sales of eating chocolate outstripped drinking chocolate sales.

Fry of Bristol

WE HAVE seen how Fry's of Bristol was at the forefront of developments in chocolate manufacturing in England in the Eighteenth and Nineteenth Centuries. It started in 1728 with Walter Churchman's shop and the granting to Churchman of Letters Patent from George II. Things accelerated in 1761 when Joseph Fry, a Quaker, physician, entrepreneur, industrialist and businessman *par excellence*, together with John Vaughan, bought Churchman's chocolate business which then became Fry, Vaughan & Co. The coffee houses in nearby fashionable Bath soon became a valuable cocoa market. About the same time, Fry and Vaughan acquired Churchman's patent rights and recipes for the manufacture of drinking chocolate. The company moved in 1777 from Newgate Street to fashionable Union Street in order to tap the wealthy clientele there. Two years later on Joseph's death, Anna Fry took over and renamed the company

A conching machine, designed by Rodolphe Lindt and manufactured by Lehmann's of Dresden, specialists in machinery for the confectionery industry.

Advertisements and show cards for Fry's cocoa and chocolate from around 1905 – note the emphasis on health giving qualities and purity. The churn became synonymous with Fry from 1925.

Anna Fry & Son. That son was Joseph Storrs Fry who assumed control in 1795. It was he who industrialised and revolutionised chocolate manufacture when he introduced the Watt steam engine into the manufacturing process. On Anna's death in 1803 a Dr Hunt joined the company, thus leading to another re-naming, Fry & Hunt. On Hunt's retirement Joseph Storr's sons, Joseph II, Francis and Richard, became partners and the company was renamed J. S. Fry & Sons – now England's largest chocolate producer. In 1835 Fry's were buying forty per cent of the cocoa imported into Britain with sales of £12,000 per annum.

Up until around 1853 French chocolate had the best reputation in Britain and it was quite unthinkable that anything British might compete. But then Fry's produced their Cream Stick – the first chocolate produced on an industrial scale. Up until then chocolate was a luxury beyond the pockets of most people but this was a 'value for money bar'. Fry's dented the popularity of French chocolate to such an extent that they even received a *brevet* appointing them manufacturers of cocoa and chocolate to the Imperial House of Napoleon III.

Discipline, on both sides of the Fry factory gates, was strict as extracts from the 1851 company rules show:

'All Day and Piece Workers are expected to attend the scripture reading at a quarter to 9 am. As soon as the bell rings for the reading, every person to go immediately into the room and the Timekeeper to bolt the door five minutes after the bell has rung … no person to use or eat any chocolate … no person to sing or make noises in the premises … it is particularly requested that every person, whether on the premises or at other places, be at all times strictly sober and that no one be in the habit of frequenting Public Houses or Beer Shops; any person known to do so will not be regarded by their employer with confidence and this knowledge will at any time be considered good reason for discharging a man or a girl … all unnecessary conversation and familiarity between men and girls is strictly prohibited.'

The warming effect of Fry's cocoa; purity is again emphasized.

So, having industrialised chocolate production with steam power and having developed eating chocolate in 1847, Fry's can claim another first when in 1866 they produced the direct descendant of Fry's Cream Stick – Fry's Chocolate Cream, a fondant cream-filled chocolate bar remoulded in 1875 to the shape it largely retains today. With deeper moulds than the standard bar the chocolate filling is tipped out to leave a thin lining and then cooled to harden. Cream is then poured in (enrobing) and cooled before a thick layer of chocolate is poured over and allowed to cool and harden again. Another crucial development was the launch in 1883 of Pure Cocoa Essence to compete with Cadbury's Cocoa Essence and Rowntree's Elect. Essence, by common consent, was where the future in cocoa was thought to lay. In 1902 Fry's Milk Chocolate was launched. It was later rechristened Fry's Five Boys. Orange Cream and Peppermint Cream came next, and Fry's Five Centre in 1934 (orange, raspberry, lime, strawberry and pineapple). Output of Chocolate Cream exceeded half-a-million units per day at one point. The famous foil wrapping and blue label was first used in 1925.

Late Victorian Fry advertisement. Associations with royalty were always much vaunted by all the chocolate companies.

Chocolate Cream was only one of many 'Specialties of the House', to be followed by Crunchie; Punch (which came in three flavours, Full Cream, Milk Chocolate, Delicious Caramel and Milky Fudge. Output was millions per month); Caramets, produced in a pack 'ideal for both pocket and handbag'; Crunch Block; Turkish Delight 'exquisitely flavoured with genuine Otto of Roses'; Five Boys – the iconic label featuring a range of facial expressions, Desperation, Pacification, Expectation, Acclamation and Realization (that it's Fry's).

In 1868 Fry's launched their highly-decorated chocolate-assortment boxes which became extremely popular at Easter and Christmas. Market research was an important facet of Fry's marketing from the start; the colour of the cups for these chocolates was chosen by eight-five per cent of informants.

By the 1870s Fry's could offer 220 different products including the first British Easter egg in 1873. Their popular and enduring Fry's Turkish Bar was introduced in 1914. In 1910 Fry's supported Captain Scott's expedition to the Antarctica with a £1,000 donation – an early example of shrewd public relations which elicited the following testimonial from Captain Scott: 'Messrs J.S. Fry and Sons supplied our Cocoa, sledging and fancy chocolate, delicious comforts excellently packed and always in good condition. Crunching those elaborate chocolates brought one nearer to civilisation than anything we experienced sledging.'

In the years leading up to the First World War, Fry's suffered badly from a lack of investment and their reputation was compromised as a result. The city centre factory was added to on a piecemeal basis but, as with the Rowntree Tanner's Moat and North Street properties, was entirely unsuitable and unpleasant. For example, the packing department was moved into a Baptist Chapel, and St Bartholomew's Church was pressed into various uses by the company. The consequence of this fall from grace in 1918, and in the face of takeover overtures from Nestlé, was a merger with Cadbury to form the the holding company British United Cocoa and Chocolate Company. Cadbury's assets were valued three times more than Fry's, so effectively making Fry a subsidiary and illustrating the perceived strengths of the two companies. Both nevertheless retained their individual corporate identities, marketing and branding of products and effectively operated as separate business entities.

Joseph Fry died in 1913, blind and a millionaire, with over two hundred benefactors named in his will, including his employees who received £42,000 between them.

Egbert (Bertie) Cadbury joined the Fry part of the business, and he and Cecil Fry managed the move to a purpose-built factory on 222 acres in Somerdale, Keynsham, in 1923 in between the River Avon and the London-Bristol main line. The 1920s saw some Cadbury-inspired streamlining in the shape of the mechanised production of fewer brands at a lower cost. Somerdale had its own power station and a railway station serving a siding linked to the Great Western Railway line.

The move from Union Street was a gradual affair lasting 12 years until 1934 when 6,000 women and men were on the payroll. The factory itself was set in parkland with poplar and chestnut trees, flower beds and lawns. *Fry's of Bristol*, an early corporate booklet, tells us that, 'The Cocoa department looks on to woodland slopes and sunlit meadows' thus giving us a flavour of the pastoral setting of Somerdale.

Cadbury of Bournville

A stunning Cadbury cocoa poster keeping drinkers at the top of their game.

THE CADBURY story opens in 1824 with John Cadbury, son of a rich Quaker, selling non-alcoholic beverages – tea, coffee and sixteen varieties of drinking chocolate – at 93 Bull Street, Birmingham, after apprenticeships first at John Cudworth's grocers in Leeds, in London at the East India Company's bonded warehouse and at the Sanderson, Fox and Company teahouse. He announced himself as follows in the *Aris Gazette* on 1 March 1824: 'JC is desirous of introducing to particular notice Cocoa Nibs, prepared by himself, an article affording a most nutritious beverage for breakfast.' In 1836 Cadbury moved to a former malt house in Crooked Lawn where he perfected techniques of coffee bean grinding to produce his cocoa, and then to a factory in Bridge Street.

John's brother Benjamin joined, and the company became known as Cadbury Brothers of Birmingham. With an office in London and a Royal Warrant, the business

This attractive poster was drawn by Cecil Aldin in 1899, famous for his animal and sport posters.

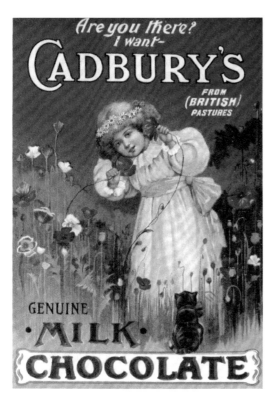

Cadbury's chocolate and cocoa advertisements and show cards. Like Fry's they promote the purity; note also the focus on the health benefits of the milk for active adults and children alike.

The facilities on offer at Bournville.

BOURNVILLE:
A WORCESTERSHIRE EDEN.

A HOP, skip, and jump across the Worcestershire border from Birmingham brings one to Bournville, and full notification of it is given to the travellers' nostrils in advance, for at Bournville are Cadbury's huge cocoa works, from which the aroma of roasted cocoa-beans is wafted for miles. Nevertheless, the present paper speaks not of cocoa and chocolate manufacture except as an incident in connection with the remarkable little colony which is springing up thereabouts. As in the main this scheme is connected with the operatives at

A CHOCOLATE PACKER.

Cadbury's works, perhaps it will be as well to follow the career of a typical female worker out of the 1400 employed there, some of whom come from villages a few miles away, for Cadbury's factories are popular with female wage-earners. Every effort is made to obtain work there; for, apart from the unusual comforts, the rate of pay is from 2s. 6d. to 2s. per week higher than at any other cocoa factory in the world, or in any other occupation for women in the Midlands.

Our typical girl arrives at 8.50 a.m., hangs up her check at the time-keeper's lodge, and proceeds to the "dressing-room"—a large, well-warmed, clean, and airy apartment—where she removes her outer

locked, so that no employé can possibly be found inside. The huge dining-hall, with eleven wide entrances and exits, containing seating room for 1600 girls, a smaller apartment for 600 men, and yet another for seventy of the clerks, are all thrown open, so our typical girl would probably go to the dining-hall and eat her meal, previously cooked for her, and supplement that from the refreshment-bar, where an exceedingly moderate tariff prevails. For example, ham, beef, or tongue, is 1d. per plate; hot fruit pies as large as a man's two clenched fists, 1d.;

A LANE IN BOURNVILLE.

three-quarters of a pint of tea or coffee, ½d.; half a pint of cocoa essence, ½d.; glass of milk, ½d.; aërated waters, 1d. per bottle; and so forth.

Just near the girls' dining-hall is the dining-room for the principals of the firm, in which is served exactly the same food as is put before the girls—indeed, the only difference is the superiority of its table services and surroundings. Still following our typical employée, in fair weather she may take her dinner at one of the convenient seats around the girls' large playground, which has an asphalted centre and pretty banks of shrubs to screen it from inquisitive eyes, or indulge

SCENE ON THE ESTATE.

garments and dons the uniform white linen costume which it is compulsory for every female employée to wear. She puts her boots to dry in a small receptacle over the hot-water pipes, and before commencing work probably washes at one of the numerous lavatories, and goes forward to another apartment to leave the dinner she brought with her to be warmed or cooked, free of charge, ready for one o'clock. At nine o'clock all assemble in the various workrooms until one o'clock, when labour ceases till two o'clock, during which hour the factory doors are

THE NURSERY.

in a sun bath under cover of the range of shades running along the southern side of the works, or stroll up the lane a hundred yards or so, where a few months hence she will be able to pass into the "Girls' Garden," of which a photograph is given, showing a corner of Bournbrook Hall in the distance. Here, with her companions, she will be able to romp to her heart's delight; or, if she prefers, seek the seclusion of the quaint little summer-house, pleasantly named "The Sylvan Arbour." The firm defrays the entire working expenses,

Aspects of life in Bournville – at home and in the chocolate factory.

A striking picture of the Bournville factory.

was to benefit from the 1853 tax reduction on cocoa, enabling them to reduce retail prices and thus bring cocoa powder to a much wider market. As a consequence, the sale of tea was abandoned and left to nephew Richard Barrow Cadbury to manage.

John Cadbury's sons Richard and George took over the company in 1868 when it was still very small with about ten employees and far from successful. By this time competition was intensifying from Rowntree, Fry and other companies such as Taylors in Spitalfields (manufacturers of more than fifty brands of cocoa and mustard), and Dunn and Hewett of Pentonville, who sold chocolate sticks and Patent Lentilised Chocolate (made from lentils, tapioca, sago or dried peas), and the somewhat over-descriptive 'Plain Chocolate Sold in Drab Paper.' Richard had joined their father soon after leaving school in 1851, while George followed in 1857 after a three-year apprenticeship with Rowntree's grocery business in the Pavement shop in York. The rules of the shop there were uncompromising and set out in a Memorandum written

The apprentices at the Pavement shop with Joseph in the centre at the front and George Cadbury on his left.

by Joseph Rowntree Snr: 'The object of the Pavement establishment is business. The young men who enter it are expected to contribute in making it successful … it affords a full opportunity for any painstaking, intelligent young man to obtain a good practical acquaintance with the tea and grocery trades … the place is not suitable for the indolent and wayward.'

Cadbury produced the first chocolate box in 1868. It was full of chocolate candles and typically sentimental for the times, featured Richard's daughter Jessica holding a kitten on the lid. Around the same time the firm produced the first Valentine's Day chocolate assortment. Traveller's samples were offered to the trade and a pledge system was set up at the factory whereby a penny was awarded to any worker who had not succumbed to the temptation of eating the manufactured product during the week.

By 1878 it was becoming increasingly urgent to find a site which made the importation of cocoa and milk easier and cheaper. The 14.5-acre Georgian Bournbrook Hall and Estate, five miles south of the city centre, fitted the bill with its access to the Birmingham West Suburban Railway and the Worcester and Birmingham Canal.

This was duly purchased and the French-sounding name of Bournville was adopted for the opening in 1879. As we have seen, the association with things French was important as *le chocolat Francais* was, by common consent, the best; taking the fight to the enemy, it was strengthened by the establishment of a depot in Paris, always something of a loss leader although it enabled the company to display the prestigious address on its stationery.

Cadbury operated a fleet of barges on the canal, in Cadbury livery, and were the first chocolate company to use powered canal boats.

The first locomotive built for Cadbury.

Milk coming in by barge on the canal

By the turn of the century, sidings were built to link the factory with the national railway network and Cadbury rolling stock was manufactured.

Horse-drawn vans were the earliest mode of road transport. In the 1920s the factory was reconstructed and the site expanded to cope with demand and new production techniques. Until the 1960s all the ancillary crafts and trades required to run a chocolate manufacturing plant were carried out on site – these included the production of boxes, cartons and tin cans, machine making, sheet-metal production, printing, joinery, advertising and marketing.

Things had not been going well though, until George Cadbury's crucial 1866 visit to van Houten in the Netherlands to acquire a press. This visit was pivotal and the installation of the equipment paved the way for a company on the verge of failure to become the successful business it soon became.

Since the recent food adulteration legislation, purity had become a key issue and the press enabled them to produce pure, unadulterated Cocoa Essence; but for it to be economical it was vital to stimulate demand and there was one way of doing just that. Eschewing any Quaker reservations about advertising, the Cadburys set about gaining medical testimonials and establishing the health-giving credentials and purity guarantees of their products, all in compliance with the terms of the Adulteration Acts. No doubt they were influenced by other manufacturers in other industries such as Pears', the soap makers, who pioneered catchy slogans and eye-catching posters featuring glamorous women and children exuding happiness and healthiness. Both the *British Medical Journal* and the *Lancet* published their approval of Cocoa Essence when launched in late 1866; the former asserting it to be 'one of the most nutritious, digestible and restorative drinks'. *Grocer* magazine chimed in, emphasising the absence of adulteration. The advertising campaign devised to capitalise on these endorsements had the slogan 'Absolutely Pure, Therefore Best. No Chemicals Used.' It promoted the 'flesh forming' (body-building) qualities and celebrated the fact that Cadbury's was twenty-one per cent pure cocoa, while others on the market had a cocoa content of around six per cent. All was not plain sailing just yet though. Just when the Cadburys must have thought they were getting a real foothold on the domestic market, van Houten spoilt everything in the early 1870s by introducing a much more chocolaty-flavoured cocoa. This was done, as we have seen, by adding alkalines into the mix. Van Houten's hold on the UK market – which they still shared with the French – was thereby sustained for the time being.

The famous chocolatier Frederic Kinchelman joined Cadbury, bringing with him more French influence, together with his successful recipes and production techniques for Nougat-Dragées, Paté Duchesse and Avelines. One of the new brands was named The Model Parish Cocoa in anticipation of the model village Cadbury were to build at Bournbrook. Sales outposts were established in Ireland, Canada, Chile and Australasia. The early 1870s also saw the launch of the exotic and luxurious, decidedly un-Quakerly, French-influenced Fancy Box, complete with silk lining and mirror. *Chemist & Druggist* described it as 'Divine. The most exquisite chocolate ever to come under our notice.' Easter eggs were introduced in 1875 and Cadbury Fingers in 1897.

But Cocoa Essence was undoubtedly their most successful line and, for the time being, Cadbury had it all to themselves in terms of domestic production. Rowntree's Elect was not launched until 1880 and Fry's competition, Pure Cocoa Essence, did not emerge until 1883.

The new technology and expertise with recipes led to the successful production of chocolate bars and, in 1898, *milk* chocolate bars made with Daniel Peter's powdered milk technique – soon to be replaced in 1905 with fresh milk. This manifested itself in Cadbury's Dairy Milk – a successful challenge to the popular Swiss milk chocolate bars. George Cadbury, a chemistry graduate from University College, London, had been working on a milk chocolate recipe since 1889. The original name was to be Dairy Maid but this was changed at the last minute after the daughter of a customer in Plymouth remarked that Dairy Milk was a 'much daintier name.' Bournville Cocoa, close in taste to van Houten's popular and successful alkalised cocoa, was launched a year later.

Cadbury soon realised that to displace the Swiss dominance in the milk chocolate market Dairy Milk had to be mass produced and advertised aggressively – a lesson they had undoubtedly learned from their experience with Essence. It was by embracing these two crucial factors that Cadbury not only went on to become the UK's largest chocolate manufacturer by displacing Fry's in 1910, but also differentiated themselves from Rowntree's who were still altogether more cautious and haphazard when it came to marketing and product development.

Cadbury was also quick to recognize the value of good public relations. They set up a Visitors' Department in 1902, and were often receiving 150,000 people a day up to 1939 – many of them on organised bus or rail excursions. A two-mile tour of the factory and Bournville awaited them, as well as refreshments and an educational film. This all had to stop though in 1970 when health and safety regulations demanded the same rigorous hygiene procedures for visitors as for production line workers. But Health and Safety were not going to get away with it. Popular demand led to the establishment of the £6 million Cadbury World in 1990 with 420,000 visitors going through the doors soon after opening. Research had shown that visitors were more likely to buy Cadbury products up to twenty years after their visit.

From 1905 the roll call of new Cadbury chocolate products is breathtaking. Dairy Milk was launched to the refrain that it contained more milk than other chocolate bar ('a glass-and-a-half of fresh milk') and became the top selling brand by 1913. 1915 saw the debut of Milk Tray – originally presented in open boxes on wooden trays (hence the name). Flake came along in 1920, made from folds of milk chocolate and 'the crumbliest, flakiest milk chocolate in the world'. Milk Tray packaging has changed almost imperceptibly over the last ninety-five years and sales are today over eight million boxes every year. The familiar purple packaging was introduced on Dairy Milk in 1920 and was chosen to reflect the noble connotations of the colour going back to Roman senators and emperors. The famous Cadbury signature was first signed in 1921.

By 1910 Cadbury had overtaken Fry as the biggest UK chocolate manufacturer with sales of £1,670,221 compared with Fry's £1,642.715 and Rowntree's £1,200,598. Creme Eggs came in 1923, (today 66,000 eggs are 'laid' every hour), Crunchie, (turned out at the rate of five miles per hour at the Somerdale factory), and Fruit & Nut arrived in 1929. Whole Nut hit the market in 1933 and Cadbury Roses Selection arrived in 1938 with its distinctive 'Dorothy Bag' carton.

A bucolic lunch time scene at Somerdale.

Other Early Chocolate Manufacturers in Britain

B UT IT wasn't all just Fry's and Cadbury's. There were a number of smaller manufacturers who made sure that the larger companies did not have it all their own way. (We will deal with Caley of Norwich and Mackintosh of Halifax later, as Caley was bought by Mackintosh and then Mackintosh merged with Rowntree. Both companies therefore inform, and become part of, the Rowntree story.)

Thornton's was established by Joseph William Thornton in 1911 when he left his job as a sales representative for the Don Confectionery Company, and opened his first Thornton's Chocolate Kabin shop on the corner of Norfolk Street and Howard Street in Sheffield. Products included Violet Cachous, Sweet-Lips, Phul-Nanas and Curiously Strong Mints. Chocolate production began in 1913 in the back room of their second shop on The Moor. Joseph William died in 1919 and his sons Norman, twenty-one-years-old, and Stanley, (who had studied Food Technology at Sheffield University), took

Packing the goods at Bournville.

over the business and formed J.W. Thornton Ltd. In 1924 Norman was pressured into buying the lease of the property. To relieve some of the financial pressure this caused, he embarked on an innovative marketing campaign which involved a twelve-feet-square neon sign, window displays which featured live chickens running amongst Easter eggs, and personalization of the eggs for individual customers. Special Toffee was launched in 1925 and soon accounted for twenty-five per cent of sales. Chocolates too, were increasingly successful, and in 1927 Thorntons moved to a factory on Penistone Road.

H.J. Packer, a former Fry's employee, began trading in 1881, making chocolate from his kitchen in Armoury Square, Bristol, under the name of Packer & Co. The workforce comprised Packer's sister and brother, and a Miss Lily Brown who was paid 2s 6d a week. The plant comprised a kitchen fire and a paraffin lamp and two saucepans and a small pan for making the chocolate and the cream centres. Sugar was bought in 14 lb loads and the finished chocolates were delivered by hand. In 1884 Packer took on H.J. Burrows – another ex- Fry's employee – and when the partnership was dissolved in 1885, it was Burrows who became owner of the business. The next year saw twenty-four year old Bruce Cole pay Burrows £950 for all plant, stock, debts and goodwill. Business began to boom from 1896, and in 1901 the company moved to a specially-commissioned, high-specification factory at Greenbank. The business grew, and between 1903 and 1912 sales increased by 250 per cent. Their strategy to sell 'Two Ounces a Penny' chocolate – good quality chocolates at a low price a child could afford – had succeeded. Packer's Chocolate Mixtures was one of their main lines.

Around the year 1908 they purchased Carson's Ltd, a prestigious confectionery firm based in Glasgow. To extend the range the company launched a new subsidiary

An early Thornton's Chocolate Kabin.

to produce high-class chocolates like the 'walnut whirl'. Bond's of Bristol chocolate products began to be produced on new production lines in the Greenbank factory alongside the Packer's brands. Success continued into the early 1920s with the company employing 2,500 workers at its peak.

The end of World War I saw a return of the low cost Packer's brand at a penny an ounce. One of the new lines, Milk Crispets was particularly popular and went on to become the company's most enduring product. By 1922 Packer's was the fourth largest chocolate manufacturer in Britain and they were the most popular low cost brand in the country. But the company was in decline from the mid 1920s through to the Second World War.

Known mainly for its confectionery, Needlers of Hull was, nevertheless, a force in the chocolate industry in the early Twentieth Century. At the age of 18 Frederick Needler, a Methodist, left the tea and coffee warehouse where he worked, and joined Edward Buckton's small confectionery manufacturing business. This he later bought for £100 with his mother's help, and set up in Anne Street south of Paragon Station in 1886. He had the equipment for making boiled sweets, a horse and a cart, a man to boil the sugar, and a lad. In 1890 he moved to a larger factory in Brook Street, and by 1900 there were ten female (including his sister Lucy) and twenty-three male employees producing a variety of lines: thirty-eight different boiled sweets, forty types of toffees, thirty-five health sweets, fourteen pralines and fifteen different labelled sticks of rock. One of his innovations was to use clear glass sweet jars rather than the standard green. This allowed customers to actually see the sweets in the jar and was a highly successful move. The company also acted as wholesalers for other firms, such as the German Quaker Stollwerk,

Raw materials for chocolate making at Packers in Bristol; note the horses and cart.

Prestigious Carson's assortments.

Cadbury, Craven of York, Taverner and Rowntree. In 1902 the firm was registered as Fred Needler Ltd, and in 1906 they moved to a purpose-built factory in Sculcoates Lane.

By 1912 the product range included 576 lines, of which seventy-four were chocolate. To cater for this, a new five-storey chocolate plant was built in 1916 at Bournemouth Street. By 1920 turnover was £570,000, comprising 650 tonnes of chocolate and 1,500 tonnes of sweets, with a range now including Christmas boxes and Easter eggs. There were 1,700 employees, mainly female, making the company one of Hull's biggest employers.

Frederick Needler was another chocolate philanthropist and a staunch Liberal. An example of his generosity was his gift of Needler Hall to Hull University College, now the University of Hull and he always donated ten per cent of his annual income to charity. The company had a strong reputation for good industrial welfare; a profit sharing scheme was introduced as early as 1911, a pension scheme in 1922 and there were excellent social and sports facilities. Needler's renowned Musical Society first tuned up in 1925. The chocolate side of the business closed in 1976.

A number of US and continental European chocolate manufacturers were exporting to, and operating in, the UK in the years when Rowntree, Terry and Craven were establishing themselves. Some of these maintained a strong presence here and eventually, in the case of Nestlé, became a major force in the industry to compete today with the companies which have since been taken over by the US Kraft Foods.

Chocolat Menier, in 1893 the world's largest manufacturer of chocolate, had opened their London office in 1870 in Southwark Street and by 1873 was turning out 500 tonnes a year.

At the end of the Nineteenth Century Swiss companies were selling 30 tonnes of milk chocolate a week in the UK, while Cadbury, for example, sold barely one tonne. In 1911 over half the chocolate eaten in the world was still made in Switzerland. Pralines (invented by one of the chefs employed by the French Marechal du Plessis Praslin in the Seventeenth Century) came over from Brussels in 1912 through Jean Neuhaus, and paved the way for Leonidas (founded 1910) and Godiva (1912).

Most famous, of course, for his revolutionary press, Dutchman Coenraad van Houten was also a significant exporter of cocoa to the UK for many years from his factory in Weesp. Amongst their products was Rova, launched in 1911 and a competitor to Rowntree's Elect and Fry's products. Like Cadbury, van Houten was an innovative and aggressive advertiser and this, along with technical innovations in the shape of the eponymous press and Dutching, ensured it was a major irritation to the UK companies, particularly Rowntrees, for many years.

Unconventional second prize-winning Ford AT5624 Needler delivery van comprising jar of sweets and chocolate box. 1920.

Miss Kathleen Singer, Yorkshire Evening News *and Scala Theatre Beauty Quest winner cashing in her last Needler coupon needed for a free box of County Chocolates; Bronchial Pastilles also available. 1925.*

A Nestlé-Cailler-Kohler-Peter advertisement from l'Illustration *December 1926.*

Frank C. Mars launched the Mar-O-Bar in 1922 with the Minneapolis-based Mar-O-Bar Company. Initially it was not a great success on account of its fragility. Milky Way followed in 1923 and was an immediate hit, being promoted as 'chocolate malted milk in a candy bar.' In 1929 the company moved to Chicago, and Frank's son, Forrest E. Mars Snr, joined the company. The Snickers bar was launched in 1930. Forrest arrived in England in 1932 with £5,000 and set up Mars Ltd in a rented factory in Slough with twelve staff. He then launched the Mars Bar. Initially the bars were coated in chocolate supplied by Cadbury ('Why ever did we do that?' Sir Adrian Cadbury wryly asked recently) and they were such a success that staff increased from twelve to over one hundred within a year. Interestingly Mars Ltd, an incredibly secretive company, demonstrated many of the philanthropic industrial welfare initiatives of the indigenous Quaker companies including a pension plan, an in-house doctor, a cafe and a company newsletter. Mars, like Cadbury and Rowntree, paid well but demanded long hours and the highest quality. Maltesers appeared in 1935.

Chemist Henri Nestlé was born in Frankfurt in 1814. In 1875, 22 years after moving to Vevey on Lake Geneva in 1843, he began production of *farine lacteé*, a baby food (*Kindermehl*), made from Alpine milk in powder form and ground cereal. As we have seen, Henri Nestlé with Daniel Peter and Jean-Jacques Kohler, his chocolate manufacturing neighbours, then went on to develop the first real milk chocolate when they combined their products to produce Chocolat au Lait Gala Peter – 'The Original Milk Chocolate' – in 1879. Henri opened a sales office in London in 1883 for the Farine Lactée Henri Nestlé Company, and in 1901 its first UK factory began production. Nestlé merged with the 1866 established Anglo–Swiss Condensed Milk Company in 1905 to form the Nestlé and Anglo-Swiss Milk Company. Sales were boosted by Nestlé's extensive use of the new vending machines which were springing up everywhere and which, in this case, dispensed 1d chocolate bars. In 1904 they made an agreement with Kohler and Cailler to import their chocolate product and thus strengthened their position in the UK market. In 1913 chocolate production began at Hayes, Middlesex.

In 1868 Jean Tobler was running a confectionery shop called Confiserie Spéciale in Bern, Switzerland, producing chocolate sweets from products supplied by other manufacturers. By 1899 Tobler's chocolates were so successful that Tobler set up his own factory, the Fabrique de Chocolat Berne, Tobler & Cie, with his sons. Theodor Tobler took over the business in 1900 and exports to countries including Britain began that year. In 1908, with his cousin Emil Baumann, he invented the unique milk chocolate bar that is Toblerone.

The name Toblerone is derived from the chocolatier's family name 'Tobler' and 'torrone', the Italian for nougat. It is thought that Theodor Tobler fashioned the shape of his unique and iconic chocolate on the mountain scenery of Switzerland – and on the Matterhorn in particular. But the truth is much more exotic. According to Theodor's sons, the bar was inspired by the red and cream-frilled line of dancers at the Folies Bergères in Paris which formed a shapely pyramid at the finale of each show.

Prudently, Theodor Tobler and Tobler AG applied for a patent in 1909 in Bern to cover the manufacture and shape of the bar, and Toblerone thus became the first patented milk chocolate bar. The official who gave the authorizing signature was one Albert Einstein who was working in the Patent Office at the time. A picture of a bear – the civic symbol of Berne – lurks in the Matterhorn mountain image on the packaging.

Such was the commercial environment in which Rowntree, Terry and Craven found themselves; important players in a highly-competitive confectionery industry. We can now look at one of the factors which Rowntree and Terry had in common with Cadbury and Fry – Quakerism.

The Quakers and the English Chocolate Industry

BOTH THE Fry and Cadbury families were of course Quakers, and like the Rowntrees and Terrys in York, one of their priorities was to provide their workers with as good working conditions as possible. Cadbury and Rowntree also provided sanitary and comfortable housing and educational, social and recreational facilities. Joseph Fry employed a nurse and a doctor to attend to the medical problems of his staff; ran 'continuation' (further education) classes for the girls, provided a gym with instructors, facilities and pitches for football, tennis, cricket and bowls, and organised the Operatic Society, the Camera Club, the Debating and Dramatic Societies. Girls leaving to get married received a copy of *Mrs Beeton's Book of Household Management*.

Fry epitomises the inextricable association of English chocolate-manufacturing with the Society of Friends, Quakerism. Friends were excluded from the only teaching universities in England at the time – Oxford and Cambridge – because of their non-conformism and the universities' association with Anglicanism. They were also debarred from Parliament and the guilds and were restricted in what they could, and could not do as lawyers because they refused to take oaths. The arts were considered frivolous and they were disqualified from the armed services because they were pacifists. One of the few alternatives left to privileged and well-to-do young Quakers was to pursue a life in industry or business, and this is what many did. They often brought with them a tradition of high-quality management, fair-trading practices, rigorous scientific research and innovative technical development, as well as an obsessive preoccupation with quality, and breathtakingly detailed attention to business administration.

One of the legacies of the frequent Meetings routinely held by the Society of Friends – and the travelling required to get to these Meetings and to spread the word – was the building up of a strong network of dependable friends and contacts. This in turn, together with intermarriage amongst Quaker families, led to a tradition of mutual assistance in business and industry, and to strong industrial partnerships, all underpinned by unfaltering service to the community at large.

It is often asked why the chocolate industry in Britain at the end of the Nineteenth Century and in the early years of the Twentieth, prospered largely under Quaker ownership: the answer seems to be mere coincidence. Quakers went into business and industry, and one of the emerging industries at the time was cocoa and chocolate. This was partly a result of increased affordability amongst the working classes who had more disposable income, lower taxes on imports which reduced prices in the shops, improvements in quality, a better taste and less adulteration. What had been a luxury was fast becoming an affordable indulgence for many.

Early concerns over the intrinsic insincerity of advertising were overcome to a greater or lesser degree, except in the case of Rowntree who harboured a long-term suspicion of what he called 'puffery'. The Quaker ethos allowed the companies to get on with building businesses, each with a largely contented workforce, enlightened industrial relations, fair dealing on both sides of the boardroom door, and all, eventually at least, in pleasant factories imbued with an air of domesticity provided by potted plants and homely pictures on the factory walls. Workers' Christian names were routinely used by managers, and the offer of housing, entertainment, sport and education to the workforce, was truly enlightened. In terms of industrial welfare generally, Fry and the other chocolate Quakers were years ahead of their time: they were providing terms of employment and working conditions which came much later in other industries – and then only after legislation made them mandatory.

Rules and guidelines were laid down as to how Quakers should conduct themselves in business. The 1738 *Advices* promoted fair dealing and absolute honesty; the 1783 *Book of Extracts* unequivocally banned paper credit; the 1833 *Rules of Discipline* reminded adherents that the root of all evil was money, and the 1861 *Doctrine, Practice and Discipline* summarised the whole code, covering debt, seeking advice from other Friends, inappropriate speculation and much more. An early company booklet, *Into the Open Country*, gives Fry's mission statement and a flavour of the corporate ethos back then: 'Fry's have kept before them two guiding principles; one, giving the public the best possible value in cocoa and chocolate manufactured under the best possible conditions; the other, of giving the workpeople the best facilities for recreation and happiness.'

At Cadbury, to add to the Bournville factory development, George Cadbury bought more land in 1893 on which to build a model village to 'alleviate the evils of more modern cramped living conditions.' This dream was inspired by, and converted into reality, by what George saw all around him: 'It is not easy to describe or imagine the dreary desolation which acre after acre of the very heart of the town presents … hundreds of leaky, damp, wretched houses, wholly unfit for human habitation. 'He realised that there was little point in allowing private interest to be involved in his scheme as this would inevitably lead to the creation of a *suburban* slum – the like of which the Cadbury's wanted their workers to escape from. George Cadbury, therefore, created a garden village next to his factory. Within seven years the new village comprised 313 sound, clean and sanitary houses, complete with front and back gardens, on 330 acres of land.

Only in the very early days were the houses provided just for Cadbury employees; the objective was to provide a village of mixed housing for a range of householders and thereby establish a mixed community. Residents were given a booklet laying down rules for keeping houses and gardens in good order, on abstaining from alcohol on the Sabbath, and the advantages of single beds for married couples. Although alcohol was not prohibited – there was provision for public houses but they were subject to strict conditions – the area was alcohol-free with no pubs and no alcohol sold in local shops until a licensed members bar opened in the Rowheath Pavilion in 1940. This abstinence reflected John Cadbury's strict temperance beliefs, and was a manifestation of his tireless work in social reform which included campaigns for warehouse reform and against industrial pollution, child labour (particularly climbing boys, or child chimney sweeps) and animal cruelty; he founded the Animals Friend Society which eventually became the RSPCA. Cadbury's own research showed that one in every thirty houses in

Birmingham was given over to the sale of alcohol, and that ten per cent of the city's 6,593 alcoholics died of alcohol-related diseases each year. The many ale houses, inns, gin shops and gin palaces unfortunately provided a ready supply of mortalities, but John and his wife Candida successfully persisted with their Total Abstinence Plan, counting even the moderate Moderation Society amongst their conquests.

Bournville was truly pioneering in all sorts of ways: socially, environmentally and architecturally in particular, but it also had great influence throughout Europe in areas as diverse as housing, urban planning, community health and local education. Visitors included architects from Krupp's in Germany, Dame Henrietta Barnett who went on to inspire the development of Hampstead Garden Suburb, William Hesketh Lever who founded Port Sunlight in 1888, and the Rowntrees who, as we shall see, established New Earswick Garden Village between Haxby and York, near their factory.

Religion was, of course, very important. Joseph Fry held a Morning Prayer meeting for all workers. George Cadbury took his advice on the matter with the result that the Cadbury morning service continued for thirty years (until sheer numbers of staff brought it to an end) and was always led by either George, Richard or Barrow Cadbury, George's nephew.

Cadbury was one of the first companies in the UK to introduce a half day on Saturday. Philanthropy and paternalism were in evidence everywhere; in the workplace with ground-breaking pension schemes, a sick club, medical services, outings, in-service education, staff committees (the Works Councils) and reasonable wages. Like the Rowntrees, George and Richard Cadbury were fervent believers in the value of education (they both taught at the Birmingham Adult Schools), and this was maintained at Bournville where Continuation Classes were set up in 1913. These provided free further education during working hours for younger employees from when they left school and joined Cadbury aged fourteen, until they were sixteen – later extended to eighteen.

The Carillon and School, Bournville.

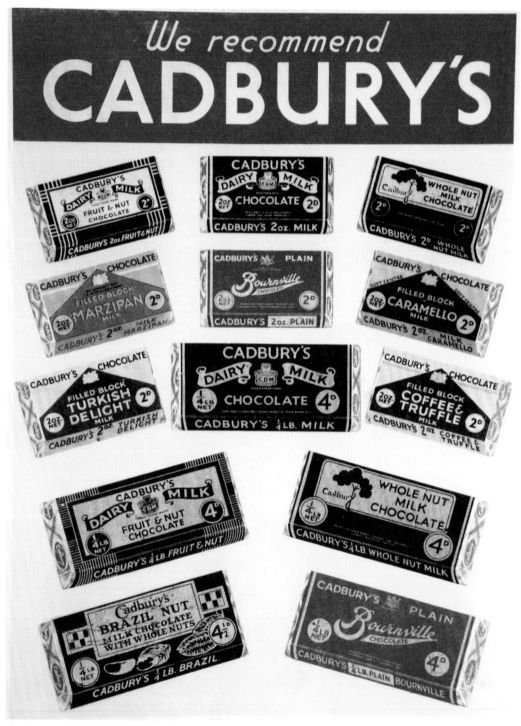

A selection of Cadbury chocolate bars.

Cadbury Bros., Ltd. Bournville Works.

Almshouses, The Quadrangle. For men or women of 60 years of age and upwards.

Bournville Hall. Formerly an old mansion. It provides a home for girls employed in the works who are orphans, or who are living at a distance from their relatives.

The almhouses and Bournville Hall.

Joseph Rowntree's office at Haxby Road.

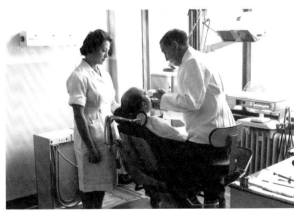

Mr Boyle the dentist about 1970.

A wide range of apprenticeships for boys and a sewing club for girls were established. Employees were, as a matter of course, treated with respect. The Works Councils, segregated until 1964, worked in concert with the trades unions which had also always been encouraged; the councils were made up of management and shop floor representatives and were primarily responsible for the company's welfare schemes. Free breakfast was given to all workers, and the industrious kitchens supplying the segregated dining rooms could, for example, produce eighty chops simultaneously within ten minutes. A workers' hostel, Bournville Hall, was set up to accommodate sixty or so girl workers who lived some distance away from their workplace.

In common with other factories of the time, male and female workers were largely segregated with separate entrances, working, rest and dining areas, and Works Councils. Technicians going in to women's areas of the factory were obliged to wear armbands showing that they had permission to be there. Married women were not employed, and girls had to leave on marriage – but not before they were presented with a bible, a carnation and a talk from one of the directors (a laudable attempt to promote sound family practice and attitudes.) It wasn't until the shortage of male workers caused by World War Two that married women were recruited.

Physical and spiritual wellbeing in the shape of social and recreational facilities, were a vital part of the Cadbury community; land was bought at Rowheath for football and hockey pitches and a running track. The pavilion opened in 1924, not just as a clubhouse and changing facility for the sportsmen and women, but also as a social venue for dinners and dances. In addition, there were bowling greens, a fishing lake and an outdoor lido. An indoor swimming pool was built in Bournville Lane; a boating lake and the cricket pitch followed. All the sports facilities were free of charge. The Bournville Village Trust was set up in 1900 and looked after, amongst other things, the primary and junior school, the School of Art and the Day Continuation School.

John Cadbury typified the Quakers' support of temperance and, in some cases, abstinence. The temperance movement took to chocolate with gusto, establishing British Workman houses to compete with alcohol-serving public houses. They even published a guide instructing how to set up and run these establishments. So began the association of temperance-promoting Quakers with chocolate. They emulated the sweet makers with their conversation lozenges and dragées carrying patriotic and romantic messages such as, 'Do you love me?' and 'No, I won't ask Mama.' But the Quakers poured sobering cold water on it all: *their* sweets carried unequivocal and uncompromising messages such as, 'Misery, sickness and poverty are the effect of drunkenness.'

The Eighteenth Century saw a massive increase in the consumption of spirits, mainly gin, rising from half-a-million gallons in 1684. to five-and-half millions in 1735. Excessive drinking continued to be rife in England in the Nineteenth Century, particularly amongst the less well off, not least because alcohol was the only really safe and easily obtainable means of quenching thirst. Water was often contaminated, and tea and coffee were expensive, cocoa prohibitively so and still hard to come by. Moreover, alcohol was thought to provide strength and stamina to set you up for hard physical work – be it harvesting, mining or factory work; its numbing effect worked well, not just with physical pain but also with the mundane grind of daily life. Inns and taverns and market squares were sociable places where news was exchanged, travellers conversed, women were solicited and locals argued and discussed the matters of the day. It was the norm, as it still is to some extent, rather than the exception, to mark all kinds of celebration – be they family or national – with a drink. The medical profession even endorsed – indeed prescribed – beer as a pickme-up, while stouts and porters gained such a reputation for being a healthy, nourishing drink that they were consumed by sportsmen and nursing mothers.

It was in this context that the temperance movement was established in the 1820s to curb chronic drinking and alcoholism. It failed, and so turned its efforts to total abstinence – teetotalism. The prohibition-focussed United Kingdom Alliance was founded in 1853, 'to procure the Total and Immediate Legislative Suppression of the Traffic in all Intoxicating Liquors'. Temperance societies sprang up everywhere. In York, for example, Joseph Rowntree was very active as Secretary in the Temperance Society which was set up in 1830. The Society's original forty subscribers grew to almost a thousand by 1936 – a huge number when you consider the city population at this time was 30,000. From 1836 there was a rival society promoting total abstinence and variously called New Temperance, Total Abstinence or Teetotal. An Association of Abstainers started in 1874.

The York Temperance Society actively campaigned against such issues as the extension of licensing hours to 11.00pm and for Sunday closing and prohibiting the sale of alcohol to children. It was also instrumental in stopping license renewals at The Golden Slipper Inn in Goodramgate and The Corporation Arms in Friargate. In Walmgate alone, there were twenty inns, according to *White's 1830 Trade Directory,* so it was nothing if not an upward battle. It has also been calculated that across the city there was an inn for every twenty-eight families. Towards the end of the century Joseph Rowntree and Arthur Sherwell, began work on their *The Temperance Problem and Social Reform,* (although even as late as 1874 records show that Rowntree may not have favoured total abstinence if an order for a case of champagne sent to his home was anything to go by.) The book was immensely popular and went on to sell 90,000 copies in nine editions. In 1841 a Temperance Coffee House opened in Colliergate; this transformed into The Commercial Temperance Hotel when it changed hands and moved to Low Ousegate in 1843. York's Temperance Hall opened in Goodramgate in 1845 at a cost of £2,500.

By 1850 the Society of Friends was relatively well established in York with a Meeting House in Castlegate, (moving in 1886 to Clifford Street), a burial ground in Bishophill, and two schools – Bootham for boys and The Mount for girls. There was also a network of Adult Schools throughout the city at which John and Joseph Rowntree were the first teachers, and, of course, regular monthly and Quarterly Meetings. Membership in York was 200 in 1855, rising to 543 in 1915. Their social welfare activities extended beyond care of the poor and the promotion of tolerance to the humane and civilized treatment of the mentally ill at The Retreat. In the usual way of Quakers, the Rowntrees – and before them the Tuke's – would have networked and interceded with other Friends in business in the city. Socially, they would have engaged with other Quakers at the many clubs that were established, for example: the Book Society, the Rowing Club, the Cycling Club and a Young Women's Friends Christian Union.

These are all factors which must have influenced the Rowntrees and Terry's in the very early days and encouraged them in their manufacture and sale of the socially and clinically harmless drink that was cocoa, and its derivatives, the chocolate assortment and the chocolate bar. The association forged with the Tukes with their shared Quakerism, the shining precedents set by Cadbury and Fry in the confectionery industry, and the success of Cravens, their neighbours in the field of toffee and sugar confectionery, must have all combined to a greater or lesser extent to propel Rowntree and Terry into industrial production, first of cocoa, and then chocolate, in the city of York in the mid Nineteenth Century.

York in the Eighteenth and Nineteenth Centuries

S O IN what commercial and industrial environment did the three fledgling companies find themselves when they started their confectionery businesses; Terry's in 1826 and Rowntrees and Craven in 1862?

In the second half of the Fourteenth Century, York, on account of its cloth trade and the ancillary industries associated with it, has been described as 'the foremost industrial town in the North of England.' This did not last, and the trade in cloth declined to such a degree that a visitor to the city in the Seventeenth Century, Thomas Fuller, remarked, 'the foreign trade is like their river, low and flat.'

According to Francis Drake in *Eboracum: or the History and Antiquities of the City of York*, York in the Eighteenth Century had precious little industry, and the only real commercial activity was butter exports, corn and wine trading. Defoe, in *A Tour Through the Whole Island of Great Britain* agrees: 'Here is no trade except such as depends upon the confluence of the gentry.' This was due to some extent to the high price of coal in York which had to be shipped from the coalfields of the West Riding, and to the restrictive, exclusive attitude of the local Merchant Adventurers who insisted that the freedom regulations, whereby all traders had to be freemen of the City, be rigorously observed. Moreover, up until 1827 when a judgement went against them, it seems that only members of the Merchant Adventurers' Company could carry out trade in imported goods. But the high price of coal would only really affect any heavy industry, and the strictures of the Merchant Adventurers would not have impeded development and progress amongst established manufacturers and traders. Some of the reason for the industrial anathema can probably laid at the door of the Corporation whose medieval constitution, financial straits and general lack of enterprise, did little to attract, promote or sustain industry or commerce at any significant level.

If the 1775 register of freemen is to be believed, only 600 enfranchised members were actually engaged in manufacturing, while more were merchants, grocers or innkeepers. York, it seems, was now destined just to work as a parochial market town supplying its own, and the surrounding area's, basic needs, goods and services, and those of the Church and the gentry who frequented the city. Communications were good by road and river and this facilitated the importation of coal – 98,000 tons annually in the 1830s – and the export of agricultural produce, for example to Leeds, which, in the same period amounted to 110,000 sheep, 53,000 cattle and 30,000 tons of grain. But by the end of the century the butter trade had declined, and York, though still a major ecclesiastical centre, was no longer the magnet for the northern gentry it had once been and the traditional trade catering for these people suffered as a result.

The only real developments were small industries such as leather making (there were tanneries in Walmgate on the Foss and at Marygate on the Ouse) and comb and horn breaking which was active mainly around Hornpot Lane off Petergate (the combmakers worked in ivory and tortoiseshell as well as in horn.) One of the more successful comb companies was Forbes and Fothergill near Toft Green. Joseph Rougier (descended from a Huguenot family of wigmakers and hairdressers) was also successful in Tanner Row. Other combmakers included B. Lund in St Andrewgate. Glass was made by Prince and Prest's Fishergate Glass Works which was established in 1797, and flour milling was in North Street and Skeldergate. The year 1780 saw the establishment of manufacturing and wholesale chemists Bleasdale Ltd behind Colliergate, while other pharmaceutical and chemical manufacturers included Wright and Prest in Pavement, Edward Wallis and Son in Bedern and Thomas Bishop at North Street Postern. Breweries were being run by the Wormald family and Thomas Hartley. A modest amount of shipbuilding came and quickly went after the construction of six brigantines outside Skeldergate Postern for butter exports around 1770, followed by a further three brigantines in 1776 and three more in 1781, 1783 and 1797. Heavy industries like iron making were limited to Stodhart in Coney Street who produced lamps and kitchen tools, John Spence in Bootham Bar, Masterman and Gibson in Manor Yard and Prince and Holmes on the River Foss.

The 1841 census gives us the following figures for the industries of any significance: Glass making: fifty-four persons employed in three firms with an average workforce of eighteen persons; flax and linen manufacture: 118 employees in eight firms with an average of fifteen; iron making: twenty-five employees, six firms, average four; chemists and druggists: seventy-six workers in thirty-eight firms averaging two people per firm; 107 comb manufacturers in nine firms averaging twelve people per firm.

Coffee houses abounded in York from 1669. There are at least thirty recorded amongst which were Parker's in Minster Yard – next to a bowling alley as shown on Horsley's 1896 map – the Garrick in Low Petergate, Wombwell and Wink's, Harrison's in Petergate (later Nessgate) Iveson's, (also in Petergate), Duke's near to the Ouse Bridge, Brigg's on the corner of Stonegate and Coffee Yard – as well as William Tuke's roasting house. As one of thirty-one York tea dealers in 1823 and importers of tea, coffee and chocolate, the Tukes were the sole holders in the north of England of a licence which permitted the processing of coffee beans and the sale of roasted coffee, tea and chocolate in the north. It is reasonable to assume that once drinking chocolate and cocoa became popular then, as elsewhere, they would have been added to the list of beverages available in York's coffee shops.

At the beginning of the Nineteenth Century the population of York (municipal borough) was 16,846; by the end of the century this had increased by over 200 per cent to 54,742, with the biggest annual increase (twenty-six per cent) coming in the 1840s soon after the arrival of the railways. Towns and cities like Leeds, Huddersfield and Bradford, which were directly affected by the Industrial Revolution, nevertheless showed much bigger increases. But the Industrial Revolution was an event which largely passed York by. Indeed, in 1851 we can appreciate the different commercial complexions of these cities when we see that York had twice as many domestic servants in employment as the other three, and an above-national average number of small artisan trades and shopkeepers: one shop for every fifty-five people; 2800 people or seventeen per cent of the city's workforce were in service (for women the figure was seventy-five per cent) and a further ninety-one (five and a half per cent) in hospitality – hotels and inns.

Temperance Society efforts to stop railway workers drinking; the coffee cart scheme was set up by Henry Rowntree in 1871.

By comparison, manufacturing accounted for 3,170 persons, or just over nineteen per cent of the economically active. Furthermore, at the dawn of the Nineteenth Century, York was England's sixteenth largest city and the fourth largest in Yorkshire after Leeds, Sheffield and Hull. By the end of the century it was the forty-first in the country and in Yorkshire, York had been surpassed by Bradford, Middlesbrough, Halifax and Huddersfield.

Before the railways, many goods were transported in and out of the city on the River Ouse. *White's* 1840 Directory had high hopes for the future: 'The formation of railways to open a better communication with the West of Yorkshire and the North and South of England, are in progress and with these improved modes of transit for goods, it is to be hoped that the trade of York will improve.' In the event, the railways may not have led to an expansion of the industrial base in York even though six main line companies were soon calling at York. But they did bring their own opportunities for employment and the obvious benefit in communication with the rest of the country, and indeed, with the world, as access to Hull and other east coast ports was improved.

The number of people employed in York on the railways increased from forty-one in 1841 to 513 in 1851, 390 of whom came for the work from other towns in the United Kingdom. Many of these were involved in engine repair and building at the railway works where there was a 1,200-strong workforce by 1855. Carriage and wagon -building followed. This all moved from Queen Street to a forty-five-acre-site at Holgate, becoming York's first large-scale industry and its biggest employer. By the end of the century there were 5,500 railway workers in the city, nearly 2,000 of whom were skilled.

The Royal Station Hotel which opened in 1878 under the ownership of LNER, as it was in the 1920s. It had 100 rooms at 14 shillings per night. It is now the Royal York Hotel.

Barges loading up with coal and sand on the River Foss in the 1950s.

Other industries in 1851 were still small fry by any comparison. The glassworks in Fishergate was ailing and was taken over by Joseph Spence, a Quaker analytical chemist, James Meek and Thomas Spence, to become the successful York Flint Glass Company. It employed 223 men turning out chemists' jars, railway lamps, beetle and wasp traps, cake shades, cruets and Daffy's Elixir bottles. The metal industry was shared between John Walker with fifty-two men, Edwin Thompson, (forty-eight men) and William Knapton, (eighteen men.) George Steward's comb manufacturing had thirty men while E.Steward had eighteen in the same industry; William Hebden, linen maker, had a workforce of thirty-five men, seven boys and one woman. In 1823 there were nine toy and household trinket manufacturers including John Barber of Coney Street, John Bell in Stonegate and John Jameson of College Street.

Chemicals, flour milling and printing were the only other industries of any size, with 150 chemical workers at the end of the century, ninety-eight millers (mainly at Leetham's in Wormald Cut in 1891 rising to 600 in 1911) and, also in 1891, almost five hundred employed in the printing and publishing trade. Printing had been established in York since the Fifteenth Century and by 1750 there were four printing houses in the city. The largest of these companies was run by the Quaker William Alexander from 1811 in Lower Ousegate and was later to be taken over in 1865 by another Quaker, William Sessions, who moved the firm to Coney Street in 1894. Alexander was following in the tradition of Thomas Gent, author and printer, who operated out of Coffee Yard from 1724 and published the first local newspaper and scores of chap books. Ben Johnson and Co Ltd was established as a lithographic printer by Johnson and John Lancaster and specialised in railway timetables and other jobs associated with the railways. Newspapers obviously also provided employment in the shape of the Whig *York Courant*, set up by Caesar Ward in the 1750s. Ward was also the publisher of the first edition of Laurence Sterne's *The Life and Opinions of Tristram Shandy*, the *York Daily Herald* (which changed from a weekly in 1874 and absorbed the *Courant* in 1848), and the 1882 *York Evening Press*, now the morning *York Press*.

Apart from Bleasdale's in the chemical and drug-making industry, there was Raimes and Company from 1818 in Micklegate, and Henry Richardson and Company, fertilizer makers founded in 1824 at Skeldergate Postern in Clementhorpe. John Walker's iron foundry was very successful and received Queen Victoria's royal warrant in 1847. In 1850 they won the contract to supply the extensive railings and gates for the British Museum and for the Sandringham Estate. In addition, much of their work was in gates and railings for the many country houses around York and at British embassies and foreign government buildings abroad, an example being the Botanical Gardens in Mauritius. The Adams Patent Sewage Lift Company Ltd was established in Peaseholme Green in 1887 to make sanitary equipment. They merged in 1919 with the 1885 iron foundry, G.W. Kirk, their biggest supplier.

Another specialist company was optical engineers, Thomas Cooke who went on to make sundials, microscopes and world renowned telescopes from 1837, and became one of York's first, if not the first, global companies. The firm moved from Stonegate to the Buckingham Works on Bishophill in 1856 and was run by Cooke's two sons after his death in 1868. By the end of the century they had diversified into clock making and employed 500 workers. Cooke also invented a steam car which carried fifteen passengers at a speed of fifteen mph, but which was outlawed by the Road Act prohibiting vehicles which travelled above four mph. His sons invented the pneumatic despatch system.

The development of flour milling in York was particularly important. Henry Leetham set up his milling industry in Hungate on the banks of the River Foss in 1850, replacing his old steam mills with state-of-the-art Hungarian steel rollers for milling the corn. In 1888 he flexed his industrial muscle by threatening to relocate to Hull if the City Corporation refused to enlarge the lock at the entry to the Foss at Castle Mills. This they duly did, and grain replaced coal as the largest river cargo. At the same time very favourable terms were negotiated for the transport of Leetham's goods. Leetham went on to build his landmark five-storey warehouse in 1896 on Wormald's Cut with its nine-storey castellated water tower linked to the Hungate Mill by bridges. At the time it was one of the largest mills in Europe. By then, the firm had operations in Hull, Newcastle and Cardiff, as well as in York and was showing handsome profits of around £50,000 per year with a wholesale customer base of around 9,000.

This then was the environment in which Mary, and then Henry Tuke, set up their chocolate, cocoa and tea business in their Castlegate shop, and in which Bayldon and Berry opened their business in St Helen's Square, and in which Mary Craven established her business in Coppergate. This was the environment in which the businesses which were to become Rowntree, Terry and Craven began their respective lives.

Significantly for us, the confectionery trade had started to emerge as a major employer – for women as well as for men. By 1851 Joseph Terry employed 127 workers in St Helen's Square, and Thomas Craven was working with 63 men and 60 boys; by the end of the century the firm employed over two hundred. There was also the York Confectionery Company founded in 1867 in Fossgate (later moving to Fenwick Street off Bishopthorpe Road), which specialized in candied peel and red and white mint rock for the seaside market. York Confectionery Company was owned by a man called Henderson of whom little is known, apart from that he suffered from dyspnoea, (shortness of breath), and that his factory became known as Puffy's as a result. Henderson went bankrupt in 1909. In 1879 Rowntrees employed 100 workers; this increased to 893 in 1894 and by 1909 had reached 4,066.

The old 1841 railway station opposite Rowntree's in Tanner's Moat within the city walls.

Rowntree: 1865–1900

MEANWHILE, 104 miles to the north east of Bournville, a remarkably similar story to the Cadbury one was unfolding. It begins with Mary Tuke who came from a famous Quaker family, and whose grandfather was jailed for his non-conformism in the 1660s. In 1725, aged 30 and a spinster, Mary established a grocery business, first in Walmgate, then Castlegate, and became embroiled in a series of commercial legal wrangles with the York Merchant Adventurers' Company. Being a woman, and a Quaker woman at that, was only the start of Mary's problems. To trade in York it was necessary to be a Freeman of the City, and the only way of achieving such status was to either pay £25 to serve an apprenticeship, or to be related to an existing Freeman. Eventually Mary did win the status of Freeman after naming her father as a deceased member. The inscription on the *Freeman's Roll of the City of York reads*: 'Maria Tuke, spinster Fil Willelmi Tuke, blacksmith.' Unfortunately, this was not enough to allow her to trade. Mary was also required to be a member of the Merchant Adventurers' Company or be granted a licence by them, but had no means of achieving either. After flouting what was essentially a pointless and outmoded law, Mary was prosecuted for trading without a licence and then went on to defy the court for a further two years. In 1728 the Merchant Adventurers relented and allowed her to trade at the pleasure of the court and on payment of ten shillings a year, and with the promise to buy all her goods locally. In 1732 Mary was allowed to trade for the rest of her life after a one off payment of £10.

Mary was joined by her nephew William in 1746 as an apprentice; he inherited the business on her death in 1752 and became a freeman grocer and member of the Merchant Adventurers. The shop specialised in the sale of coffee, chicory and drinking chocolate; his son Henry, at that time halfway through a medical degree, gave it all up in 1785 in a typically Quakerish act and joined the business. They branched out to sell tea and to manufacture cocoa and chocolate themselves. Brands such Tukes' Rich Cocoa, Tukes' Plain Chocolate, British Cocoa Coffee and Tukes' Milk Chocolate (not milk chocolate as we know it but chocolate used for mixing with milk) were brought to market.

In 1796 William went on to establish The Retreat in York which was a revolutionary and humane new way of treating the mentally ill. It was in direct contrast to existing methods which saw such patients chained up as criminals and treated like prisoners rather than patients. In William's own words he wanted 'an institution for the care and proper treatment of those labouring under that most afflictive dispensation, the loss of reason.' The thirty-bed Retreat was the result of William's resolve: 'A habitation for persons in a state of lunacy', and it laid the foundations for the modern treatment of psychiatric disorders. Another legacy of William's was the establishment of Trinity Lane Girl's School, later to become the Mount School.

The 1895 Leetham's Mill taken over by Rowntree from Spiller's in 1937 for cocoa bean storage.

Henry's son, Samuel, joined the firm in 1805. He was a good friend of fellow Quaker Joseph Rowntree I, as well as being related to him through marriage. Joseph had come to York from Scarborough where his father ran a grocer's shop and where Joseph had worked since the age of eleven. Joseph, too, was now a grocer with a shop in Pavement; its

An advertisement for the Rowntree shop at No 10 (?) Pavement showing the range of goods.

apprentices, as we have seen, included George Cadbury. Samuel's sons, meanwhile, were more preoccupied with building up a business in banking with their relatives the Barclays, and had no interest in the York business, leaving it to a manager, Henry Hipsley, to run. Another partner John Casson, was appointed, and the firm was renamed Tuke and Casson.

The Pavement shop was bought in 1822 by Joseph I on his twenty-first birthday at auction at the Elephant & Castle Inn in Skeldergate, (the auctioneer was so drunk that Joseph and his friend, James Backhouse, had to plunge his head in a barrel of cold water so that he could proceed with the sale.) Joseph refurbished the shop – his mahogany counters, iron grilles, full length curtains upstairs and elaborate fire guards being considered somewhat fancy by Quaker standards. Not unusually for the times, hours were long: 7.00 am or 7.30 to 8.00 pm, six days a week, with late-night opening on market days until 10.00 pm, and two days' holiday – Good Friday and Christmas Day. It is worth quoting more from Mr Rowntree's fearsome memorandum: 'Punctuality in the time of rising etc is important in each member otherwise the thoughtless or ease-loving individual wastes the time of the others ... without neglecting business much may be done ... to prevent the needless extension of meal-taking a gratuity of 26 shillings per year is allowed to the punctual.'

The Pavement shop was to give Joseph's son, the younger Joseph Rowntree, a sound and invaluable seventeen-year apprenticeship in retail and business management, particularly with regard to the grocery business. This, and an earlier period of work as a wholesale grocer near Fenchurch Street in London from 1857, provided a priceless foundation for the next stage of his career when he joined his brother at the cocoa works in Tanner's Moat.

The shop at No 28 Pavement .

Early advertisers' attempts to appeal to children.

William Tuke moved the tea dealership part of his business – which he had started in 1835 – to London, and eventually, in 1862, sold it to John Casson. In July 1862 Joseph Rowntree's elder son, Henry Isaac Rowntree, bought the Tukes' cocoa and chocolate business. Henry had served his apprenticeship at his father's grocery shop in Scarborough, then at the family shop in Pavement, and finally at Tuke's from 1860 where he was manager at the time. The notice posted by William Tuke read as follows: 'We have to inform you that we have relinquished the manufacture of cocoa, chocolate and chicory in favour of our friend, H.I. Rowntree, who has been for some time practically engaged on the concern, and whose knowledge of the business in its several departments enables us with confidence to recommend him to the notice of our connections.' Henry, in turn, circulated the following sales letter to his customers: 'The genuine Rock Cocoa introduced by my predecessors, and which from its superiority commands an exclusive sale. I shall continue to supply in its integrity and purity my special attention will be directed to this branch of the business with a view to the introduction of such improvements in the manufacture as may present themselves. My representative Richard Wilson expects to have the pleasure of waiting upon you about the usual time your orders will at all oblige and receive my careful and prompt attention'.

New and improved machinery to enable the new owner to fulfil all orders was promised to customers. The cocoa and chocolate firm was relatively small, with about twelve staff, including the sales representative, Richard Wilson, and with sales of about £3,000 – ten per cent of Cadbury sales and five per cent of Fry sales at the time. Nevertheless, this was the genesis of the Rowntree chocolate company in York.

The bulk of the output was Tukes's Superior Rock Cocoa, later to become Rowntree's Prize Medal Rock Cocoa. This, at nine pence a pound, was a blend of pure cocoa and sugar – made using pre-van Houten technology – into fine ground cakes. Unfortunately, the cakes suffered from the oiliness that is characteristic of the manufacturing process, but Henry remained optimistic and often quoted *Deuteronomy* 32 in its defence: 'Their Rock is not as our Rock, even our enemies themselves being judges'. As one would expect from a Quaker, high standards of quality were of the essence even from these very early days, and Henry would not make false claims about his products – a characteristic soon to be shared with Joseph Rowntree II.

Henry relocated the firm from Castlegate to an old iron-foundry, a row of cottages and an inn at Tanner's Moat, which he bought for £1,000 in 1864. However, the combination of Henry's preoccupation with Quaker-related activities, his publishing of the *York Weekly Press*, old cocoa technology, and small scale, short-run manufacturing techniques, compromised any real progress and, like Cadbury's at the time, the business was ailing. Sales in 1862, for example, were less than £3000, the payroll comprised twelve men, and output was 1200 hundredweight of cocoa per week. The Pavement shop was taken over by T.Coning and Sons, and continued as a grocer's shop where the new owners made and sold their own cocoa.

In 1869 Henry was joined by his thirty-three-year-old brother, Joseph Rowntree II, the man we most associate with the company, and the firm H. I. Rowntree & Co was established. Joseph brought much-needed capital to Tanner's Moat. Just as importantly though, he brought a good deal of experience and business acumen to the company, focusing on the financial and sales side, and leaving the manufacturing to Henry. Joseph soon began building up the sales force, and by 1897, 'Sales' was an official department of the company. In effect, he probably saved the 'hopelessly embarrassed' company from a decidedly un-Quakerly bankruptcy, bailing out a brother who 'knew next to nothing of the business.' Joseph had cut his teeth in statistics and accountancy with his earlier work at Pavement and with the Quakers in their various campaigns – in particular, his own extensive research into poverty in England had given him a mastery of statistics and a meticulousness which manifested itself not just in his accounts, but even in the handwriting with which he transcribed those accounts and other aspects of the company's business.

The jumble of improvised buildings at Tanner's Moat was nothing if not full of character; apart from the resident parrot there was a somewhat temperamental donkey which was obedient to one man and one man only and a serious peril to everyone else. On its dismissal, deliveries were relegated to a hand cart. Night-shift workers were sustained by cocoa and pork pies on the firm, and most communications to and from Joseph Rowntree were through a trapdoor in the floor of his Lendal Bridge-facing office. Hanks the foreman paid the wages each week from a hat full of silver and coppers. Employees would be asked how many hours they had worked and were duly paid the going rate from the contents of the hat. Girls aged about fourteen would have got around three shillings per week, boys a shilling more. Men earned eighteen shillings at most – fairly standard money for the times. The purchase of a horse and wagonette in 1874 proved injudicious and an overhead the company could ill afford for food, farriers' and veterinary bills, and tolls amounted to twelve shillings and seven pence three-farthings per week. The horse was duly sold and the wagonette mothballed. Production was steam driven, but hampered by the use of different machines for each of the processes involved (grinding, sifting, roasting and so on) with raw materials laboriously manhandled between machines.

A combination of Joseph's meticulousness, increased product lines, and a rise in demand, raised the company's fortunes. They were, of course, also influenced by market trends. Cocoa prices had been falling from 1873 to 1879, signifying something of a depression, and foreign competition was increasing. But between 1870 and 1890, cocoa consumption in the UK increased from nearly seven million pounds weight to over 20 million pounds, with a rise in consumption per capita from 0.22 pounds weight to 0.53. From a personal point of view, Joseph may have realised he was at the point of no return career-wise. On his third child's birth certificate in 1875, he no longer described himself as a master grocer, but as a cocoa manufacturer. Until then, grocery was the trade in which he had spent all of his working life so far but cocoa and chocolate were to be his life from now on.

In 1876 Homoeopathic Cocoa was launched, riding on the popularity of the medicinal content ascribed to arrowroot. Other products included Iceland Moss, Hexagon Cocoa, Pearl Cocoa, Farinaceous Cocoa, Shield Chocolate, Shilling Chocolate, Flake Cocoa, Chocolate Creams, Chocolate Balls, Chocolate Beans and Chocolate Drops. More diverse lines included a granular effervescent citrate of magnesia fruit sauce and the agency for Neaves' Farinaceous Infant Food – early competition for Nestlé products.

While others in the industry were embracing marketing and advertising, Joseph was very uncomfortable with it. He preferred to let the quality of his cocoa speak for itself, delivering goods to wholesalers and retailers unbranded with just a formal sales letter and, indeed, supplying labels bearing the name of the customer which tended to give the impression that the customer was the producer rather than Rowntrees. We know that Joseph would rather delay an order than send out substandard goods to his customers. When Seebohm once pointed out that a wholesaler had been waiting six weeks for an order Joseph responded by saying the delay was due to a manufacturing fault and that a further fortnight's delay was possible, 'but when he does get it, it will be what he ordered.' A letter from the mid 1870s shows just how unequivocal Joseph was: 'As we do not advertise we are enabled to give greater value for money than those firms whose sales depend on advertisements. We prefer to trust to quality … steadily increasing sales strengthens our opinion that this is a sound method of doing business.'

To Joseph, as with others in the trade, being a grocer was a dignified and skilled business catering for the better off. He would not sell down to the mass market which began to emerge and which slowly, but surely, formed the ever-growing core market for his business. To Joseph, as with some other Quakers and to some extent shopkeeper-manufacturers generally, advertising, and attractive, alluring shop windows smacked of disingenuousness and implied substandard goods. This scepticism was partly fuelled by the extensive use of advertising by companies selling patent, 'quack' remedies and medicines – a massive £2million was spent by this sector in 1914 – and the distrust, before 1890, of advertising agencies which were largely seen as being concerned solely with cynically selling space in newspapers, with none of the associated expertise in design and copywriting, sales projections or even circulation or readership figures.

The unfortunate and inevitable consequence of the lack of advertising was that none of the Rowntree lines was particularly successful and, although between 1870 and 1879 sales rose from £7,384 to £30,890, margins remained tight, and losses were recorded in

An early eating chocolate Rowntree sign.

Iceland Moss under Henry's name.

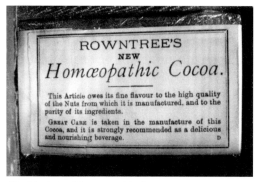

Health-giving Homoeopathic Cocoa.

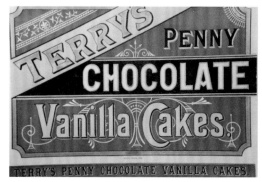

Chocolate Vanilla Cakes.

1873 (£500) and 1876. Only four out of nineteen lines were profitable, although these did account for seventy per cent of sales.

The meagre staff had to learn versatility; they shared the tasks of grinding and roasting the cocoa on the two available machines, and of heaving the sugar around. Hanks ran the chocolate cream department assisted by one girl. He was also night watchman (he lived next door to the factory) and, as we have seen, wages clerk. His wages would have been about 16 shillings per week. This musical chairs method of staffing persisted into the 1880s and 1890s; an employee originally hired as a timekeeper moved on to general manager and then took charge of the *mélangeur* and cake room departments. Another man hired as a junior clerk transferred to the cream rooms as manager to twenty staff. On retirement he was responsible for nearly one thousand workers.

The friendship between George Cadbury and Joseph Rowntree during their Pavement apprenticeship, and of course the bond created by Cadbury, Rowntree and Fry being Quakers, were the driving forces responsible for the agreements the three companies forged together in 1872, 1889, 1895 and 1900, coordinating prices on chocolate and other confectioneries, but not on cocoa – the main product at that time. The cartel also limited trade discounts and shop point of sale in order to maintain decent margins for all the companies. In 1918 they signed what became known as the Cheltenham Agreements. Non-Quaker Caley in Norwich was also involved in some of these arrangements, as were

Clarke, Nicholl and Coombes (Clarnico) of London. In 1935 neighbours Terry and then Nestlé joined to form a Five Firm Agreement for chocolate.

But it was cocoa essence as pioneered by Cadbury, which eventually led Fry, Cadbury and Rowntree out of their respective difficult times. The year 1872 also saw Joseph Rowntree paying fact-finding visits to Fry's, Taylor's, Dunn and Hewitt, the Quaker Stollwerk in Cologne and Menier in Paris, to learn more about their production processes and recipes. He visited the Cadburys in 1875, the Netherlands twice in 1877, and spent his holidays with the Cadbury's in Switzerland.

The Quaker belief in the value of the individual, and refusal to see the factory worker just as a means to an end, led to a paternalistic and fair, virtually non-hierarchical relationship with the workforce. Their innate pacifism generated a preoccupation with the welfare of their employees extending to social activities, sick pay, loans and pensions of sorts. Mutual trust, loyalty and respect were the order of the day. But if Quakerism was largely responsible for philanthropy and enlightened industrial relations within the industry (Bryant & May and Huntley & Palmers were to some extent exceptions within the faith) and a paternalistic approach towards employees, it was by no means a cohesive force when it came to advertising. Joseph Fry had been advertising in the press since the 1830s, and their marketing spend in 1866 was about £2,000. More significantly, it was an intensive marketing campaign which assured and confirmed the success of Cadbury's new van Houten generated-product Cocoa Essence, in 1866. Advertising, apart from drawing the attention of a rapidly growing consumer market to the product, also enabled the manufacturer to promote other qualities, often at the expense of the competition. Cadbury actively promoted their essence as pure, safe and compliant under the terms of the 1872 and 1875 Food Adulteration Acts (whereby all ingredients in cocoa had to be revealed), thus tapping into a growing public awareness of food safety and purity. By contrast, Rowntree was much more conservative, sticking with their Rock Cocoa and largely refraining from advertising and branding.

A sales call by Claude Gaget in 1879 had a significant and lasting impact on Rowntrees. Gaget was working out of the London office of Compagnie Française, a Parisian confectioners who specialized in gums and pastilles which, up until then, were the preserve of the French manufacturers. The samples he presented that day eventually led to Rowntrees' manufacture in 1881 (but only when the product they made was of the highest quality) of their famous Crystallized Gum Pastilles – in 4lb unbranded wooden boxes at a penny per ounce.

They were an immediate success with sales of the pastilles enabling the company to expand into Simpson's flour mill in North Street, adjacent to Tanner's Moat. By 1885 four tonnes were being produced every week. Staff, too, doubled to 200 in 1883, and sales more than doubled from 1880 (£44,000) to 1889 (£99,000); net profits increased five-fold from around £372 (0.85 per cent) in 1879 to £1649 (1.67 per cent) in 1889, although they were still poor. These sweets were of course the precursors of Rowntrees Fruit Gums and Fruit Pastilles.

Henry's death from peritonitis in 1883 coincided with another fall in the price of cocoa, and pressing annual mortgage repayments of £12,000 on recently-bought premises in Foss Islands and North Street. All this led to Joseph's two eldest sons joining the firm; John Wilhelm in 1885, aged seventeen, and Benjamin Seebohm (Seebohm was his mother's German family name) in 1888. Seebohm had graduated in chemistry from

Tanner's Moat and North Street mills.

Owen's College at the University of Manchester and had established the company's first laboratory in 1897, as well as appointing the firm's first food chemist, Samuel H. Davies, another Quaker. John Wilhelm reorganised the cocoa and chocolate departments and managed the travellers. The company was now offering about one hundred lines and producing four tons of gums and pastilles each week. By 1887 a horse drawn truck was needed to take the goods to the station each day.

We have seen how the per capita consumption of cocoa expanded dramatically during these years. This was reflected in Rowntrees sales: Between 1870 and 1890 they grew from £7,384 to £114,529 increasing to £463,199 in 1900. The comparative figures for Cadbury were £54,790 – £515,371 and £1,226,552; and for Fry, £143,750 – £761,969 and £1,326,312. In 1870 Rowntree had four per cent of the UK market, increasing to 15 per cent by 1900, and Cadbury was at twenty-seven per cent in 1870, rising to forty-one per cent in 1900. All this was at the expense of Fry, whose share declined from seventy per cent to forty-four per cent over the same period.

The success of fruit pastilles enabled Joseph to invest in more property – this time in nearby Queen Street – and to refurbish or extend existing properties including the North Street flour mill and the Tanner's Moat cottages. It also allowed him to purchase new machinery in 1880: a refrigerator and better machines for cleaning the beans and turning out the nibs. But the *pièce de résistance* was undoubtedly a van Houten press which paved the way for the production and launch in 1880 of cocoa essence Rowntrees Elect, 'more than a drink, a food' and made from top quality cocoa. The name Elect was borrowed from the apothecary trade, where it signified a particularly

An early Rowntree's pastilles stockist.

efficacious drug. It was described as 'an extremely light powder, the essential product of the cocoa bean after it had been roasted and ground and the fat (cocoa butter) taken out by hydraulic pressure.' But despite the new technology and increased demand, output remained low. In 1893 Elect still only accounted for six per cent of sales and two and a half per cent of output. Company profits were unimpressive at two-and-a half-per cent of turnover in 1888. In 1885 a Dutchman, Cornelius Hollander, was appointed, mainly, it seems, to perfect Elect because he was understood to know the original van Houten essence recipe. It appears that the secretive and querulous Hollander was not as useful as had first been assumed. Elect was re-launched anyway in 1887 after Hollander's secure North Street room was broken into and the recipe revealed. On Hollander's dismissal, James Archer, the company engineer, was given control of the Elect Department.

Notwithstanding, and no doubt with an eye of Cadbury's achievements at Bournville, Joseph persisted with his enlightened attitude towards his workforce, and in 1885 stocked and opened a library for his staff. He put in £10 of his own money and this was matched by a grant from the company's Pure Literature Society. One penny was deducted from the weekly wages of all employees – a not inconsiderable amount (over one per cent of wages in some cases) for someone earning the average wage of £1 per week.

The increasing size of the company was starting to diminish Joseph's personal relationship with his workers and so he set about compensating for this by creating what might be seen as extensions of himself. A girl's welfare officer, Miss Wood, was appointed in 1891 to look after the health, moral upbringing and behaviour of female

Rowntrees Gums in trays.

Rowntrees Gums in boxes and tubes – as essential as a road map to a motor car journey.

staff, some of whom were as young as thirteen. This was something of a pioneering move in British industry, even though an 1864 Factory Inspector's report had recommended that firms which employed a large number of females should 'take on a married female of mature age to act as an 'onlooker''. One of the problems which Joseph Rowntree had identified was that there were few, if any, women in the firm of any maturity as his female workforce left at a relatively young age to get married, start families – and never return. His lady, among other things, instituted a sober dress code of black dresses and no skirts or blouses. This was provoked when one young lady presented for work in a blouse which left her throat exposed; the reaction of the Rowntree's 'onlooker' was to exclaim that such immodesty 'might easily draw a man's attention to you.' Notwithstanding, the appointment was obviously a success as within a year an assistant 'onlooker' was hired.

A work's outing to Whitby was even more decadent but less successful. Some of the party left the specially-chartered train at Goathland on the North York Moors, planning to walk the rest of the way and meet the main group for an afternoon stroll on the beach at their destination. A rain storm intervened and diverted the walkers into a public house for shelter. When they emerged again many of them were so drunk that they had to be escorted to the station by the Whitby police. There were no more outings for a number of years. Joseph, nevertheless, did continue with the regular 'concerts' – lavish meals in the Bootham Exhibition Buildings to which the whole workforce were invited – a rare treat in those days for most. Office staff (the equivalent of management) were frequently invited to Joseph's house for 'social evenings.' *Cocoa Works Magazine (CWM)* was launched in 1902 as a vehicle to maintain communication and impart company and employee's news at all levels.

William Laycock with his rulley and horse about to leave for the station with the day's production; Laycock made the journey from 1877 until 1911.

Miss Wood's department took over the hiring of girls. Day one started with the supervisor meeting with the girl's mother to assure her that her daughter's welfare was paramount and every girl was given a 'companion' or mentor to train her on the job. Often the homes of applicants of both sexes were visited to confirm that they were 'clean and respectable.' Girls and boys, men and women, were of course segregated as far as possible with separate dining rooms and women only corridors. Boys were a constant problem due to their high turnover and the negative effects this had on production, and so it was in 1900, D.S. Crichton, a Congregationalist Minister, was hired to look after the boys' pastoral care. Many young men had to leave when they reached twenty-one as the jobs they were doing would only be cost-effective if Rowntree paid child rather than adult rates of pay. Crichton tried to minimize this by strategically placing boys in jobs where there was a likelihood of continuing work.

Quaker thinking naturally permeated the company and came to bear on many other, non-welfare related aspects of factory life. Gambling, for example, was rife until it was banned in 1904, and the company never knowingly employed anyone who had a liquor licence. Mothers of children born out of wedlock were likewise excluded, and any man who 'got a girl into trouble' was denied the usual three-day honeymoon holiday on marriage. Sick pay was not paid to anyone absent from work due to a sexually transmitted infection, and indeed, many sufferers were dismissed as a precaution against contagion amongst the workforce. York Races were always a problem and requests for time off to attend were routinely turned down. Things came to a head in 1914 though, when 1,200 staff protested *en masse*, with 754 men voting to have time off, 619 voting not to and 188 abstaining. Amongst the women, 283 voted in favour, 666 not and 150 abstained.

Building the roof of the Haxby Road factory in 1904; the 'Rowntree' sign was already in place. Each letter measured ten feet in height; the distance between the 'R' and the 'E' in the name was 112 feet.

Seebohm Rowntree relented and agreed to take requests for time off. In all, 2,477 workers – or forty-nine per cent of the workforce – applied, but only the men were permitted leave of absence for a half day at the May and August meetings.

Joseph's 'philanthropy' was not entirely altruistic – it was driven by an enlightened business vision which identified and cultivated the benefits afforded by a contented work force working in a reasonably pleasant environment.

This is seen in 1890 when Joseph bought a twenty-acre site to the north of the city centre on Haxby Road, with a view to building a more efficient and ergonomic factory which would enable the firm to improve production techniques and transportation, and meet the growing demand for their products in a pleasant working environment.

In Joseph's own words he wanted a workplace where his workers could 'develop all that is best and worthy in themselves … healthful conditions of labour are not luxuries to be adopted or dispensed at will. They are conditions necessary for success.' Tanner's Moat was inadequate in every way. Seebohm in later life said of it, 'Tanner's Moat was Hell.' Coming from a man not usually given over to such language these were strong words indeed. The new factory would be an efficient and congenial place to work – and

Locomotive Number 3 at the halt.

so it transpired. For example, the offices were lit by electricity powered by a generator and the factory had its own North Eastern Railway goods branch line and halt – to expedite transportation.

The manufacture of clear gums began in 1893, permitted by the extra space in Haxby Road. The Fruit Room and Gums were first to transfer, and by 1898, all production was on the new site.

Two more members of the family joined the firm. First in 1892, came Arnold, a son of Joseph's brother John, then a year later Henry Isaac's son Frank. They thus helped to reinforce the Quaker tendency to populate the higher echelons of their companies with their own, thus ensuring a degree of continuity and consolidation at the top. The number of employees in 1884 was 182; by 1899 this had risen to 1613, and by 1902 it stood at over 2000. Fry and Cadbury had seen equally dramatic increases from 250 to 4500 and 230 to 2683 over a similar period.

Haxby Road and the increasing headcount coincided with a necessary change in attitude in industrial relations. As we have noted, gone were the opportunities for familiarity and personal contact with staff. Rules and regulations more appropriate to a large company had to be introduced, and that is what happened from 1892. The time system was tightened up with doors opening at 6.00 am. Anyone not inside within five minutes was excluded until 8.25 by which time a quarter of a day's pay would have been lost. Two 'lates' in one week was punished with a week's suspension. Late-coming after breakfast and dinner were likewise not tolerated. Inventory controls were set up to minimise wastage and improve requisitioning. Later, the working week was reduced

An awestruck Prince of Wales surveys the Haxby Road factory from the air in 1923.

to forty-eight hours, and the working day was changed from 7.30am to 5.00 pm with an hour for dinner. There was no reduction in pay; instead the savings made in fuel compensated. The late start also obviated the need to provide breakfast. Latecomers were docked half a day's pay.

Advertising was still minimal and suspect, despite the fact that the other players in the market – Fry, Cadbury, van Houten and Cailler – were all advertising their products aggressively. John Wilhelm and his cousin, Arnold Stephenson Rowntree, were both rather more enthusiastic about advertising than Joseph. They succeeded in doubling the advertising budget in 1892 to £4,000, largely spent on Elect, and grandiloquently announced thus in a letter to the travellers: 'In connection with our Advertising, we are considering the question of an important forward mover in the coming year, and of entering upon National Advertisements, as distinguished from the localised advertisements, which are all we have hitherto attempted.' The adverts in national newspapers featured a 1d voucher and coupon which could be redeemed for a sample of Elect. The slogan read, 'A cup of cocoa and your morning paper for nothing.' Unfortunately, this foray into advertising was short-lived, although in 1893 the first tentative steps towards branding took place with the registering of the famous Rowntree and Co. signature. This was the very signature that decorated the foot of the letter quoted above. But it was not until 1897 that Rowntree's embarked on a cohesive and resourced marketing campaign for its Elect Cocoa, championed by John Wilhelm. Space was taken in two quality magazines, *Tit-Bits* and *Answers* at roughly £35 a page. The importance of Elect, even if not reflected in actual sales, can be seen by the fact that Elect staff now numbered 240 and output was at twenty-six tons per week. Advertising staff, though, still only amounted to one headcount in 1899.

In 1897 Rowntrees became a limited company and the name changed to Rowntree & Co Ltd. It nevertheless remained a family concern with Joseph Chairman of the Board and sons John Wilhelm and Seebohm and nephews Arnold and Frank and J. Bowes Morrell, directors, with Arnold's brother, Theodore, Company Secretary. Joseph apart, they were all under thirty years of age. Morrell, fellow Quaker and Bootham School old boy, was the first outsider to gain entry to the upper echelons of the firm as Finance Director. He was the son of the owner of the York City and County Bank which provided some of the finance for Haxby Road.

Advertising stunts came in the late 1890s – surprising when you consider Joseph's antipathy – when Joseph Rowntree's nephew Arnold organised one of those new fangled motor cars to tour the country with a giant nine-foot Elect Cocoa tin lashed on the back. On windy days it was shipped to its destination by train. The car replaced a pony pulling a delivery cart. Nothing could have been more out of character from a company so opposed to advertising, but it had its desired effect, breaking down at one point in Sheffield city centre in a blaze of publicity, with the driver escaping prosecution on condition that he drove at a maximum speed of three mph. Arnold later went on to have a barge covered in Elect posters and towed by a brace of mechanical swans cross the Thames on the course of the 1897 Oxford and Cambridge Boat Race. From this bizarre, but no doubt extremely effective stunt, samples of Elect were generously distributed.

More conventional marketing came with the appointment of S.H. Benson as advertising agent, a man noted for his integrity and values. He embarked on a campaign to heighten the profile of Elect in the marketplace and to make it easier for the Rowntree travellers to get a foot in the door. It was called the *Daily Telegraph* Scheme and was achieved largely through sampling. Coupons were placed in the *Telegraph* which were redeemable for a 1d stamp and a tin of Elect. This led to the opening of thousands of new trade accounts to meet the demand. Elect adverts appeared on London buses with appropriately attired conductors. and women readers of the *Daily Mail* were invited to hop on board and receive a tin of Elect. 'Have you had your ride on a Rowntree Bus?' the *Daily Mail* demanded. So successful was it that the police were on the point of halting the exercise to preserve public order. One way or another, 20,000 samples were given away at the end of 1897. In addition to this, 20,000 boxes of chocolates were given away to anyone introducing six new Elect customers, and 1898 calendars were offered free with a tin of Elect. The health-giving qualities of Elect were emphasized, particularly its benefits to the nervous system and as a cure for anaemia. The great advantage of Benson's innovative campaigns was that the consumer could actually taste (and smell) the product for themselves, rather than just see a picture of it on the page and be obliged to believe the advertiser's claims. In 1902, 500,000 tins of cake chocolate were given away to London's poor as part of the Coronation celebrations, as well as 60,000 additional tins to stewards serving the meal, 'as they would be of greater importance to us socially than the 500,000 poor.' Benson's were also responsible for commissioning the world- famous but commercially unsuccessful Beggarstaff J. & W. posters in 1896.

IMPORTANT.

TIME OFFICE RULES

ABSENCE WITHOUT LE.	SUSPENSION
1. Morning or afternoon, more than once a week.	THREE DAYS.
2. Morning or afternoon, once in a week and once in the following week.	TWO DAYS.
3. One day's absence without satisfactory explanation sent in writing to timekeeper during that day.	ONE DAY.
4. At work in the morning but absent without leave in the afternoon.	ONE DAY.
5. Two or more days' consecutive absence without satisfactory explanation in writing to the timekeeper within two days.	ONE WEEK.
6. Absence without leave on Saturday.	SUSPENDED ON FOLLOWING MONDAY.
7. IMPORTANT. To obtain leave of absence, a written permit must be procured from the overlooker stating time for leaving, and length of absence desired, and this permit must be given	

Rules and penalties in the early Haxby Road days.

Cocoa Works Magazine

THE *Cocoa Works Magazine,* or *CWM,* to give it its proper name, was first published in March 1902 and the last issue was in May 1986. Over that time it provides a fascinating and detailed record of life at Rowntree from the board to the shop floor. Its subtitle was *A Journal in the Interest of the Employees of Rowntree & Co Ltd, York.* Its purpose in up to forty pages per issue was quite simply to provide a means of communication within the company to keep everyone informed about what was going on at all levels. Joseph Rowntree and his colleagues on the board could no longer maintain the personal, one to one communication he in particular had nurtured; there were just too many people now and *CWM* was seen as one way in which that the company could compensate for the loss of that personal touch. Joseph Rowntree says as much in his letter to D.S. Crichton in the inaugural issue, explaining the impossibility of keeping

The inaugural issue of CWM, *1902.*

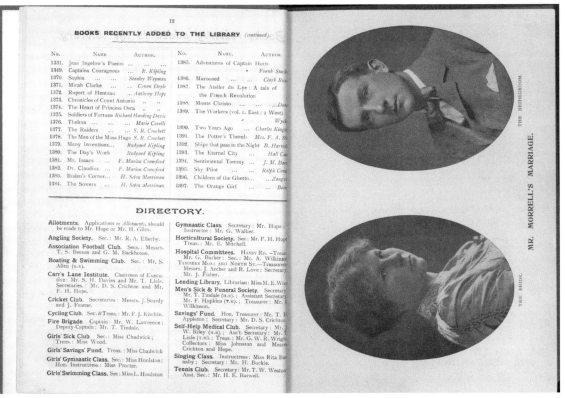

BOOKS RECENTLY ADDED TO THE LIBRARY *(continued).*

No.	NAME	AUTHOR.	No.	NAME.	AUTHOR.
1331.	Jean Ingelow's Poems		1385.	Adventures of Captain Horn	
1349.	Captains Courageous ...	*R. Kipling*			*Frank Stock...*
1370.	Sophia	*Stanley Weyman*	1386.	Marooned	*Clark Rus...*
1371.	Micah Clarke	*Conan Doyle*	1387.	The Atelier du Lys : A tale of	
1372.	Rupert of Hentzau	*...Anthony Hope*		the French Revolution	
1373.	Chronicles of Count Antonio	,, ,,	1388.	Monte Christo	*...Dun...*
1374.	The Heart of Princess Osra	,, ,,	1389.	The Workers (vol. 1. East ; 2 West)	
1375.	Soldiers of Fortune	*Richard Harding Davis*		,,	*Wyck...*
1376.	Thelma	*Marie Corelli*	1390.	Two Years Ago ...	*Charles Kings...*
1377.	The Raiders	*S. R. Crockett*	1391.	The Potter's Thumb	*Mrs. F. A. St...*
1378.	The Men of the Moss Hags	*S. R. Crockett*	1392.	Ships that pass in the Night	*B. Harrab...*
1379.	Many Inventions...	*Rudyard Kipling*	1393.	The Eternal City ...	*Hall Cai...*
1380.	The Day's Work	*Rudyard Kipling*	1394.	Sentimental Tommy ...	*J. M. Barr...*
1381.	Mr. Isaacs ...	*F. Marion Crawford*	1395.	Sky Pilot	*Ralph Conn...*
1382.	Dr. Claudius ...	*F. Marion Crawford*	1396.	Children of the Ghetto...	*...Zangwi...*
1383.	Roden's Corner...	*H. Seton Merriman*	1397.	The Orange Girl ...	*Bes...*
1384.	The Sowers ...	*H. Seton Merriman*			

DIRECTORY.

Allotments. Applications *re Allotments*, should be made to Mr. Hope or Mr. H. Giles.

Angling Society. Sec.: Mr. R. A. Ellerby.

Association Football Club. Secs.: Messrs. T. S. Beeson and G. M. Backhouse.

Boating & Swimming Club. Sec.: Mr. S. Allen (H.R.).

Carr's Lane Institute. Chairmen of Executive: Mr. S. H. Davies and Mr. T. Lisle. Secretaries.: Mr. D. S. Crichton and Mr. F. H. Hope.

Cricket Club. Secretaries : Messrs. J. Sturdy and J. Fearne.

Cycling Club. Sec. & Treas.: Mr. F. J. Kitchin.

Fire Brigade. Captain: Mr. W. Lawrence ; Deputy-Captain: Mr. T. Tindale.

Girls' Sick Club. Sec.: Miss Chadwick ; Treas.: Miss Wood.

Girls' Savings' Fund. Treas.: Miss Chadwick

Girls' Gymnastic Class. Sec.: Miss Houlston ; Hon. Instructress : Miss Procter.

Girls' Swimming Class. Sec.: Miss L. Houlston

Gymnastic Class. Secretary : Mr. Hope ; Instructor : Mr. G. Walker.

Horticultural Society. Sec.: Mr. F. H. Hope Treas.: Mr. E. Mitchell.

Hospital Committees. HAXBY RD. —Treas. Mr. G. Barker ; Sec.: Mr. A. Wilkinson TANNERS MOAT and NORTH ST.—Treasurers Messrs. J. Archer and R. Love ; Secretary Mr. J. Fisher.

Lending Library. Librarian: Miss M. E. Woo

Men's Sick & Funeral Society. Secretary Mr. T. Tindale (H.R.).; Assistant Secretary Mr. F. Hopkins (T.M.).; Treasurer : Mr. Wilkinson.

Savings' Fund. Hon. Treasurer : Mr. T. F Appleton ; Secretary : Mr. D. S. Crichton

Self-Help Medical Club. Secretary : Mr. W. Riley (H.R.).; Ass't. Secretary : Mr. Lisle (T.M.).; Treas.: Mr. G. W. R. Wright Collectors : Miss Johnston and Messr Crichton and Hope.

Singing Class. Instructress : Miss Rita Bu naby ; Secretary : Mr. H. Buckle.

Tennis Club. Secretary : Mr. T. W. Weston Asst. Sec.: Mr. H. E. Barwell.

THE BRIDEGROOM.

MR. MORRELL'S MARRIAGE.

THE BRIDE.

Pages from CWM *showing books recently added to the library; details about various clubs and the marriage of Mr and Mrs Morrell.*

up a personal acquaintance with the staff as fully as was the case in the earlier years, particularly as there were now three mills on different sites: Haxby Road, Tanner's Moat and North Street, and the company was becoming increasingly departmentalized with self-contained units.

Joseph wanted 'the entire body of workers to be animated by a common aim' and the magazine to be 'a periodical devoted to matters of common interest.' It also featured a suggestion scheme, unique at the time, for which prizes would be given for anything '*no matter how small*' that was adopted to improve 'manufacturing or packing goods, for improvement in the quality of goods; for quicker or more economical methods of manufacture, or of carrying on any work undertaken by the Firm; for improvements in machinery etc, for improvements in the conditions under which work is conducted; any other matters which affect the welfare of the Firm and of the Employees.'

In the inaugural issue Joseph Rowntree also draws attention to the new bowling green and rose garden, and takes the opportunity to warn 'some of the young people' not to allow their rooms (such as the men's new dining room) 'to get into a dirty and slatternly condition'; otherwise 'there is little inducement to add to what has already been done.'

The first *CWM* also featured an account of the explosion on the Royal Mail Steamer *Para* by John Wilhelm Rowntree when he and his wife had the misfortune to be on board the vessel which was bringing cocoa back from Trinidad and Granada: 'There was an appalling roar, a momentary flash followed by blinding darkness. Mrs R and myself found ourselves hurled into the air … ship's officers and crew behaved as Englishmen

The marriage of Mr and Mrs Lewis in Jamaica along with a native worker.

28

valley our view extends to the sea coast. There is no flat land on the whole estate.

Big slopes and undulating tracts, each 20 to 30 acres in extent have been cleared and planted, first with bananas then with cocoa.

The banana springs up quickly; its broad green leaves form an admirable shade for the young cocoa plants, which are planted in intermediate rows. After fifteen months a crop of bananas is obtained. When the fruit is cut, the whole plant is chopped down, one

of a huge American Fruit Trust, which ships millions of bunches annually to the States.

Every Monday, you may see the labourers at the Vinery, under Mr. Macdonald's supervision, loading up mules with the precious bunches, wrapped in dry leaves until little but the heads and tails of the animals can be seen. These pack mules convey the fruit to the coast road, whence it is carried to Annotto Bay in carts, joining the stream of traffic which sets in on steamer days.

MR. AND MRS. LEWIS.

A COCOA DRYING-TRAY.

Photos. by Mr. G. Thompson, Liverpool.

of the young suckers from the same root taking its place. Thus a yearly crop of bananas is obtained until the cocoa trees are fully grown and no longer require shade. The bananas are then rooted out, and thus an orchard of young cocoa trees is established.

Every Monday and Tuesday there is a ready sale of bananas at the coast towns, to the agents

There is much work to be done on the estate: we employ about one hundred men and women. In the early days, the forest has to be cleared. Then the cultivations must be frequently weeded and the ground forked if a good crop of bananas is desired. Two hundred acres of land have been cleared and planted within the last two years.

should ... the captain, while in the air, shouted for the Fire Brigade.' The explosion was caused by an experimental shipment of bananas. One of the parties on board was attempting to see if, by extracting oxygen from the containers holding the bananas, deterioration could be avoided or minimized. The result was catastrophic with three dead and others injured, one of whom was 'in delirium'.

Issue 1 included a list of new books added to the staff library which now contained 1,200 volumes, 400 of which were in circulation at any one time. The librarian, Mr M.E.Woods added some book reviews. *Garden Notes* were provided by Roughway; news was given of the progress of the Hospital Fund, the Savings Fund, the Sick Benefit Club and the Medical Aid Society, along with financials. Reports were published from the Singing Class (thirty members); the Angling Club (forty members); the Bowling Club (recruiting) and the Football team which had reached the semi-final of the Faber Cup and still were in with a chance of winning the York and District League.

A touching moment in "Quality Street" by the Actors' Club

THE ROWNTREE PLAYERS

By the time the magazine appears, "La Vie Parisienne" will have run its course and have brought to a successful conclusion the very long and arduous preparation for it. For months beforehand the thirty members of the caste and chorus had been hard at work under the direction of E. Mitchell Learmonth. All this hard work has its compensating side in the comradeship which it develops as well as the educational value of the rehearsals. All those who take part in the Rowntree Players' productions will tell you how much they enjoy their work.

Next year we are going out for an increase in the number of paying members, but we want also a large increase in the number of playing members. The wonderful reception of our play, "And So To Bed," shows that we can put on the play and get the audiences. This particular play was hailed as the best amateur production of the season, so we hope that all employees who are interested in amateur productions will join up next season.

Miss Doreen Pearson, age 18, daughter of Mr. F. W. Pearson, Traffic Department, was successful in a recent public speaking competition held in Leeds under the auspices of the Electrical Development Association. She gained the 1st Prize of £5 and a Certificate.

THE SWIMMING CLUB

The Swimming Club will renew its Summer activities soon now, and the programme promises to be a full one. Hull and York Police have been invited to send teams to compete with the Rowntree Club on June 1st, and we are anxious to be in good training for them. It is hoped to be able to send teams to London again to take part in the Confectionery and Allied Trades' Swimming Sports in September, and there is a new section this year for sons of members.

Members will be glad to learn that Mr. Peter Rowntree (President of the Club) was elected president of the new York and District Amateur Swimming Association. Mr. W. Lockhart was elected vice-chairman and Mr. C. Southwood, hon. secretary. The following clubs have already joined the Association:—City Police, L.N.E.R., Rowntree's, Terry's, York City.

Mr. R. A. Castle (Transport Dept.), who is leaving York to take up the post of Depot Manager in Southampton.

The Boys' Page

The Annual Camp

We have again booked last year's site at Bridlington for our Annual Camp and are anticipating another enjoyable holiday.

Some Good News for Campers

The question of camp fees has been very carefully considered, and it has been decided that for this year the cost to each lad will be reduced by 5/-. This can only be made possible by a larger number of lads joining the camp, and 120 to 150 are required. We want every one of you at the Works to think carefully about his holiday this year and then give your name to Mr. J. Greatorex, Boys' Gymnasium, if you decide on a camping holiday at Bridlington. A reduction of 5/- is quite a substantial one and the fees will now be:—

					s.	d.
Lads 14 years and under 15	on July 1st		20	0
,, 15	,,	16	,,	22	6
,, 16	,,	17	,,	25	0
,, 17	,,	18	,,	27	6
,, 18	,,	19	,,	30	0

This fee includes railway fare, board and lodgings for a whole week.

From now to the annual holiday, there are just fourteen weeks and the best way to save up is to put a small amount in the Boys' bank each week.

You will, of course, need a little pocket money at camp, so that if you could spare another 6d. per week, you would have 7/- to jingle in your pocket.

Last year, quite a number of letters were written home containing an S.O.S. for pocket money. This year we want to avoid this, so put every available penny into the Boys' Bank each week and you'll then have enough to see you through the holiday. Mr. Greatorex has the bank-book ready; his fountain pen is filled, and money can be deposited any time.

Now lads, come along with us to camp and have a week of laughter, fun and frolic.

Here is the menu for one day at camp:—

Breakfast	Porridge, Eggs and Bacon, Bread and Butter, Jam, Tea.
Dinner ..	Roast Beef, Potatoes and Peas ; Plum Pudding and Custard.
Tea ..	Hot Fish and Potatoes, Bread and Butter, Cake, Jam, Tea.
Supper ..	Cocoa or Tea, Stew, Potatoes, Bread and Butter and Jam.

Some lads like camping every week-end as soon as the weather permits the usual week-end camps at Poppleton are being arranged. The "all-in" cost from Friday evening until Sunday afternoon is only 3/6d., and there's room for thirty lads. Several lads have already given in their names for the first week, so book up without delay.

The 1938 Motto is—"COME ALONG."

Mark Twain said that when he was a boy of fourteen his father was so ignorant he could hardly stand to have the old man around ; but when he got to be twenty-one he was astonished at how much the old man had learned in seven years.

The "A" and "B" Football teams which have done so well in the York Minor League

---

A Rowntrees Players production reviewed in CWM.

We are reminded that Miss Wood engages girls every Tuesday and Friday at 10.00 am at Tanner's Moat, while Mr Crichton does likewise for boys on Mondays and Thursdays at 9.30 am. The girls' Gymnastic Class is 7.30pm every Monday evening and members 'are expected to wear a very becoming costume of dark blue and red, about 5 shillings … any overstrain is carefully guarded against.' At the Dressmaking Class the penny fee per night 'is paid whether the member is present or not.' Commons sketches also featured.

Issue 2 finds Roughway describing how to cultivate kale, mint and gladiolus; births, deaths and marriages are introduced – the most high profile of the marriages being that between J.B. Morrell and Bertha Spence Watson. Presents to Mr Morrell included *Green's Short History of the English People*, *Grote's History of Greece* and Gibbon's *Decline and Fall of the Roman Empire*. *An Ostrich Story* was written for the children, and the Fur and Feather Society, and the Boating and Swimming Society both reported.

The third issue had an article on the Rowntree-owned Jamaica Cocoa Curing Station at Dover, Jamaica, with a photograph of Mr Lewis (second in charge at Dover) with his bride, the daughter of Mr Supersangsingh, owner of the Dover estate. There was 'much music and jollity' at the wedding. *Cookery Notes* included recipes for milk soup, hot pot and feather buns. In the next issue the focus was on 'Invalid Cooking' with advice on beef tea to the effect that 'the most juicy and inferior parts of the buttock yield the richest tea, not the leg or shins.' Other recipes for the invalid included beef

Visitors from Siberia.

1705   **"THE C.W.M."**

The Camera Club.

Taking advantage of the Works' Holiday, our members spent the morning of Saturday, June 27th, in visiting the Museum Gardens and Ruins of St. Mary's Abbey. Although our numbers were small, we spent a most interesting and enjoyable time. Many plates were exposed on various portions of the ruins and surroundings, and incidentally we understand with good results, which we hope to have the pleasure of seeing later in competition and at our Exhibition.

The competition for the month will be for the best picture of St. Mary's Abbey, which may include negatives taken during the above visit or from any taken by members at any other time.

Subscriptions for 1914 are now due, and the Secretary is ready to receive same at any time.

P.D.

THE SIBERIAN DELEGATES AT THE WORKS.   *Photo by P. Davy.*

Our Visitors from Siberia.

We have many visitors at the Cocoa Works, and they come from many climes, but the party of Siberian peasant farmers, to whom Mr. Joseph Rowntree gave a cordial welcome on July 2nd, came from a quarter of the globe which, we believe, has not previously been represented. The members of the party were delegates from the Union of Siberian Co-operative Associations, in connection with which are 850 butter-making associations and 640 consuming shops. The Association last year exported 40,000 tons of butter in addition to considerable quantities of bacon, eggs and cheese. The delegates, some of whom had seen the sea for the first time on their journey to England, had come to find out if the British farmers could give them any valuable hints on co-operative farming, etc. We do not know that their visit to York added greatly to their knowledge in this respect, but they were evidently very much pleased with what they saw both at the Cocoa Works and at New Earswick. Unfortunately the heavy rain interfered with their inspection of New Earswick, but they found shelter in the village school, and were greatly interested in the work

jelly and canary pudding. The Girls Temperance Society and the Drum and Fife Band both made their first appearances; small ads for items for sale and exchange started, and information was given on the company holidays for the year.

In 1910 Captain Robert Falcon Scott visited nearby Bootham School to give a talk prior to the ill-fated British Antarctic Expedition's 1910 attempt at the South Pole. This was reported in *CWM* along with an announcement that a fund had been established to pay for a Rowntree sledge for the expedition.

In April 1914 the 'very dangerous practice of wearing unprotected hat-pins' was highlighted: 'In January during the first few days, one girl has had her eye pierced, another her eye badly scratched … since then 14 accidents have happened in the clock room and corridors through unguarded pins'. Hat pin protectors were made available

A typical view of Joe Dickinson's wonderful Rowntree museum showing Mr York at the bottom, the fine, original cabinet to the left and the famous 1896 Beggarstaff posters on the right.

for sale at 1d each. Later, in June that year, there was a report on the visit from Siberia of a group of peasant farmers – delegates from the Union of Siberian Co-operative Association representing 550 butter-making associations and 640 butter-buying shops – between them responsible for 40,000 tons of Russian butter exports. Dr Tchaykovsky was in charge and was the interpreter. The final issue of the year reports Sir Robert Baden Powell's visit to the works, and publishes his morale-boosting message. During the First World War casualty reports became a sad but regular feature; perhaps the most high profile of these was the death of L.E. Rowntree, son of John Wilhelm, reported in the December 1917 issue.

The Easter 1938 issue – just over a year before the Second World War breaks out – announces a company holiday to the Rhineland and Black Forest – fourteen nights at £12.10s per head. Two issues later we learn that it was a great success in every respect and that 'the friendship we met with everywhere will be our most lasting impression.' That same year we read that the Actor's Club put on a production of *Quality Street*. Little did they, or the audiences know that around thirty years later some of them and their successors would be part of the company which produced and sold the famous assortment named after J.M.Barrie's play.

During the war *CWM* became more sporadic, smaller, and reduced to six pages on account of paper shortages. A suitably sombre note was introduced in the Summer 1939 issue with a specially-commissioned article, *How British Policy has Changed* by Sir Ralph Norman Angell, Labour MP, Nobel Peace Prize Winner, and executive for the World Committee against War and Fascism. From that issue on until the end of the war, the

"THE FALLEN."

"THE FALLEN."

Sergeant R. Vause (Melangeur). Killed by explosion of shell, Oct. 29th, 1915.

Pte. W. N. Young (Offices). Killed, Oct. 11th, 1915.

Pte. D. McNichol (Gum). Killed, Nov. 18th, 1915.

Pte. G. H. Foster (Melangeur). Killed at Hulluch, Sept. 25th, 1915.

Pte. J. Allen (Melangeur). Killed, June 15th, 1915.

Pte. H. Wilcock (Cream). Killed, August 20th, 1915.

Pte. L. Lea (Gum). Died of Dysentery, Nov. 7th, 1915.

Pte. J. T. Nelson (Saw Mill). Died in Hospital.

The ongoing toll of the First World War.

News from the Front and a much travelled card in CWM.

thoughts by informing you that our dug-outs are fitted up with beds (wood and trellis work), tables, chairs, mirrors, lamps and stoves. In fact we are living in greater luxury than when in England, and, of course, the food supply is perfect. I have been in the trenches and seen the German lines, but a modern battlefield is not a sight for an artist.

I was nearly satisfied that the R.F.A. was the best regiment, but now I am perfectly satisfied. The best part of the job is when you are ordered " Battery fire, one second." Then all our guns " plonk " the Germans with one second interval between shots. Most of the villages around here have been nearly demolished by shell fire. It is a great thing for us that water separates us from the Continent.

The Germans, to-day, made a gas attack on the division on our left, which we were expecting too, but probably they know who we are, at any rate, the gas attack did not come off on our front.

There is a good deal of aerial activity on our front, but our aviators are the most daring. I have not much doubt about the issue of the war, for, although we are not moving the Germans now, when the summer comes I think we can, with a little sacrifice, get them on the run.

W. NICHOLSON (Engineers).

ANOTHER CHEERY EPISTLE FROM " DARKIE " SULLENS.

I hope you will excuse my writing as I am in a barn and I can't find nothing handy to write on just now so I am writing these few lines the best I can. I am laid flat on my stomach that's how we have to do when the shells are spreading over us. Well that tin of Rowntree's Elect came in handy. I was in a horse box one night and 2 days and we only had our water bottles full of cold water and when we got to some station we pulled up to water our poor horses I said to my mate " You water my horses and I will nip and get a drop of boiling water as I have a tin of Rowntree's Elect Cocoa "; he said " What about the sugar ? " I said to him " Rowntree's Elect Cocoa is always handy ain't it old chum." So I made two water bottles full and almost all the troop asked me for a drink of Elect Cocoa that's how it came in so very handy. New Year's Day the postman shouted out " Darkie Sullens some more Rowntree's chocolate for you hurry up and get the

parcel opened out." So I did and even the sergeants came around and had some as well and they all said it was the best chocolate and cocoa they had ever tasted in all their life. I always know when I have a parcel from the old firm on it is labelled Rowntree. Well I hope you will excuse my writing as my stomach aches laying here in this old barn and my water bottle is not a very good writing desk. I thank you one and all for my famous Christmas present but I got it on New Year's Day. May God bless you one and all roll on when the war is over, then we will come back again some day.

From DARKIE SULLENS (Estate).

ADVICE TO RECRUITS.

I have been very busy studying for a musketry examination, and have had very little time for writing. You may, perhaps, be rather surprised to hear of a soldier studying, but I am at the present time an assistant instructor in musketry, and my job is to train raw recruits to use a rifle as it should be used. I had no idea when I joined the army that I should have so much " swotting " to do, but I have found that in the army, as in civil life, to get on means work and very much work.

We are experiencing wretched weather just now, and the camp is a foot deep in mud. We live in mud ; to get our meals we have to wade through slush, our drill is more mud drill than platoon drill, and we go to rest with muddy boards a few inches below our noses. However, we manage to keep cheerful, although it is a bit trying when, after having polished your buttons and cleaned your equipment and rifle, you side-slip in a patch of muck and glide a couple of yards on your face.

I don't know if you have heard of Clipstone Camp before, but it is a fairly large camp, just outside Mansfield. The life is vastly different from that on the Lincolnshire Coast, where we were billeted in barns, sheds, etc., and had all our food cooked on field kitchens. Here we sport the luxury of a large cookhouse for each regiment, and our homes are wooden huts, warmed by stoves and lit by electricity. In Clipstone, also, we eat our food on plates and use knives and forks, whilst in Lincs. we often had to get through our meals à la savage. Can you imagine a clerk at the Cocoa Works at his breakfast of dry bread and bacon, holding a lump of fat bacon in one hand and an inch-thick

piece of bread in the other, taking alternate bites ? We drank our tea out of all sorts of utensils, mine being an empty 2-lb. jam jar.

COLIN CARTER (Offices).

FROM THE FRONT LINE OF TRENCHES.

I am afraid that we who are on active service are apt to forget, for the time being, the services those at home who are unable to take up the rifle and bayonet for various reasons are also rendering, but I do believe that in whatever

The Cocoa Works, York. November, 1915.

The girls have assembled to send their greetings to you!

We all join with them wishing you good health and the best of fortune.

To [...] S. CRICHTON HORNER.

In case of non-delivery please return to Rowntree & Co., York.

POST CARD

THE ADDRESS TO BE WRITTEN HERE

A MUCH-TRAVELLED CARD.

Memo. to our Boys in Khaki.—Don't forget to keep us posted with every change of address.

particular branch one is serving, we are all doing our best to bring this terrible war to an early conclusion. Well, this is somewhat different to being on leave in peaceful old York. We are having another turn in the front line, and my duty takes me up and down our particular sector several times during the day and night, and the thing that strikes me most is that knowing there are thousands of troops in the vicinity, we only see a few men dotted about in the trenches. We look over the parapet and occasionally see one of the enemy, who are only from 15 to 40 yards away, trying to improve his trench by throwing the mud out. Suddenly

a small shell just skims over our heads and knocks the enemy's parapet down. Exit Fritz !

Of course, we have a fair amount of water and mud to contend with, but, fortunately, we hold the high ground here, and we simply drain our trenches towards the Hun. Our lads say, " If he won't fight, we'll drown him."

(The following extracts are taken from a series of interesting letters written from the trenches by 2nd-Lieut. W. Tatham, of the 13th Cheshire Regt., who is one of the Firm's travellers.]

The weather hasn't improved, and in the trenches we are really having a terrible time. Unfortunately, as it is my duty as platoon commander to lead my platoon into the trenches allotted to us, I have each time had the bad luck to fall into waist-deep water, and the last time I went into a sump hole, goodness knows how deep, and I had to swim for it, so that gives some idea as to the state the trenches are in. Pumps are kept going day and night, but they don't seem to be very effective. The river Lys

Rowntree's Cycling Club assembling in Wigginton Road.

pages of *CWM* featured listings of employees on military or national service, news from Rowntree workers serving overseas, and letters from prisoners of war. As with issues published in the First World War, these were soon complemented by lists of the firm's casualties and those servicemen reported missing.

CWM was succeeded in 1986 by *RM News* after the merger with Mackintosh; this in turn was replaced by *Nestlé Group News* in 1992 on the arrival of Nestlé.

Some avid note-taking at a Rowntree Junior Induction Course in 1969.

An impressive range of Rowntree products from 1969.

Rowntree: 1901–1914

THE BIG challenge in the late 1890s and in early years of the Twentieth Century was to break the dominance of the foreign manufacturers operating in the UK, not just in the essence market but also in the increasingly popular milk chocolate market. Van Houten had set up sales agencies in London, Leeds, Liverpool, Edinburgh, Glasgow and Dublin for its alkalised essence, and Cailler was the leader in milk chocolate. French gums were still being imported on a large scale and the French were still the biggest sellers of chocolate assortments or creams. We have seen how Cadbury's Dairy Milk started to make inroads on Cailler's, Nestlé's and Lindt's market share from 1906, but Rowntree never really competed in this increasingly lucrative market; their first attempt at a milk chocolate block, Swiss Milk Chocolate, in 1899, failed, largely on account of the fact that it used powdered milk rather than condensed milk in the best Swiss style. Another factor may well have been Joseph Rowntree's misguided belief that the 'rage' for milk chocolate may be little more than 'a passing phase.' The Swiss hold on the market tightened even more in 1904 when Nestlé started importing milk chocolate made by Kohler and Cailler.

Rowntrees did, nevertheless, see the real need to ratchet up their sales efforts. After consulting Reckitt's – the Quaker chemical company based in Hull – a sales manager, J. Bromilow, was appointed in 1892 and the important Co-operative accounts were made the responsibility of one traveller, a Mr S. Cartwright. Between 1890 and 1897 the sales force grew from fourteen to thirty three, largely under the management of John Wilhelm and his cousin, Arnold Stephenson Rowntree. In 1901 Rowntree's launched their famous and enduring line of jellies.

Product development remained decidedly haphazard with approval based largely on tastings held at Directors' Conferences. The number of lines just kept increasing with no significant successes anywhere to be seen. Further attempts at milk chocolate were made from 1904 to 1910 but Mountain Milk Chocolate, Alpine Milk Chocolate (a copy of a Cailler brand) and Malted Milk Chocolate all failed. Bulgarian Soured Milk Chocolates were developed to cash in on the fashion for chocolates containing supposedly life extending microbes. These were much in demand from apothecaries as well as confectioners.

A pension scheme for the 4,000 workers was set up in 1905 and signalled another example of enlightened social vision and progressive industrial relations. Joseph knew that poverty in old age was a major problem and a reliable pension was one wasy of limiting this. Workers over the age of twenty-one contributed between two and five per cent of their pay with the company paying seventy-five percent of contributions for men and eighty percent for women (forty-seven percent of the work force). Sickness benefit was also paid for the first thirteen weeks of illness. The Company put in a lump sum of £9,000 with Joseph Rowntree contributing a further £10,000 of his own money. Employees nearing the end of their working lives were also accommodated so that they too benefitted in equal measure; the initial investments allowed the scheme to proceed on a profitable basis from the start. It later also provided for widows whose husbands had been killed in action in the First World War. A fund had been started in 1911 to compensate widows with £50 on the death of their husbands; this was doubled in later years. The Widows Benefit Fund was established during the war to allow a pension to widows aged fifty or over (later changed to forty-five) on the death of the husband. Joseph Rowntree was determined to see these measures through, as can be seen from the minutes of a 1917 Board Meeting: 'I am so much impressed with the need and value to our people of the proposed arrangement that I ask the Board to accept the principle before discussing the cost.' Counter-intuitive as it was to the financially meticulous Joseph, it demonstrates very clearly to us, as it must have to the Board that day, just how fervently he believed in this benefit. His fervour even led to a battle with the Inspector of Taxes who had claimed that the firm's contribution was not allowable as a business expense, Joseph won.

A later example of concern for the welfare of retirees was the opening in 1946 of the Dunollie convalescent home in Scarborough where employees might go to enjoy the revivifying sea air in what was twenty-five-bedroom home by the sea. Its popularity can be measured by the fact that it had had 4,000 visitors by 1955. The City of York benefitted from Rowntree's sense of civic responsibility and philanthropy in 1909 when

Traveller with van ready to go...

the Yearsley Road swimming baths next to the Haxby Road factory were donated to the people of York. Rowntree Park was given to York by Rowntree in 1921, at the end of the First World War, as a memorial to the company's staff who lost their lives or suffered during the War. The Park was York's first municipal park. A set of listed gates were added to the park in memory of those who fell in the Second World War. Bronze plaques mark both occasions within the Lych Gate. Situated, somewhat ironically, on Terry Avenue, on the banks of the River Ouse, the thirty-acre park has recently benefitted from a £1.8 million refurbishment restoring it to its original splendour.

A profit-sharing scheme had been mooted in 1907 but, due to the almost universal opposition within and without Rowntrees, it was shelved until 1916. Then, after much research, the ground was laid for a scheme which finally started in 1923 and which, by any standard, was immensely popular; although payouts were minimal up until 1938, between 1943 and 1953 around £1.5m was distributed. As at Cadbury's, Works Councils were set up to give employees a voice in the running of the company. The councils – one for women, another for men – comprised equal numbers of administrative staff appointed by management, and shop floor workers nominated by themselves through ballot. Again, Rowntree anticipated the government, in this case the Whitley Committee, which recommended that such committees be set up industry wide. One of the ways in which the Councils were effective was when they were invited in 1919 to participate in a revision of 'Works Rules' and a longer five-day weekday was introduced in lieu of Saturday morning working. A week's paid holiday was granted every year from 1918, the latter anticipating the Act of Parliament which made this statutory for all workers by some nineteen years. In 1921 the Appeals Committee was set up, the first impartial industrial tribunal in the UK. In effect, this allowed workers the right of appeal against allegedly unjust disciplinary action or punishment for breaking Works rules; the employee could have his or her case heard before the Committee – made up of two workers and two members appointed by the directors with a chairman voted for by the other four. Of the thirty-one cases heard between 1921 and 1938, fifteen involved theft, ten of which failed. Of the others, four had their penalties reduced and one had all charges dismissed. There were sixteen other appeals involving management decisions: seven were upheld, three had a penalty reduction and six found in favour of the appellant. Justice was being done and, in the cases here, seven lives were saved from being wrongly blighted. From 1923, workers were also given a say in who was to be their foreman or forewoman, approving or disapproving the management nomination and suggesting an alternative where they disapproved. Although the Company reserved the right to have the casting vote if no outright decision could be made, by 1938, according to Seebohm Rowntree, they never once had to exercise that right.

Another pioneering innovation successfully designed to improve communication was what we would today call the Company Meeting. Every year after the customary address to the shareholders, another meeting would be convened which was attended by all the workers. This would comprise a detailed survey of the year's developments, changes and results.

On the social side, numerous clubs sprang up covering all manner of sport, culture and entertainment, from cricket to singing, from angling to photography, from literature to tennis.

In 1904 Rowntree's emulated Cadbury's once more when they appointed a company doctor to provide free medical care. Dr Peter Macdonald, who had married Agnes,

A busy day at Yearsley; before these baths were opened swimming was in the adjacent River Foss, open air and for men only, as many of the poorer men swam naked. The river bed was concreted over for about 100 yards.

Men and women's tennis for Rowntree staff around 1910.

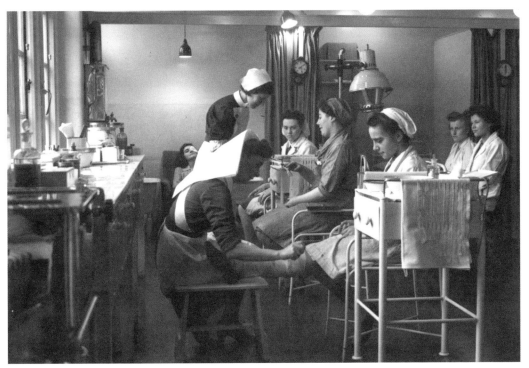

A busy day in the female session at the Rowntree medical department.

The world famous Shackleton cocoa tin and...

the label for the tin.

Joseph's elder daughter, was the first to hold the post. One of MacDonald's first observations was that much of the staff's ill health was caused, or exacerbated by, poor dental health, and so it was that a staff dentist was duly appointed. Joseph Rowntree justified these important steps as follows: 'Healthful conditions of labour are not luxuries to be adopted or dispensed with at will; they are conditions necessary for success. In keen international competition the vigour and intelligence of the workmen are likely to be determining factor.' An optician was appointed in 1919 followed by a female doctor in 1925.

Concerned for the girls who spent most of their waking hours in his factory with little time left to prepare themselves for later life, Rowntree set up a domestic school staffed with teachers to train all girls joining the firm before they were seventeen, in household management and cookery – two hours per week, paid. It was justified as follows in the *Cocoa Works Magazine:* 'The contention that factory life unfits a girl for home duties by allowing her neither time nor opportunity for learning what is necessary for the management of a home.' For boys, Swedish physical education began in 1907, as well as classes in mathematics, woodwork and English.

Sir Joseph Rowntree at Scarborough.

On the sales and marketing front, things were slowly starting to change. By 1906, forty men were working in the advertising department and there were eighty-five or so commercial salesmen.

In 1905 John Wilhelm died in New York from pneumonia and a kidney infection; this was after a long period of increasing illness which removed him from the centre of the company's activities. The sad irony of this lay in the fact that he was in New York to consult an ophthalmologist about his failing eyesight, a further disability to add to his lifelong deafness. His brothers Joseph Stephenson and Oscar joined the board soon after.

In 1911 the City of York conferred on Joseph Rowntree a rare honour – Honorary Freeman of the City. Since 1746, only twenty-three others had been made Honorary Freemen. The Very Reverend Dean Pury-Cust, who was similarly honoured on the same day, summed up Joseph's, and Rowntree's, contribution to York and its confectionery industry, saying he 'had done so much to promote the commercial prosperity of the city, and whose efforts to advance the welfare of all classes are recognised and appreciated by us all.'

Two fascinating Rowntree exhibits from the early Twentieth Century can be seen in the Castle Museum in York. The first is an advertisement for Elect in the form of a smirking red cat with a green bow-tie covered in Rowntree 'R's. The second is a Rowntree's cocoa tin which Ernest Shackleton took to the Antarctic with him on his 1908–1909 *Nimrod* expedition. Unused, it was brought back to England with other supplies when Shackleton and three colleagues got within ninety-seven miles of the South Pole before turning back.

The cocoa tin was donated to the museum by a woman from Sydenham who had been given the tin by one of Shackleton's sisters. The handwritten label on the tin reads, 'This tin of cocoa is one of the unused stores brought back by Sir Ernest Shackleton's expedition from the Antarctic.' It was privileged to have been chosen as one of the top museum objects from the North Yorkshire region as part of the BBC's *History of the World* project.

New Earswick

THE CROWNING achievement of Joseph Rowntree's pragmatism and sense of social justice lay in the social experiment that was New Earswick. In 1904 Rowntree emulated the Cadburys by establishing a series of Trusts: the Social Service Trust, the Charitable Trust and the Village Trust. The beneficiary of this last was the building of New Earswick at the turn of the century. The first two were concerned with supporting social research and surveys, adult education and work connected with the Quakers – in effect ensuring the continuation of the work which Joseph had spent much of his life on so far. In acting thus, Joseph Rowntree handed over half of his own fortune by giving the Trusts almost fifty-two-and-a half-per cent of voting shares in his company.

Packing for the 1952 Himalaya Expedition to Cho Oyu organised by the Joint Himalayan Committee of the Alpine Club and the Royal Geographical Society. Cho Oyu is the world's sixth highest mountain.

Early plans for New Earswick.

Poverty around Hungate in York at the end of the Nineteenth Century.

1 and 2. Residential roads in New Earswick, the Rowntree village near York.   3. Norton Way South, a Letchworth thoroughfare.   4 and 5. Factories in Letchworth.   6. A road in Bournville.   7. The shopping centre of Letchworth. 8. A corner in Hampstead Garden Suburb

GARDEN CITY: TRIUMPHS OF MODERN TOWN PLANNING IN BRITAIN
By courtesy of The Garden Cities and Town Planning Assoc.

New Earswick and other model villages – Letchworth, Bournville and Hampstead Garden Suburb.

The objective of the Village Trust was to provide the worker on a wage of about twenty-five shillings per week with a new type of house that was 'artistic in appearance', was clean, sanitary, and solidly built. In other words, a place to live which was not a slum.

Rowntree's deep concern for the welfare of his workers, the research findings and solutions proposed by Seebohm into local poverty and the plight of the urban poor, in his ground-breaking and influential *Poverty: A Study of Town Life,* his own Quaker beliefs, Cadbury's achievements at Bournville, and the pioneering work on garden cities by Ebenezer Howard, manifested later in Letchworth in 1903, Saltaire – Titus Salt's model village, aspects of William Lever's Port Sunlight – all combined to see the establishment of New Earswick just north of the city of York, and minutes away from the Haxby Road factory. By 1924 the population of News Earswick was about 2,000; 850 of these people worked for Rowntree.

There was a variety of houses: some were in groups of seven with an access passage between the third and fourth houses. They cost £318 7s 11d to build; rent was 6s 3d per week. The architect was Raymond Unwin whose brief from the Trust was nothing if not challenging: to provide high quality housing at affordable rents with adequate living space within restricted floor space. The building programme was as follows: 1902 – 123 houses; 1902–1904 – 28; 1904–1919 – 229; 1919–1936 – 259. Total spend on land, houses and services was £450,000.

To meet his brief, Unwin used some of the indoor floor space as a bicycle and coal store, obviating the need for outhouses and thus reducing costs and allowing upstairs space for a third bedroom. The toilet was downstairs and the bath was in the kitchen under a hinged table flap. A black range was in the living room with a pantry. The first

The range in a typical New Earswick house.

houses had earth closets which were replaced in 1906 with a water system. By 1948 ninety-three per cent of the 530 houses had three bedrooms; one had two and the rest four or five. Separate bathrooms came in thirty new houses built in 1954. The houses did not all front on to the street, as the living room was always situated to capture maximum sunlight, and so very often looked out to the back. Floors in New Earswick were typically linoleum and red quarry tiles; taps and door knobs were all brass. Also, the twelve bungalows for older residents featured a large room which could be used as a living room/bedroom or as two separate rooms (with obvious social advantages and financial benefits on heating costs). In addition, they were fitted with alarm bells connected to a qualified nurses' rent-free residence for emergencies. When the television age dawned, New Earswick was one of the very few places in Britain where roof television aerials were banned, on the grounds that they were not aesthetically pleasing. Instead, they were installed in the lofts. All evidence that, socially and environmentally, New Earswick was years ahead of its time.

As in Bournville, there were shops for the residents: in the 1930s these included Howard's haberdashery, Mrs Farrell's sweet shop, Ernie Wood's chemist, Fred Wiley the cobbler, the Co-op butchers, Burrell's bakers and Coning's wet fish shop. The houses in Chestnut Avenue were built in 1917 in blocks of four with a central passageway for access. Chestnut Avenue, then and now epitomized the ethos of the village: tree lined virtually traffic-free avenues which were, and are, pleasant to live and play in. The cost to build was £309. 15s 7d, and rent was 6s per week if the bath was in the scullery; if it was upstairs it was 6s 8d. Later, Nurse Atkinson lived in nearby Rowan Avenue. She was the village District Nurse and midwife from 1944 until her retirement in 1969, during

The parade of shops at New Earswick. The balconies have since been removed.

which time she estimates that she delivered about one thousand babies. Dr Riddols was the village doctor and President of the Nursing Association, and one of his duties was to collect the 2d per week from residents to pay for Nurse Atkinson.

White Rose Dairy opened in 1904 and was the inspiration of Seebohm Rowntree who established the dairy to ensure the provision of clean milk to village residents in the knowledge that contaminated milk was a major factor in the generally high infant mortality rate. To do this he brought in a Dane, Wilfred Sorensen, (known locally and geographically inaccurately as Oslo), from the Manchester Pure Milk Co and bought some land for him to build a farm on and to develop a herd. For the time, unusually high levels of hygiene were adopted and the milk was filtered and cooled to destroy bacteria.

The Folk Hall was the centre of New Earswick's busy social life and one of its prime purposes was to offer societies and clubs a place in which to run activities reflecting the interests of the residents. It was built in 1907 at a cost of £2,278 15s 1½d. Joseph Rowntree actively encouraged women to get out of the home and use the many facilities offered there: 'In this country it seems to be the thought that women do not need recreation' he pondered, citing the example of Germany where it was and still is today the norm for families to go out together as families, with the children. During World War I, the hall was used to offer hospitality to Belgian refugees. The village library was here from 1908 with the first 100 books donated by Joseph Rowntree. Of course, one of the other main functions of the Hall was as a place of worship – for all faiths. However, over time a separate Wesleyan Chapel and a place for Anglican worship were established while the Society of Friends and Roman Catholics continued to use the Hall. It was given Meeting status for the Quakers in 1917; a Sunday school followed in 1918. From 1945 it was home to the village nursery until its move to the primary school in 1997. At its opening, there were thirty children between the ages of two and five, each paying 1s per week, mornings only.

New Earswick's Folk Hall – the centre of social and religious life, as it is to this day.

The New Earswick Musical Society was a regular user of the hall. The society was founded in 1914 (out of the 1912 Choral Society) as the New Earswick Dramatic Society, and ninety-seven years later still performs two shows every year, now in the Joseph Rowntree Theatre in Haxby Road. In 1933 the Society had 260 active members and performed a staggering twenty-four productions – Gilbert and Sullivan plays and operas – one every two weeks. Recent repertoires are much more diverse and have included *The Railway Children, High Society, Oliver* and *Hello, Dolly!* In 1935 the success of the society helped drive through a new hall with seating for 450, a well lit stage and dressing rooms. Seebohm Rowntree's opening speech revealed the wide range of societies and organisations using the Hall: the Library Committee, the Women's Guild, the Orchestral Society, the Dramatic Society, the Village Council, the Rose Carnival, the Children's Welfare Centre, the Musical Society and the Men's Social Club, as well as all the sports societies.

The first football club was formed in 1912, soon followed by the cricket club. Initially, both played on the green opposite the shops in Hawthorne Terrace, but Westfield Beck proved a hazard and the shop windows provided too tempting target practice for the batsmen. So, from 1923, both teams were able to play on pitches on the newly developed sixteen-acre sports fields. There were also tennis courts and a bowling green and a sports pavilion. In the late 1940s the Hall took 1,075 lettings in one year bringing in £710 with highly profitable Saturday night dances proving particularly popular. The many adult education courses espoused by the Rowntrees took place at the Folk Hall.

In developing New Earswick, Joseph Rowntree was heavily influenced by Ebenezer Howard's (1850–1928) vision of a kind of utopian city where citizens lived in harmony

A 1930s New Earswick Musical Society production.

A 2010 NEMS production of Sugar, *adapted from* Some Like it Hot.

with nature, as expounded in his 1898 *Tomorrow: A Peaceful Path to Real Reform*, (retitled *Garden Cities of Tomorrow* in 1902.) Howard's towns were to be slum free and largely managed and financed by the residents who had a financial interest. They combined the best of town and country life. Equal opportunity, good wages, entertainment, low rents, beauty, fresh air were the aim. We can recognise some of these elements in Joseph Rowntree's New Earswick.

The first 'school' was in the Folk Hall, set up in 1909 for twenty-five infants. The first permanent school was built in 1912 for 352 five to fourteen-year-olds to save them the trek to Haxby Road School about a mile-and-a-half away; the school (the 'Open Air School') was another model of enlightenment: boys and girls were taught the same subjects (science teaching was usually the preserve of boys) and all the full length windows faced south, opened to an extent of eighteen feet and were at head level to maximise natural daylight. Each child had a notional fifteen square feet of floor area which meant ample space in between desks – fifty per cent more than was stipulated by the Board of Education then. Class sizes were limited to thirty pupils, although at the time in York, classes of between fifty and sixty were not uncommon. As the authorities could not be reasonably expected to make exceptions in the case of New Earswick, the Trustees paid for an extra teacher, later increasing to three. The importance of attracting good teachers was never underestimated, probably a result of the Rowntree family's own experience of teaching in the York Adult Schools: 'The most potent influence will no

The White Rose Dairy.

doubt come from the teachers, this will make itself felt in many ways. New Earswick School is coeducational throughout, sewing and cooking will not be neglected for the girls, we want the girls when they grow up to be able to enter marriage with intelligent understanding so that they may be true and helpful companions to their husbands and able wisely to guide the minds of children.'

Scholarships to a nearby grammar school were set up to cater for those children who were likely to benefit from a secondary education. The scholarship also included a grant for books and, where necessary, a maintenance allowance for their parents; 185 children benefitted from this over the years, sixty of whom went on to join one of the professions. Discipline though was never compromised: two extracts from the *Punishment Book*: '28th February 1927: L. Smith age 10 – running home (twice warned) 2 strokes – hand; 12th December 1938: N. Peacock 11 – stealing 3 shillings – 3 strokes – hand at mother's request.'

The fine clock on the cupola was donated by Joseph Stephenson Rowntree. The opening ceremony, attended by local dignitaries led by Joseph Rowntree, attracted a number of suffragettes who threw bricks through the windows; Miss Violet Key Jones jumped on the running board of Sir Walter Worsley's car and went on to the Folk Hall to scatter pamphlets urging 'Votes for Women.'

The first Joseph Rowntree secondary School was opened on 12 January 1942 by Rab Butler and catered for 480 children (in classes of forty) from age eleven who lived in

722

would have been a great pleasure to me to have been able by my presence to express my sense of the deep debt which we owe to the great German nation, and the desire which I have, in common with my fellow-countrymen, to do everything to join with them in an ever closer tie of common service to the cause of human progress. I hope that the interchange of ideals and experience between you and them in regard to the deeply-interesting and important question of the planning of our towns may be happy and fruitful.

"Yours very truly,
"COSMO EBOR."

These messages and all the subsequent

and far-seeing schemes which you have carried out with so much success in great cities such as Berlin and Düsseldorf. Indeed, it is doubtful whether our municipalities have yet realised what you so fully understand—that for the successful carrying out of any large scheme of town planning it is of the first importance that the municipalities should acquire and hold large quantities of land in the immediate neighbourhood of their towns. If we in England, and especially if we in our experiment at Earswick have anything that is likely to be of special interest to you, it will probably be in the character and arrangement of individual houses. As you know, the people of this country do not like the flat system, and do not adopt it unless through circumstances

TRIUMPHAL ARCH AT NEW EARSWICK,
"A HEARTY WELCOME TO OUR GERMAN COUSINS."

proceedings were translated into excellent German by Mr. Lasker, of New Earswick.

Then followed the reading by the Chairman of a letter from Mr. Joseph Rowntree, which had been translated into German. Mr. Rowntree said :—

"You have come to this country to enquire into the housing question, and our little village of New Earswick has the honour of your first visit. We think you will probably return to your own country with a feeling that we in England have more to learn from Germany than you can possibly learn from us, especially in the question of town planning. We have nothing to compare with the large

they are almost driven to it. English people like to have their own separate houses. Our object at New Earswick has been to build convenient and wholesome, and at the same time attractive cottages in which the decencies of life can be well maintained, and to do this at a price which working men are able to pay, and, of course, to have these houses associated in every case with garden ground. Our architects have continually presented us with plans of houses more beautiful than those we have erected, but again and again we have rejected them because the houses would have been too costly. We have felt that the value of the Earswick experiment would greatly depend upon whether we could show that cottages such as we have erected can be made to pay a moderate but still a commercial rate of interest. If this can be shown, the experiment is more likely to be imitated elsewhere than it would be if the undertaking were not upon a sound business basis,

723

"I have said that we have rejected many plans of cottages more beautiful than those we have erected, but we think our architect has, in spite of all the difficulties we have put in his way, succeeded in making a pretty village. You will observe that we have avoided long, monotonous rows of houses—that the village, in fact, consists of small groups of houses, and also that the back of the houses, as well as the front, is pleasant to the eye. We have done away with the unsightly outbuildings which disfigure so much of the cottage property in this country, and have done so without any disregard of sanitary conditions. Each group of houses is so placed that the living room shall receive abundant sunshine. To secure this end we have

not hesitated, when necessary, to make the back of the house face the street. Experience shows that the gardens are greatly valued, and in almost every case are carefully cultivated, and by the tenants themselves. Where vegetables are grown the produce is of sensible value in the weekly budget.

Within the last three months not only has an English housing deputation visited Germany, but our statesmen have enquired into your system of old age pensions, of your provision for invalidity, of your wonderful system of national education, both in its elementary and advanced forms. Nothing can exceed the hospitality with which these visitors were received, nor the thoughtfulness and unstinted kindness with which information was supplied. In all endeavours for the uplifting of the people, for the widening of intelligence, and for mitigating the sorrows incident to humanity each country gladly learns what the other has to teach. In efforts of this kind there cannot be too keen a rivalry between one country and

another. Your visit to England is one proof among many others that in these matters of supreme importance there is a growing unity of thought and purpose between our two nations, and inspire the faith that at no far distant date the great rivalry between your country and ours will be in those things only that make for the cause of human progress."

The President of the German Garden City Association responded in German.

The party was driven to New Earswick in an imposing cavalcade of char-a-bancs and

"TO THE BROTHERHOOD OF MAN!—AUF WIEDERSEHEN!"

carriages, in all some 50 vehicles. Horses and drivers were decorated with the German colours. On either side of Haxby Road, near the Council school, over one thousand boys and girls lined the road, and cheered the visitors to their intense delight.

A triumphal arch was thrown across the roadway at the entrance to the village, bearing a greeting to the Germans in their own language. The arch was built of timber by Mr. G. B. Brown and his staff, and decorated with long laurel streamers and wreaths made

Welcoming the German Garden Association to New Earswick in 1909.

A lesson in gardening at New Earswick school.

the village and surrounding area. As with the primary school it was highly innovative for its time, taking advice, for example, from the National Institute of Industrial Psychology on ergonomic matters such as ventilation, heating and lighting. From the very start, practical skills were valued and taught in equal measure to academic subjects. Printing and typography were part of the curriculum, a reflection perhaps of the traditional importance of printing and publishing in York, with Quaker companies like Sessions just down the road in Huntington. Adult education was encouraged too, in line with the Rowntree philosophy, with an Evening Institute of 350 students. The garden comprised two-and-a-half acres, and included a demonstration orchard to teach the principles of fruit cultivation; there were two further acres for raising livestock and an apiary.

The cost of the first school was £30,395 (excluding extra costs arising from war conditions) giving a per pupil cost of £63. The staff comprised the Head and seven men and seven women – each qualified in a particular subject. Special needs pupils were catered for. The school was designed as an open-air building and innovations included very large south-facing windows which were low enough for pupils to see out of when at their desks. They were 'capable of any required degree of opening', depending on the weather or time of year to provide optimum ventilation and lighting. There were ceiling heating panels and 'the long principal corridor [which] is slightly curved so as to minimise noise transmission by means of skin friction.' Equipment included an electric kiln, a printing press and aquaria. Mechanical engineering included the conversion of an old car into a runabout truck.

Domestic science at Joseph Rowntree School in the 1940s.

An ancient history lesson at the first Joseph Rowntree school in the 1940s.

The superb, new Joseph Rowntree school, May 2010, three months after opening.

Domestic science featured cooking by electricity, gas or coal, working in the domestic flat adjacent to the department and used by the Domestic Subjects Mistress, assisting in the village Nursery School, and feeding the animals.

The gym had room for a full-sized boxing ring when required, and had a radiogram and piano for use during folk dancing.

One hundred or so years later, the new Joseph Rowntree School is a fitting early Twenty-First Century testament to Joseph Rowntree's early Twentieth Century vision. It cost £29 million and opened for lessons in February 2010. The long-term benefits to present and future pupils are inestimable. Like its predecessors, it is innovative. One of the key features is a centre for autistic children offering specialist teaching and care for all children on the autistic spectrum. In November 2009 a time capsule containing a school uniform, a prospectus and dried pasta, was buried by Year 11 pupils under a paving slab at the entrance to the new school. The new lecture theatre seats 120 students and has a 12'x9' 3D cinema screen and demonstration bench. The main hall doubles as a theatre with tiered seating and a flexible stage area. The sports hall in the new school has a wooden-sprung floor, and can be set up for a wide range of sports including volleyball and tennis, within its 595 square metres. There is also a fifty-seven square metre multi-gym with cardiovascular machines and free weights. These are complemented by six outdoor tennis or netball courts.

Chocolate in the First World War

CHOCOLATE has often played an important role in more recent wars – either as a ration for servicemen, as a gift to liberated civilians, or as a peace offering to the vanquished. As we know, in 1780 Fry was commissioned to supply the Royal Navy with a ration of chocolate in cocoa slab form for its sailors to replace rum and to provide them with something a little more nutritious to go with their ship's biscuit. In the 1850s Fry's tins were sent to the troops fighting in the Crimean War. Chocolate played a role during the Boer War when Queen Victoria instructed George Cadbury to send 120,000 tins of chocolate to the troops in 1900. At first he refused, citing his Quakerly aversion to war as the reason; the Queen responded by pointing that this was

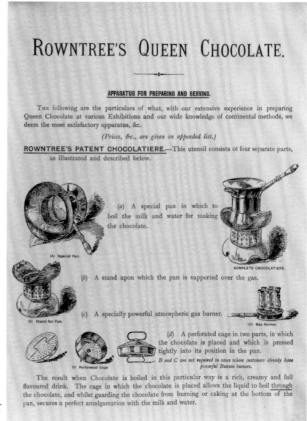

Everything you need to know about making Rowntree's Queen chocolate.

not a request but a royal command. The issue was resolved by sharing the order with Fry and Rowntree, and the tins were sent out unbranded to obscure their origin: each tin contained a half block of vanilla chocolate. George Cadbury then salved his conscience by producing and distributing over one million anti-war pamphlets. Rowntree shelved an idea to celebrate its royal warrant with Queen's Gift Tins in 1899 because the gesture may have been misconstrued as 'pandering to some degree to the present war fever.'

The importance of chocolate in military circles was highlighted by the 1905 issue of *War OfficeTimes and Naval Review:* 'Now chocolate is the sweetmeat of the Services: on the march, at manoeuvres, or on any special occasion where staying power is needed.' Chocolate was now official; chocolate would now be regular issue.

Fourteen years after the Boer War, confectionery tins containing sweets, chocolates and, in a compartment at the base of Rowntrees' tins, a set of postcards, were sent to the troops in the trenches. Initially, at least, the fall off in demand caused by the privations of the First World War had little impact on sales and profits – it was amply compensated for by government orders for the supply of chocolate for rations. Nevertheless, tariffs on cocoa and sugar had been increased and postal charges and general taxation had gone up. The naval blockade created by German submarines focused the government on providing essential foods such as milk and cocoa which helped the chocolate companies. Sugar shortages, though, led to the suspension of many brands and the adaptation of recipes for others. Serious manpower shortages occurred as men left for the front. At Cadbury alone, 1,700 out of 3,000 men departed for the army and navy (218 did not return), with another 700 leaving for munitions work. At Rowntree, 193 men left to take up their role as Territorial Army reservists – just when the company needed them most to meet the increasing demand.

Rowntree did not, for obvious reasons, comply with the current policy of dismissing conscientious objectors. However, in 1916 the company did stop employing objectors on account of the ill feeling they caused amongst the rest of the workforce. Pension contributions of workers on active service were paid in full by the company and, as we know, provision was made for war widows. By May 1915, 750 Rowntree men had signed up with further 'losses' resulting from trained fitters and turners moving over to the armaments industry under the terms of the Munitions Act. So many had left, that the factory would have had to close had not the Ministry of Munitions conferred reserved occupation status on those remaining. To compensate for the shortfall in workers, the company rescinded its policy of not hiring men aged over thirty-five. Belgian refugees were taken on, although Hindus were rejected on the grounds that 'it would not do to employ [them] in any of the general rooms, or where there were girls.' Between April 1916 and March 1917, the number of male employees fell from 2,644 to 1,855 while the number of women fell from 3,341 to 2,655 over the same period.

Cadbury's provided books and clothing for the troops and Caley's Marching Chocolate was issued to British troops under the name of 'Marcho'. Special wrappers were produced showing soldiers presenting arms (but unfortunately the rifles were drawn on the wrong shoulder). After the war it was marketed at, and became popular with, sportsmen and outdoor enthusiasts receiving plaudits from such popular heroes as Jack Hobbs, the Surrey and England batsman.

Throughout the war *Cocoa Works Magazine* published a litany of casualty announcements and photographs. Lawrence, John Wilhelm's only son, was killed in action in 1917.

The Rowntree Women's Dining Room – soon to be requisitioned.

Taking chocolate near the front; Jean-Etienne Liotard's famous 1743 Beautiful Chocolate Girl *is on the wall.*

LAWRENCE E. ROWNTREE.

The notice of L.E. Rowntree's death in CWM.

We deeply regret to record the death of SEC.-LIEUT. LAWRENCE E. ROWNTREE, only son of the late John Wilhelm Rowntree, and grandson of Mr. Joseph.

Cocoa Block turned military hospital.

the regions above, now in the hands of the military. Everywhere "B.P." was recognized, and was given three hearty cheers on descending the staircase. Although one of the busiest men in the country, "B.P." kindly sent the following message to the "Cocoa Boys" :—

You who read this are hoping to have a happy Christmas, I expect. You probably look forward

act of kindness or politeness—if it is only to smile at them ; it need not cost you much, but you will find that it repays you. You will feel all the happier for having done it. In this way you will find that it depends on yourself to make happiness for yourself by just making someone else happy. Try it this Christmas Day.

THE GIRLS' DINING-ROOM.—AS IT WAS, AND

to somebody giving you a present or a treat of some kind. Supposing they don't do it ? Where will you be ? Your Christmas won't be so "merry and bright" as you had thought it would be. Well, I can give you a tip for guarding against this : instead of waiting for somebody to do you a good turn, do the good turn yourself, to somebody. Lend a helping hand to somebody needing it ; do some little

And after that, whenever you may feel a little down on your luck, you will have a sure cure for it—you will only have to turn to and do a good turn to someone and you'll be as right as a trivet.

Good luck to you, and a very happy Christmas.

THE ALLOTMENTS—ANNUAL REPORT.

Mr. Redington's report for the season 1914 has been received, and copies distributed among holders of plots. Mr. Redington is struck with the number of tenants who "have risen to the occasion to do their best to meet the prospective need for additional food supply, under present emergencies. On the occasions of our last two visits this was very noticeable, and at the present time one can safely say there never has been such a good supply of winter and spring vegetables. This is all the more satisfactory when

AS IT IS.

it is remembered that the management of this section of vegetables is one of the most difficult parts of the management of the kitchen garden.

On the whole, the season has been a very successful and satisfactory one, although in the early part considerable difficulty was experienced through the late frosts, especially with the early potatoes. It was, however, fortunate that the

plants seemed to recover from the check much better than they usually do, afterwards yielding very good crops.

PRIZE LIST.

ADULTS.

Class 1.—The garden that is best managed throughout the year, regard being paid to the cultivation of the soil, arrangement, neatness and cleanliness, also successional, useful and varied cropping, together with the appearance by the use of flowers.

1. W. Davis (Landing Stage), 2 A. C. Winter (Melangeur), 3 J. Kendrew (Gardeners), 4 B. Harrison (Store), 5 J. Richmond (Almond Paste).

Class 2.—The garden that has the best proportion of well-grown useful vegetables, salads and herbs cropped so as to come in at seasonable intervals throughout the year, cleanliness and neatness also being considered.

The Girl's Dining Room, before the war … and during, with billeted troops.

OFFICE.—Continued.

Taylor, H. E.	(T.)	Wells, S.	(V.)		
Toes, R. G.	(T.)	Walker, E. W.	(T.)		
Welburn, C. E.	(V.)	Weatherley, L.	(T.)		
Wood, W. H.	(V.)	Williamson, F.	(T.)		
Ward, H.	(R.)				

SAWMILL.

Archer, C.	(V.)	Linfoot, A.	(V.)
Brown, A.	(V.)	Lee, A.	(T.)
Brown, F.	(V.)	Linley, F.	(V.)
Bycroft, J.	(T.)	Lickley, A.	(V.)
Barker, D.	(V.)	Nash, G.	(V.)
Cade, H.	(R.)	Newby, R.	(V.)
Carter, H.	(V.)	Neale, H.	(T.)
Cleveland, C. B.	(V.)	Noble, W.	(T.)
Cade, W.	(V.)	Pickard, F.	(V.)
Gell, W.	(V.)	Precious, C. W.	(V.)
Harneis, G.	(V.)	Richardson, S.	(R.)
Harrison, J. W.	(V.)	Tillott, N.	(T.)
Jackson, A.	(T.)	Topham, A.	(V.)
Linfoot, N.	(V.)	Taylor, H. J.	(V.)

CARDBOARD BOX DEPARTMENT.

Ward, W.	(V.)	Halder, B. (Naval R.)	

ESTATE DEPARTMENT.

Isaacs, H.	(T.)	Simpson, C.	(V.)
Sullens, E.	(V.)	Whitehead	(R.)

JOINERS DEPARTMENT.

Bewsher, G.	(R.)	Jackson, J. G.	(T.)
Culliford, R. W.	(R.)	Wordsworth, A.	(T.)

FRUIT AND ALMOND DEPARTMENT.

Barker, F.	(T.)	Manion, T.	(V.)
Bilham, A.	(T.)	Pattison, H.	(V.)
Chapman, W	(T.)	Walker, R.	(T.)
Kershaw, W.	(T.)	Walker, T.	(T.)
Marriner, M.	(V.)		

ELECT DEPARTMENT.

De Barre, S.	(T.)	Muldoon, J. (Nat. R.)	
Hawley, A.	(T.)	North, E. (Nat. R.)	
Johnson, W.	(T.)		

FIRE STATION.

Ovenden, G.	(R.)		

SOCIAL DEPARTMENT.

Dr. M. D. Ferguson.

BUILDING DEPARTMENT.

Brownbridge, G.	(R.)	Exelby, T.	(V.)
Calpin, J. F.	(R.)	Leadley, W.	(T.)
Calpin, W.	(V.)	Lickley, W.	(T.)
Calpin, Jas.	(V.)	McNulty, J.	(V.)
Diggles, W.	(V.)	Normington, J.	(R.)

THE COCOA WORKS AND THE BELGIAN REFUGEES.

Perhaps the saddest feature of this terrible war is the devastation of Belgium and the flight of the population to Holland, France and England. Immediately the streams of refugees began to reach our shores a movement was set on foot at the Works to provide hospitality for a number of these innocent sufferers from Prussian brutality. On October 13th, a meeting was called in the Lecture Room, by Mr. A. Wilkinson, to consider ways and means. Mr. S. H. Sidney and Mr. G. T. Dawson laid proposals before the meeting, and after much discussion it was agreed to call a further meeting of all employees inertested on October 20th. At this gathering it

was decided to invite the works-people to contribute 1d. weekly per head towards the support of a definite number of Belgian families. The Directors kindly placed nine houses at New Earswick at our disposal rent free, and one of these was allotted to the Engineering Department. The following Committee was appointed to proceed immediately with all necessary arrangements :—

Mr. A. Wilkinson (Hon. Secretary), Mr. C. Horner (Chairman and Hon. Treasurer), Mrs. Bean, Mrs. Moses, Mrs. Wilson, Mrs. Earnshaw, Mrs. Walters, Miss Craven, Miss Wales, Miss Barker, Miss Penrose, Miss Nelson, Miss M. Lister,

Miss M. Umpleby, Miss E. Calvert, Miss Houlston, Miss M. Lunn, Miss F. Dinsdale, Miss Masser, Miss Foggin, Miss Holt, Miss Harrison, Miss Hughes, Miss Gray, Miss Archer, Miss A. Walker, Miss L. Yates, Miss J. Aston, Miss E. Barker, Miss M. Josh, Miss A. Wright, Miss Ward, Mr. Jarvis, Mr. R. Porter, Mr. Oldfield, Mr. Hardgraves, Mr. Pinchbeck, Mr. Marsden, Mr. J. E. Oglesby, Mr. E. Smallwood, Mr. H. Pawson, Mr. O. Brooks, Mr. P. J. Woods, Mr. J. Drinkell, Mr. W. Gott, Mr. W. Grantham, Mr. G. P. Johnson, Mr. T. H. Nutbrown, Mr. M. Flatley, Mr. J. Robinson, Mr. Barham,

MONSIEUR AND MADAME VAN EECKHOUT, CELINE, FANNY AND MARIE.

Mr. Howard, Mr. G. Kirby, Mr. A. G. Illingworth, Mr. F. J. Kitchin, Mr. W. W. Milburn.

Auditors to the Fund :—Mr. Geo. Walker and Mr. W. W. Milburn.

The following executive committee was elected to deal with matters of urgency :—

Officers, and Miss Kendrew, Miss Stockley, Mrs. M. Wood, Mr. T. D. Randles, Mr. Harris, Mr. G. Wilkie.

Those of our readers who are married know something of the task of furnishing a home,

but the problem of completely furnishing nine houses in as many weeks was certainly a formidable one, and our thanks are due to Messrs. F. Harris and T. Randles, who attended every furniture sale in York during that period, and arranged for the transport of goods bought to the village. The Committee also wish to thank Mrs. Harris for considerable help in furnishing these houses. We are grateful also to many kind friends at the Works and outside who generously gave or lent various articles that go to the furnishing of a home. Space only prevents us giving a complete list. Many departments

also helped in various ways to oil the wheels of our organization, and the Committee would like to express their indebtedness to Messrs. J. Crossland, W. Mawson, G. Shepherd, G. W. R. Wright, T. Addinall, Purnell, P. J. Woods and Bruce ; also to Messrs. I. Neville, J. Wardropper and A. Maude for help in various directions.

The generous response of the Works to the appeal of the homeless Belgians is shown below the figures being the total amount subscribed in each department from October 24th to the time of going to press :—

The dining room in the Cocoa Block was requisitioned as billets for the 1,000 or so men of the 8th Battalion, the West Yorkshire Regiment (Territorials). In 1915, the Leeds Rifles came and went, to be replaced by men of the King's Own Yorkshire Light Infantry. The block was later converted into a temporary military hospital.

Belgian refugees were accommodated in New Earswick, some of whom offered French lessons to local residents. A fund was set up for 1d per head to support the refugees, described as 'innocent sufferers of Prussian brutality,' and nine houses were hastily furnished and provided rent free for nine families. Joseph Rowntree announced in the Christmas 1914 edition of *Cocoa Works Magazine* that 500 men had joined up, with two already killed. All 500 were dignified by being listed by name and by department.

One amazing story published in *Cocoa Works Magazine* in 1915 was headlined 'Elect Cocoa Saves a Soldier's Life' and was sent in by Sgt. T.J. Williams of the 5th King's Own Lancashire Regiment. His letter began, 'to inform you what good service one of your tins cocoa did for me,' and went on to relate how, during the Battle of St Julien, he received a one-pound tin of Elect, which he duly put in his emergency ration pack along with a tin of tea and sugar: 'Advancing under heavy fire and now and again dropping flat on the ground a bullet entered my valise .[it] had gone through the tin containing the tea and sugar, the tin of Rowntrees had been penetrated on one side and not the other. What luck! If it had gone through it would have penetrated my back. It speaks well as to the strength of the tin but more so for the strength of the cocoa. Ha! Ha!'

As we have seen, the war brought with it restrictions on the use of sugar, all of which was normally imported, and two thirds of which came from Germany and

1774   "THE C.W.M."

A Tin of "Elect" that Saved a Soldier's Life.

Elect Cocoa Saves a Soldier's Life.

Extract from letter from Sergt. T. J. Williams 5th K.O., Royal Lancaster Regt. 25/5/15

I am writing these few lines just to inform you what good service one of your tins of cocoa did for me.

I was present at the battle of St. Julien, and no doubt you read an account of the same—a very warm corner, I can assure you. Well, I had, two days previous to this engagement, received from home a 1-lb. tin of your Rowntree's Cocoa, as I always found it to be very strengthening, and I have made many a good drink whilst in the trenches. Well, however, I placed this fresh tin in what we call the emergency ration bag, along with a tin of tea and sugar, etc. Now I will tell you what happened. We were advancing across an open field under very heavy fire, and now and again dropping flat on the ground. Well, I had just got down when a bullet entered my valise or pack as the boys call it. The next man to me said, "Are you hit, Sergeant?" I said, "No." However, we

had no time to think about this at the time; as long as I wasn't hit all was right, but imagine the surprise I got the next day when I looked into my ration bag. First of all I found the bullet had gone through the tin containing the tea and sugar, then I noticed the tin of Rowntree's was penetrated on one side and not on the other. "What luck!" The bullet had lodged in the cocoa, thereby saving my life. If it had gone through the tin of Rowntree's it would have penetrated my back. So I consider myself lucky, and I shall always keep the tin and the bullet, and if you care to have a look at the same I would be only too pleased to send it along, on condition you sent it back to me. It speaks well as to the strength of the tin, but more so for the strength of the cocoa. "Ha! Ha!"

Partial Amendment of Rules
of the
York Cocoa Works Friendly Society.
(Reg. No. 5097 York.)

RULE 11, as amended 1913, at the end add :—

"(17) Members serving their country in His Majesty's Forces, shall not be liable for their contributions during the War, or such period after their discharge, or the proclamation of peace, as the Committee may determine.

Unless otherwise decided by the Committee of Management, Members who have been in His Majesty's Forces shall recommence payment of their contributions immediately after their discharge.

Should any of the aforesaid Members require sick benefit before they have recommenced payment of contributions, they shall be entitled to the same, but the Society shall deduct their weekly contributions from their Sick Pay."

"THE C.W.M."   1775

RULE 13, at the end :—

"In the event of a Member losing his life while in the service of his country, the death claim shall be allowed."

ARTHUR CALVERT,
GEORGE T. DAWSON, } 3 Members.
WILLIAM THOMAS,
G. WALKER, Secretary.

Register No. 5097 Yorks. Partial Amendment. Acknowledgment of Registry of Amendments of Rules.

The foregoing Amendment of the Rules of the York Cocoa Works Friendly Society, is registered under the Friendly Societies Act, 1896, this 9th day of July, 1915.

Copy kept G.S.R.

Cream Packers Camping Out.
G. Lawn,
B. Haigh.   L. Pink.
M. Jennings.

UNDER CANVAS.

The camping-out habit, always popular with the boys, has this season extended to the other sex, and we take off our hats to the four pioneers—Misses G. Lawn, B. Haigh, L. Pink and M. Jennings, of No. 1 Cream Packing, who have been sleeping out (*not* without visible means of support) near Poppleton, all the summer. Although the night and morning air is keen, they firmly intend going on—perhaps till Christmas! They rise at 5.30 a.m., two cycling to the Factory, and two walking (unless they get a lift in a milk cart).

They appear to have had some amusing and exciting experiences, which are best left in their own words :—"The first night we did not sleep. The cows would persist in trying to get in the tent, so we had barbed wire put round to keep

them out. The chain in the photograph is the gate. The wasps were our biggest trouble, all having been stung. One morning, whilst having our breakfast, we killed 18. One of the girls went for one that was on her jam and bread with a mallet ; the bread and jam were left sticking to the mallet.

"One morning, being rather late, going down the road, one of the girls complained of being deaf ; she had forgotten to take the cotton-wool out of her ears, which is put in as a protection against earwigs. Every night we went with a mallet and a candle killing them. Sunday was our visiting day. We generally had about 10 to tea ; the worst part of it was they forgot to bring their own mugs."

US FOUR.

P.S.—*We have never slept in once.*

Austria-Hungary. Syrups were used as a replacement. In 1915 Rowntrees established Confectionery Ingredients Ltd in King's Lynn with flavourings and essence makers Strange and Graham, to develop vanillin, a cheap substitute for vanilla. Research into saccharin followed, and by 1917 it was being produced in bulk and sold to third parties at good margins. With Nestlé virtually excluded from the UK market, the door was open for Cadbury, not Rowntree, to fill the void in the milk chocolate market and it was at this time that milk chocolate, synonymous now with Cadbury's Dairy Milk, superseded cocoa as the main product of the chocolate industry.

By the end of the war Rowntrees had lost 179 men. On 12 September 1920, Seebohm Rowntree unveiled an oak memorial to the fallen which cost £179.17s 5d and was funded by employee contributions. Joseph Rowntree donated a further £800 which had recently been collected for his and Mrs Rowntree's golden wedding celebrations.

Rowntree Between the Wars

FOR THE next fifteen years or so after the end of the First World War, the company languished in the doldrums. The Depression, a lack of clear policy, a tendency to produce a lot of short-run unprofitable lines, the failure to compete with Cadbury's Dairy Milk, and the persistent suspicion of advertising and marketing all contributed. Sales had increased by seventy per cent between 1918 and 1920 – the boom following the war – but the wage bill had simultaneously ballooned by nearly 300 per cent as the company and the economy generally faced the inevitable bust. Pay cuts followed, agreed between Rowntree and Cadbury-Fry who between them employed fifty-six per cent of the nation's chocolate industry workers. Savings were fed back into the company to help reduce the price of chocolates in the shops. From 1918, Rowntree had to face the combined competition of a merged Cadbury-Fry and even though a tripartite merger was considered by the Rowntree board, the idea was soon rejected.

The newer industries of the time, including food and confectionery, had fuelled demand by introducing more efficient mechanisation and transportation which in turn helped reduce the cost and therefore the price of their goods; this coincided with an increase in disposable income which itself added to the demand. Advertising was becoming more affordable in successful companies and indeed, more necessary, if companies were to increase product awareness, counter the claims of competitors and establish brand recognition – the latter facilitated by the 1875 Trade Marks Act. Branding also allowed a company to differentiate its product in the market and this was largely responsible for the dichotomy which existed in the confectionery marketplace: high quality proprietary brands versus low quality nameless products. Advertising had been a powerful tool in convincing consumers your products were pure and unadulterated – an increasingly important issue in the minds of consumers who had put up with all manner of additives before the 1872 legislation. But increasingly, advertisements and posters were used to tell consumers how a product fitted effortlessly and essentially into their lives, and how it affected their lifestyle; this opened the way for pithy slogans and eye-catching pictures. Again, such developments were anathema to members of the Rowntree board. In 1919 they were concerned that the new type of advertising was appealing to 'the cinema type of mind' rather than to the more cerebral customer, whom they still saw as their target. But the need, of course, was to aim at the working class customer who, due to rises in wages and disposable income, was now the socioeconomic group responsible for the increases in consumption.

Finally, in 1920, the Rowntree board accepted that the only way to change their fortunes in the market was, in part, to advertise their way out the crisis. They were behind Nestlé and Cadbury in milk chocolate, behind Cadbury's Bournville in cocoa, and behind Terry's in assortments. A marketing budget of £133,000 was approved for the first half of 1921, getting closer to but still some way off Cadbury's figure of £200,000. This was set against a changing inter-war years market; annual consumption of milk chocolate rose by sixty-six per cent, wages increased by over fifteen-and-a-half per cent, and consumer spend on food grew by forty per cent, while food costs decreased by sixty-five per cent . These factors, in association with improved production and economies of scale, resulted in a large fall in the price of milk chocolate in the shops: from 4s 2d to 1s 4d per lb. From now on, chocolate was no longer a luxury but a routine purchase by the man and woman in the street. Weekly per capita confectionery consumption grew in 1920, 1930 and 1938 from 4.7 oz to 5.7 and 7.1, with chocolate accounting for roughly half of this.

In February 1923 Seebohm Rowntree succeeded his father as Chairman of the company but, despite root and branch investigations into all aspects of the company's operations, little actually changed, and most significantly little actually changed in marketing. And

Fry chimes with the bulldog spirit in this Strand Magazine *advertisement.*

Inside the Joseph Rowntree Memorial Library.

this at a time when sales of confectionery sold loose in grocer shops and tobacconists were declining in the face of packaged sweets and chocolates with branded wrappers and containers.

Joseph Rowntree died on 24 February 1925. His grave, along with others of his family, is in the Quaker cemetery in the grounds of The Retreat on Heslington Road. The Joseph Rowntree Memorial Library was erected in 1927 in Haxby Road in gratitude for a life of devoted service. It was designed by Fred Rowntree and housed the company library which was previously inside the factory. Some of the books were also from Joseph's personal collection, presented to the firm by his children. The interior decorations were financed by employees of the company.

Rowntree's bought the London-based Lockhart's with its six restaurants and thirty-nine shops, Fuller and Maynard's Black Boy shops, and bought into the Scottish company Gray, Dunn, (boiled sweet and chocolate biscuit manufacturers) in 1924. The marketing inertia was relieved to some extent by two new products. In 1925 they launched Plain York Chocolate bar – promoted with the repetitious and alliterative slogan: '*Plain Mr York of York, Yorkshire.*'

Joe Dickinson, author of a chapter in this book and keeper of the largest collection of Rowntree memorabilia, at Joseph Rowntree's graveside.

Avuncular Mr York was a chip off the Sunny Jim Force cereal and Johnny Walker whisky blocks in the branding world; his intrinsic plainness reflected the chocolate's main quality – plainness and its pure and honest simplicity. The anything but plain fruit and nut block, Motoring, followed with its milk or plain chocolate variations containing almonds and raisins. Sold as a snack suitable for a long journey, it tapped in to the increasing popularity of motoring amongst a well to do sector of the market. Both Motoring and Plain York were advertised with scenes from everyday life to drive home the message that eating (Rowntrees) chocolate was now an inextricable feature our daily lives. The Cocoa Nibs also saw the first light of day around this time and were very popular with children, particularly in the promotional games and models in which they regularly featured.

Unsuccessful overtures were made to acquire York neighbours Cravens, the chocolate and confectionery manufacturers. This ultimately led to the formation of York Confectionery Company to allow Rowntree to compete at the cheaper end of the market through a subsidiary company which would not detract from Rowntree's reputation as a manufacturer of quality. York Milk was launched in 1927, but this suffered by comparison with Cadbury's Dairy Milk because it was made from powdered milk and had none of the taste and health advantages of an aggressively advertised and marketed as the 'glass and a half' health-giving milk chocolate bar. Tried Favourites came in 1927, but these assortments faced strong competition from Rowntrees' other York neighbours, Terry's, the market leaders in chocolate assortments. Tried Favourites ultimately failed. That same year, Rowntree bought into the chewing gum market by joining forces with

Mr York selling in style and anything but 'plain'.

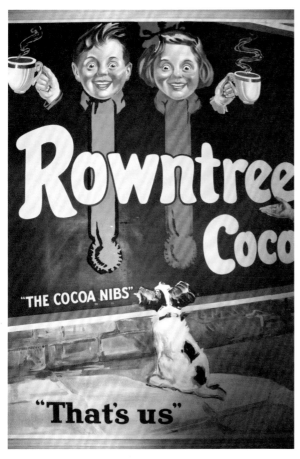

The Cocoa Nibs, scaring the animals...

US manufacturer Beech Nut to form Beech Nut Sweets (England) Ltd with sales rights in Britain and the Empire. After the installation of packaging machinery, tubed fruit pastilles were launched in 1928 and York Milk, packaged like and riding on the relative success of Plain York, soon followed. Chocolate, though, was still a disappointment in the overall company finances and gums and pastilles accounted for seventy-five per cent of profits in 1928, an indication of the lower level of competition in this market where, accordingly, advertising was significantly less crucial. Intensive advertising campaigns and damaging price competition from Cadbury, coupled with the 1929 Wall Street Crash, meant an uncomfortable end to the decade for Rowntree's. Indeed, to make matters worse, both gums and cocoa were themselves under threat; the former from toffee from companies like Mackintosh and Craven, and the latter from new products such as Ovaltine and Horlicks.

The company had to act, and its first significant action was bringing together marketing (product development, advertising, pricing, and profit forecasting), and distribution under Frederick Fryer. Such a marriage of departments was then relatively rare in the UK and was imported from the USA, where it had been enjoying success in a number of large organisations since 1918. The constitution of the Board was changed too, to something more dynamic, when it was decided that all directors would be working executives and membership would not guaranteed through nepotism. Retirement at sixty-five became mandatory. J. Walter Thompson took over as advertising agents in 1931, bringing with them expertise gleaned from US clients Wrigley and Beech Nut and from working with Cadbury, for whom they provided the famous 'glass and a half' slogan. One of their first moves was to initiate campaigns for the fruit gum and pastille range which they gradually steered away from a focus on the medicinal qualities (they purportedly cured sore throats caused by colds or by smoking), towards the appeal to children and their parents by playing the purity and healthy fruit content cards.

It was, however, the appointment and subsequent rise and rise of sales manager, marketing director and future chairman George Harris, which began to make a real difference. Significantly, Harris was a friend of Forrest Mars, of Simon Marks of Marks & Spencer and of John Sainsbury. He married in to the Rowntree family, but his own skills and experience account for his success. The experience (not always successful, but invaluable all the same), he brought of American marketing methods, consumer research, product development, branding and advertising with Chufru Gums, and a five-year stint running their London office, eventually led Rowntree to change from a conservative, production-led company to a brand and market-driven one. He was dynamic, hard working, and critical of the amateurism he saw around him. Most importantly though, he could spot and develop a market opportunity and inculcate similar vision in others. He also recognised that the long-term road to success for Rowntree lay in challenging Cadbury head on in the milk chocolate market. Although this challenge was never really met with a Rowntree version of Dairy Milk, his vision ultimately resulted in the launch of KitKat, Black Magic, Aero, Dairy Box, Smarties, Rolo in the 1930s. Harris could see what we nowadays call 'the bigger picture' and he could obviously, to modify today's parlance, 'think outside the chocolate box.' His US experience may well have allowed him to observe what is obvious to us today: that the newer industries emerging in the UK – food, drink, tobacco, electrical and motor – depended much more on consumer marketing and branding in the face of intense competition. The marketing objectives of the older industries – textiles, coal, steel, shipbuilding and the like – were very different. Indeed,

Harris only had to look as far south as Bournville to see how consumer advertising and market research had lifted and consolidated sales of Cadbury's flagship product lines. On a smaller scale, Caley had probably managed what was a disproportionate share of the market for their output because of their innovative and eye catching advertising. Harris championed and embraced marketing and branding and it is this, in concert with a stellar list of new products launched just before the onset of another world war, which brought Rowntrees out of the doldrums and into the limelight.

In the meantime, the company increased its no-name product business with Woolworth and Marks & Spencer – by 1934 these two accounted for ten per cent and fifty per cent respectively of their non-proprietary business. Products included cocoa, jelly, blancmange and custard powder – even a wine jelly – to the consternation of some people.

Harris's business acumen was, of course, not the only reason for the reversal of fortunes. The dominance of the foreign importers was well and truly broken by now and a combination of lower prices and the inter-war years' increase in wages for those in work, meant higher disposable income which could be spent on 'luxuries' like confectionery and tobacco. It was during this period that chocolate replaced cocoa as the industry's leading product. Indeed, between 1920 and 1939, wages increased by over fifteen per cent and consumer expenditure by thirty-two per cent. Outlets for confectionery, too, increased from 100,000 in 1914 to over 250,000 in 1939, thus making chocolate widely available and affordable to about ninety per cent of the population. Market demand was met by all the leading manufacturers, with increased output fuelled by efficiencies in production and distribution to make the British the biggest per capita consumers of chocolate. What had hitherto been something of a luxury enjoyed by the better off had now become a staple. In 1920 the average chocolate consumption was around 1.5 ounces in a week; by 1938 the figure had nearly doubled to 2.7 ounces, rising to 3.5 ounces in 1954 one year after the end of rationing.

Attempts in 1931 to form an alliance with Halifax toffee firm, Mackintosh, came to nothing for Rowntrees, but it did lead to Harold Mackintosh's purchase of Caley from Unilever. The focus was still on producing a competitor to Dairy Milk. Cadbury was still turning out something like ten times the number of chocolate bars that were coming out of Rowntrees; and attempts to remedy this gave birth to Extra Creamy Milk in 1933. In 1935 Rowntree started advertising their jellies on Radio Luxembourg. Cocoa advertisements soon followed on the radio.

During the late twenties and the thirties, Rowntree, like Cadbury, was receiving a large number of visitors to the works – 7,500 in 1929 alone. Dedicated guides were assigned to show these visitors around and to ensure that they were as well informed as possible about the company and the industry generally. *The Guide's Booklet* was produced in the thirties and was full of information which they could impart to visitors. From it we learn that 709,000 gallons of water are used every week to drive the steam powered machinery; 4,500 calls per day are taken in the telephone exchange, and 200 tons of ice are made daily for the various refrigeration units and air conditioning. Each week 500 tons of coal was used up and every year three million feet of ribbon tied up fourteen million chocolate boxes which were wrapped in one million miles of transparent paper.

The Haxby Road halt in the factory had two platforms with space for three locomotives and thirty-six wagons, and there were three miles of railway track around the factory. The company had a fleet of about 100 delivery vans. The female dining room could

Rowntree's impressive stand at Olympia in 1934 – the same year that Oswald Mosley addresses 12,000 fascists in the same hall.

```
      THE GUIDE'S BOOKLET.


     The object of this booklet
is to help you in replying to the
many and varied questions asked
by visitors, and to give you some
main talking points concerning
the Factory.

     Keep it in the pocket of your
overall ready for reference.

     The complete satisfaction of
every visitor is our ideal, and,
if this is obtained, will con-
siderably influence their decision
when purchasing confectionery etc.
Our endeavour must be to impress
them so favourably with their visit
that they will always ask for

          "ROWNTREE'S"
```

The introduction to the Rowntree guides' vade mecum.

seat 2,500 while the men's accommodated 600. Dinner was sevenpence halfpenny. The main corridor is 750 feet long; and there were eighty-four time clocks. There were now three libraries. The Staff Library held 10,000 books, half of which were fiction, 4,000 non-fiction and 1,000 juvenile; the Lad's Library had 250 books for the Boy's Club, and the Technical Library kept 7,000 books and 8,000 pamphlets, as well as having 300 subscriptions to magazines and journals. The company fire brigade comprised eighteen full-time staff and they had a fire engine, a steamer and an ambulance. The first BBC broadcast at the company took place in 1926 and featured girls singing at work, no doubt for a programme of *Worker's Playtime*.

On the chocolate assortment front, Black Magic was launched in 1933, 'the first chocolate assortment ever made to order for a mass market.' Market research was, at last, being embraced. The twelve chocolates in Black Magic boxes were only decided on after interviews with 2,500 shopkeepers and 7,000 consumers and the striking packaging was instrumental in stimulating impulse sales. Black Magic was advertised on the radio. Also of significance is the fact that the company name was subordinated to the brand name in the Black Magic marketing. The hard, soft and praline centres were aimed squarely at the best selling assortment box of the day, Cadbury's King George Assortment. Sales of Black Magic were very encouraging. However, the Dairy Milk competitor, Extra Creamy Milk, flopped soon after it was launched in 1933, even though it did contain more milk than Dairy Milk. The seemingly-endless quest for a viable competitor went on, now with

The intrepid Rowntree Cocoa Works fire brigade and fire fighting equipment.

all eyes on the success enjoyed at Mars, first with their Mars Bar and then with Milky Way. Two products were, however, waiting in the wings for launch approval. The first was Wafer Crisp, loosely based on a similar Huntley and Palmers line.

But it was Aero, an aerated rather than a solid chocolate, that provided the first real success in the milk chocolate battle for Rowntrees in 1935. Aero was originally to be called Airways to reflect the popular increase in jet travel in the 1930s, but Rowntrees settled on using a name originally registered with Cadbury though discarded by them and transferred over. Aero soon started to eat into Dairy Milk's market share and demonstrated a sixty per cent customer preference against Dairy Milk's thirty per cent, amongst polls of eighteen to thirty year olds. Seebohm Rowntree saw Aero, patented in 1936, as the most significant development in the chocolate market since Henri Nestlé's mixing of milk with chocolate. Launched in the North of England, Aero was soon rolled out to the rest of the nation as polls continued to support the initial preference ratings. Early promotions focussed on its unique texture, easy digestibility, and the 'lift' it gave. Aggressive advertising was at last being deployed with straight-to-the- point, critical copy asserting ' It digests twice as quickly as old-fashioned milk chocolate', and 'there are no lumps in Aero.' Short-lived Nut and Fruit and Nut Aeros followed, partly in response to Fry's launch of the aerated, honeycombed Crunchie.

At about the same time, Wafer Crisp, was rebranded as Chocolate Crisp, later KitKat Chocolate Crisp, and then launched as just KitKat. It sold (from 1939) with the slogan 'give yourself a break at tea time ', and was launched on a meagre budget of £1,750. Other tags included 'the biggest little meal' and 'the best companion to a cup of tea.' The simple, enduring rationale behind it was to produce 'A chocolate bar that a man could take to work in his pack up' – a concept which came from a Rowntree's employee via *CWM's* suggestions columns. The KitKat name first appeared on a box of assorted chocolates in the 1920s (it had been trademarked in 1911), was derived from the Eighteenth Century Whig literary club and featured its proprietor, pie-shop owner Christopher Catling (aka Kit Cat), on the box. In 1931 the old Kit Cat assortment became a casualty of a product review. Profit forecasts for 1935 were revised upwards from £80,000 to £200,000, although this was tempered slightly by a rise in advertising costs from ten per cent of sales in 1930 to thirteen per cent.

One of the team involved in the KitKat research and subsequent launch was Thomas Thompson. His retirement notice in *Cocoa Works Magazine* in 1965 highlights the key role he played in bringing it to market: 'He is, of course, best remembered for his contribution to the development of lines which have been established and are now household names throughout the world. It would be impracticable to mention all of the new lines with which he was concerned but perhaps Kit Kat requires special mention for here his personal efforts probably tipped the scales in the right direction when its very future was in the balance. Thomas Thompson worked in Cream Manufacturing Experimental (later to be known as Product Development) where he used the experience that he had gained in Time Study Sales Department, of which he was a founder member, to estimate the probable future outputs for lines which were then in their very early stages and enabled very accurate assessments of costs and value to be made.'

His nephew, Peter Stanhope, adds: 'It seems that the Directors of the Company were not at all sure in the early stages of the future success of their Rowntrees Chocolate Crisp new line and were ready to abandon it. It was Tom who did the research into manufacturing costs set against his predictions of future sales potential, that finally persuaded the Board to give it a second chance and, out of the ashes of 'Chocolate Crisp' rose Kit Kat which is now renowned and enjoyed around the world.'

Early press advertisement copy was nothing, if not didactic. No one after reading this virtual essay could go away ill informed about KitKat – what it lacks in the pithiness of the later 'have a break…' slogan, it more than makes up for with this long-winded, almost technical, copy: 'When you have a break in your work, there's nothing else quite like a KitKat. Crisp, golden-baked wafer biscuit, moulded into a block with delicious milk chocolate. The wafer and the chocolate are a pair – not a mixture. You can see them, quite separate, when you snap off a piece from your Kit Kat – feel them, quite separate, in your mouth. You can taste them, still quite separate, as you crunch them up. Two splendid foods, with two wonderful flavours, each doubling the enjoyment of the other. Crisp wafer – milk chocolate – KitKat Chocolate Crisp made by Rowntrees and sold by confectioners and cafes. Price 2d.'

Dairy Assortment – later Dairy Box – was launched in 1936 against Cadbury's Milk Tray, with the advantage that Dairy Assortment was packaged, while Milk Tray was still being sold loose. Chocolate Beans, later Smarties, came in 1938 – originally sold loose but soon in their iconic tubes – an imitation of the established French *dragée*. The familiar letter stamped on the cap as 'an attractive plaything for children' was introduced in 1959. On the confectionery side, Polo mints were launched in 1939, based on the American Lifesaver sweet. Polo fruits followed in 1953.

Chocolate in the Second World War

I N THE Second World War chocolate was rationed from 1942, with three ounces allowed per person per week – less than half the average pre-war consumption of just over seven ounces was divided between no fewer than 181 companies. Chocolate companies were either closed – for example Mars in Slough – transformed into completely different companies helping the war effort where capital costs and anticipated profits were paid for and compensated for by the government (for example, Rowntree's County Industries Ltd), or else they hosted other war manufacturers. Rowntree, for example, produced Oxford Marmalade on behalf of Frank Cooper Ltd – so good a fit was this that they tried to buy them out in 1944.

Because of manpower restrictions and the zoning of production, 120 tons per week of Cadbury output was transferred to York. Zoning was the national system whereby distribution was confined to the zone in which the product was manufactured. Rowntree

A Rowntree (Aka County Industries) fuse worker.

supplied the Eastern sector and some places in Scotland. Nevertheless, despite this and orders for NAAFI supplies and for rations, Rowntree sales had halved by 1945 from their pre-war levels with assortments like Black Magic and Dairy Milk the first to go. Importation of raw materials was seriously compromised. The subsequent shortages which developed as a result, together with the diversion of the domestic supply of milk, had a serious affect on the quality of major brands. Rowntrees, for example, responded by manufacturing a kind of ersatz KitKat (then called Chocolate Crisp) and exchanging the distinctive red wrapper for a blue one denoting which key ingredients were missing. The strategy was that if any adverse public reaction came from this debasement, then the original name and wrapper could be restored with impunity when normal production was resumed. In the end, KitKat's wartime production ceased altogether. Dairy Milk disappeared from the shops when milk was prohibited for manufacturing use in 1941 (Ration Chocolate replaced it, made from skimmed milk powder.) The massive changes the war brought to British industry is well captured in the post war publication *The Cocoa Works in War-time* published by Rowntree in 1947: 'Lathes, machines and conveyor belts were worked and fed for the first time in British history by women' adding 'even a new language was formed: human beings became "mobile workers", who were sent to "scarlet areas"; "dilutees" were accepted in many craft industries.'

To support the war effort Cadbury turned out aircraft seats, and part of the Bournville factory was let to Austin for the production of aircraft gun magazines and helmets, and to Lucas to enable them to increase rotating gun turret and Sten gun magazine production. Bournville Utilities Ltd was established in 1940 and 2,000 employees were transferred to the new company. The Moulding Department produced gun doors for Spitfires, air-intake and super-charger controls for Stirlings, and flare cases for other aeroplanes. Packing made gas masks, while Metals turned out pilots' seats for Defiants, junction boxes for Wellingtons, and upper-mid gun turrets for Stirlings. Other departments churned out jerry cans, fuel tanks for Spitfires, Beaufighters, Lancasters, and Vosper motor torpedo boats. Anti-aircraft rockets were filled with explosives, and 600 workers produced over five million gas masks and six million canisters. Only fifteen of these were men; the work best suited to the 'nimble fingers'

A reproduction of the wartime KitKat.

of women. Sheep grazed on the green, Bournville was shrouded in wire camouflage netting, 'mercy vans' carrying hot cocoa were sent into the Birmingham city centre during raids, the recreation fields were dug for Victory, and the Cadbury Home Guard was formed.

IN May 1940, when the Allied armies were in full retreat in the west, the Secretary of State for War, Mr. Anthony Eden, appealed to men of all ages to volunteer for home defence. In our own city of York, the response was immediate. In consultation with Brigadier-Gen. P. V. Kelly, C.M.G., D.S.O., who had been appointed to organize the defence of the City, it was agreed by the directors that the Cocoa Works would organize a company of Local Defence Volunteers, and would provide all possible facilities. A few days later, "No. 3 Company," as the Works' Company was called, had been formed. It quickly grew in strength and skill, thanks especially to the experience and enthusiasm of the men at the Works who had served in World War I.

In a very short time supplies of Denim overalls, caps, rifles and ammunition were obtained. Firing practices were carried out on the range at Fulford Barracks, and, by the courtesy of St. Peter's School, on the School's miniature rifle range. Night patrols were soon operating and covered Haxby Road, Haley's Terrace, Huntington Road, New Lane, Malton Road, Stockton Lane, Tang Hall Lane and the Central Electricity Board Grid Station at Osbaldwick. The tower on the A.B.X. Block was used as a look-out post. Strong points were built, slit trenches dug (and oh, how wet they were!) and pill boxes erected on the perimeter defence line.

Well-earned honours awarded to members include:—
British Empire Medal—Lieut. D. Battle (Gum Department).
Certificate of Merit—Lieut. J. Delaney (Sales Stat.).
C.Q.M.S. H. R. Cockerill (Card Box Mill).
Sgt. W. Vassie (Engineers).
Pte. T. Wright (Cake Department).

Practice with the Northover Projector on Rowntree's Sports Ground.

A page from The Cocoa Works in War-time.

Fry's were able to make a positive contribution to the war effort by giving up factory floor space to the production of Rolls Royce Merlin engines. Somerdale became the Bristol Aeroplane Company.

Both York and Norwich were among the historical cities targeted by Goering in the notorious 1942 Baedecker raids, launched in reprisal for the RAF's destruction of the fine town of Lübeck. Rowntree in York survived largely intact, although the North Street warehouse was destroyed by incendiaries and other sites in other locations suffered. The London depot and Shuttleworth, the London subsidiary, were bombed out, as were the Southampton depot and Hughes in Birmingham, the company's biscuit makers. Caley's factory in Norwich was completely destroyed.

Branding and packaging reflected the conditions and times. On the confectionery front in the 1940s there was Mackay's ARP toffee whose wrappers showed barrage balloons and anti-aircraft guns, while Cadbury's had their Ration Chocolate. Indeed, because of the shortage of full cream milk, separated milk was used to produce blended chocolate, as manufactured by Nestlé and Cadbury. Apart from its obvious nutritional and energy benefits to World War II troops, the chocolate that was sent out to them had other uses, not least as civilizing gifts and peace offerings to liberated populations and as 'romantic gestures' to local girls and women. KitKat, in its downgraded form, was a vital food during the war and was advertised as 'What active people need.'

At Rowntree, 13,000 square feet of floor space in the new office block was put at the disposal of 300 clerks of the Royal Army Pay Corps. The Fruit Gum Department, at the request of the Ministry Of Food, manufactured jams and marmalade for Frank Cooper Ltd of Oxford. Part of the Almond Block extension was used by York firm Cooke, Troughton and Simms for the manufacture of optical instruments. From the Cream Department came National Milk Cocoa, Ryvita, Household Milk and Dried Egg. The site next to the sports ground was chosen for the storage of explosives for County Industries Ltd (C.I.L), a company set up mainly to produce shell and mine fuses and housed in the Smarties block. The Card Box Mill replaced its production of fancy boxes to become a main supply depot for the R.A.S.C. Northern Command. The rest centre in the Dining Block was a refuge for blitzed families, particularly in the aftermath of the Baedecker raid when it was requisitioned for five nights. A VAD hospital with 100 or so beds occupied the rest of the building. The nursery was also in there and this allowed mothers of children aged six months to five years of age to come to work. At any one time sixty children were looked after. Cots and other furniture were made by the work's joiners and the orchard behind the Dining Block became the playground.

The target for C.I.L. set by the Ministry Of Supply was 100,000 fuses per week, made mainly for the shells used in twenty-five pounder guns. This was exceeded. By the end of the war they had also turned out four million anti-tank mine fuses. Workers in contact with explosive powder had to protect their skin and so 'make up' rooms were set up where special face powder and topical creams were made available for their use. The girls and women were advised to drink milk rather than tea or coffee at their mid-shift break. The sixty men and 850 women here worked alternate day and night shifts, and were under the management of the aptly named Mr N.G. Sparkes. Most of them had been transferred from production work in the Cocoa Works.

Most of the work was done by County Industries Ltd. There was a contract for a subsidiary company to make flare lanyards. These consisted of cord wound on to an iron bracket and were used to effect delayed action to make the dropping of flares safer. The Card Box Department, housed in the main factory, undertook two contracts for the Ministry Of Supply for exploder bags used in the manufacture of high explosives. More than two million tubes were made from special waxed paper which had to be rolled and sealed. Later, rubberised material became available, and this was substituted for the

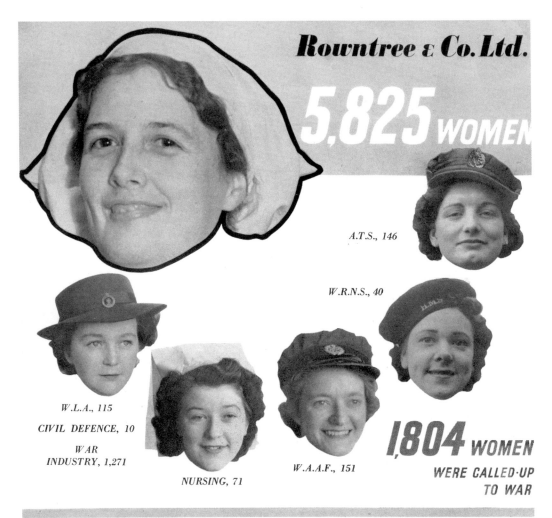

Rowntree & Co. Ltd.

5,825 WOMEN

A.T.S., 146

W.R.N.S., 40

W.L.A., 115

CIVIL DEFENCE, 10

WAR INDUSTRY, 1,271

NURSING, 71

W.A.A.F., 151

1,804 WOMEN WERE CALLED-UP TO WAR

DISTRIBUTION OF RANKS (Male Employees)

Royal Navy		Army		Royal Air Force		Civil Defence
incldg. Royal Marines		Pte. · · · 1,325		A.C.1, A.C.2 · 94		*(Full Time)*
		L/Cpl. · · · 141		L.A.C. · · · 201		
O/Seaman · · 155		Cpl. · · · 167		Cpl. · · · 74		15
A/Seaman · · 135		Sgt. · · · 147		Sgt. · · · 34		
L/Seaman · · 49		S/Sgt. · · · 6		F/Sgt. · · · 6		
Petty Officer · 35		W.O.II · · · 39		W.O. · · · 11		War Industries
Chief Petty Officer 4		W.O.I. · · · 1		P.O. · · · 6		
S/Lt. · · · 2		2nd/Lt. · · · 3		F.O. · · · 10		293
Lt. · · · 6		Lt. · · · 14		F/Lt. · · · 11		
Capt. (R.M.) · 1		Capt. · · · 22		S/Ldr. · · · 2		
		Major · · · 12				
		Lt.-Col. · · 1				
		Brigadier · · 1				
Total 387		Total 1,879		Total 449		Grand Total 3,023

24

waxed paper. As in the case of C.I.L. fuses, the work had to reach a very high standard before it was passed by the Government inspectors.

Special wooden cases were made in the Sawmill for the Ministry Of Supply; some were used for smoke generator cases, others were for fuses produced by C.I.L. The White Tile Heaters Company was also allocated space in the Sawmill for work carried out for the

7 *Shutter stemming machine.*

8 *Spinning the magazine.*

9 *The "Emergency."*

10 *Mr. C. Lambert, B.E.M., technical foreman.*

11 *Waterproofing and stabbing the centrifugal bolt hole plug.*

Bomb damage in York in 1941.

Ministry Of Aircraft Production. Sea markers had to be filled, assembled and made air and watertight, and flame floats and land mines were also made; the latter involving the welding of components, assembling, checking for accurate functioning, and packing into wooden cases with special fittings and frame-work made by the Sawmill.

ARP work included the construction of three underground tunnel shelters in the orchard, rose garden and near the Wigginton Road entrance. The fire brigade comprised twenty-three full time and eighty part-time staff, complemented by 145 fire guards. The air-raid siren was on the top of the Elect Cocoa Block – throughout the war it sounded 140 times in blasts that lasted for 209 hours in total.

The Estates Department was busy digging for victory and between 1939 and 1945 eight tons each of tomatoes, cabbage and onions, three tons of leeks, two tons of Brussels sprouts and 13,000 heads of lettuce along with smaller quantities of other vegetables were produced.

One of the most productive departments in the factory was the Cake (Chocolate Moulding) Department which was engaged in the production of various types of war-time chocolate. Vitaminised plain chocolate was made for army rations and for distribution by U.N.R.R.A. for the relief of starving children in Europe. Blended chocolate and vitaminised Plain York Chocolate was made for prisoner-of-war parcels. At Christmas, these were sent out with special wrappers.

Special chocolate 'Naps' in sealed tins were supplied to the Ministry of War Transport as emergency rations for use on ships, lifeboats and rafts. Pacific and Jungle chocolate was specially produced to withstand high temperatures for troops and sailors in tropical climates. A similar type of chocolate is still produced in Australian chocolate factories today. Oatmeal Block and Fruit Bar was made for the servicemen in the Far East. U.S. Army Field Ration Vitaminised chocolate, known as ration D, was specially packed for the American forces. An Army Emergency Ration Special Chocolate that was hermetically

The Caley factory after the Baedecker raid.

Part of the CIL wartime workforce.

Bournville cocoa as rations.

sealed in tins was also manufactured, along with special chocolate rations for use by air crew after they have baled out. All the war-time products had special wrapping materials including glascine, silver foil and heat sealed cellophane for the tropical chocolate.

By 1940, the company was looking for a site for cocoa essence production that was less vulnerable to air raid damage or destruction. An old cotton mill was found at Walsden in the Pennines, on the border of Lancashire and Yorkshire. Under the supervision of Mr R.C.E. Cable a staff of some fifty men and forty women was assembled, and between September 1941 and the end of the war in Europe, several thousand tons of cocoa were produced there. The Cream Department back in York carried out various activities including the packing of seven-and-a-half million tins of household milk and nine million tins of dried egg, as well as assembling and despatching of over four million anti-tank mine fuses. In February 1941, after a raid on Birmingham destroyed the Ryvita factory, part of Ryvita biscuit production was transferred to the York Cream Department.

But it wasn't all work and no play. The Rowntree Roundup entertainers gave over three hundred performances at locations which included anti-aircraft posts and searchlight units; sometimes from a specially converted bus. The Ballet Rambert and the BBC Northern Orchestra under Charles Groves also gave a performance at the factory.

Rowntree & Co Ltd staff called up to war numbered 1,804 out of 5,825 women and 3,023 out of 6,009 men. They went to the Royal Navy (387 including eight officers), Army (1879 including fifty-three officers with one Lieutenant Colonel and one Brigadier), Royal Air Force (449, including two Squadron Leaders), or Civil Defence (fifteen), or were directed to war industries (293). The women went to seven different destinations – most (1,271) to other war industries; 146 joined the ATS, 151 the WAAF, 115 the Land

Rations produced by Rowntree, including those for Frank Cooper.

Army, forty to the WRNS, and seventy-one became nurses. The 200-strong Rowntree Local Defence Volunteers was formed and later became 'C' Company the 14th West Riding Home Guard Battalion.

Honours and awards were plentiful. One Military Cross; one Air Force Cross; three Distinguished Conduct Medals; six Military Medals; three Distinguished Flying Medals; five British Empire Medals (three Military and two Civil Division) and fourteen Mentions in Dispatches. £5,989 was raised for the Red Cross during the course of the war by Rowntree employees.

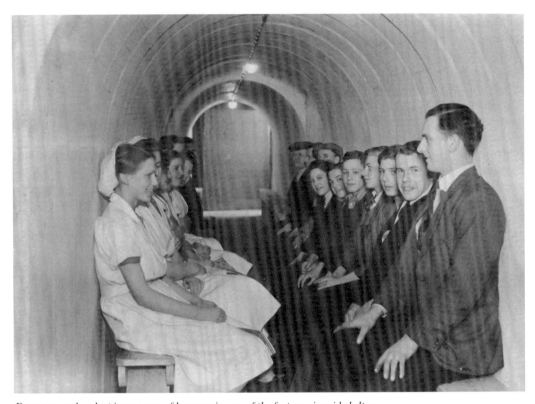

Rowntree workers keeping a sense of humour in one of the factory air raid shelters.

Rowntree: 1946–1969

AFTER THE Second World War the privations suffered by the chocolate companies were to continue until 1953 when rationing was finally ended. To make matters worse, cocoa disease in 1948 wiped out sixteen per cent of the world's cocoa supply, thus pushing up the price to £237 per tonne – six times the pre-war price. It was a period of consolidation for all the companies.

One of Rowntree's first post war acts was to resume the interrupted launch of Polo Digestive Mints which eventually took place in 1948. The word 'digestive' was soon removed from the brand name and from advertising, as no scientific evidence could be found for its alleged action as an antacid. Instead, the launch slogan 'the mint with the hole' was eventually adopted. The wording 'Made by Rowntrees' on the sweet itself was sacrificed to deflect any litigation that may arise from the very similar US product Lifesaver. A competitor to Fry's Crunchie was also launched around this time under the name Cracknel Block – but without success.

In January 1952 George Harris left the company. He was seen by many as having played a major part in delivering much of the company's success in the thirties, and positioning it for the role it was to play in the world chocolate industry in the second half of the century. William Wallace was his successor to be followed by Lloyd Owen in 1957.

Confectionery consumption peaked in 1954 – the year after rationing ended – at 9.4 oz per head, falling back to 8.3 oz by 1962. National sales were £251.1m and £290.8m for those years. As a percentage of consumer expenditure it was steady at around one-and-a half-per cent. Riding on the success of Polo Mints, Polo Fruits were launched in 1954, although these faced stiff opposition from Mars' Spangles. KitKat, facing competition from Terry's Waifa and MacDonald's Penguin, was repositioned in the market place to take maximum advantage of its attraction as a mid-morning snack. As a consequence, the famous slogan 'Have a break have a KitKat' was introduced in May 1957, along with the broken bar image – all playing, of course, on the word 'break.' The Nux Bar – a combination of chocolate, hazelnuts and Rice Krispies – was introduced in 1957, and production started on St Michael's Wafers for Marks & Spencer, using KitKat off-cuts in the factory at Tunbridge Wells.

It is no surprise that confectionery companies were amongst the early advertisers on commercial television on its launch in 1955. The first to show were Gibbs with SR Toothpaste, followed by offerings from Cross & Blackwell, and Persil from Unilever. Rowntree was prepared for this revolution with a budget of £50,000. Some of the more memorable confectionery slogans include: Beecham's Murraymints – 'the too-good-to-hurry-mints' and, for Rowntree's Fruit Gums: 'Don't forget the fruit gums, mum.'

Music While you Work—at the Cocoa Works 40 years ago

ROWNTREE SWIMMING CLUB

It is hoped to restart after Easter. All who are interested in swimming are invited to send names, check numbers, and departments to the Joint Secretaries—Miss U. F. Schwabe, Women's Social Dept., and Mr. W. Payne, Melangeur Dept.

THE MOOR AND FELL CLUB

In spite of restrictions placed upon activities by war conditions, we succeed in having a walk every month.

During the last few months there were excursions around Leavening, Pond Head and Gilling Castle, and a cross-country walk from Thirsk to Helmsley.

" . . . .
*All at once I saw a crowd,
A host of golden daffodils ;
Beside the lake, beneath the trees,
Fluttering and dancing in the breeze."*
        —*Wordsworth.*

(*Photo taken at Moorlands, near Wiggington, by J. R. Ridges*)

COCOA WORKS' WAR MEMORIAL FUND

As it is some time since particulars of this special fund were published, we reprint below the official notice to remind employees of its existence and its purpose.

The object of the Fund shall be to assist certain employees of the Company and the widows and dependants of such employees.

The Fund shall be applied by the Committee in any one or more of the following ways :—

(a) In assisting employees who have been disabled or partially disabled in the course of their duties whilst serving in His Majesty's Forces or in a Civil Defence Organisation by supplementing any State help they may receive, providing special surgical aids, providing medical and/or convalescent treatment, and making grants and giving any other assistance they may think fit with a view to assisting such employees to earn a livelihood.

(b) In assisting widows and/or dependants of employees who have been killed or who have died as a result of injury or disease contracted in the course of their duties whilst serving in His Majesty's Forces or a Civil Defence Organisation who may be in special distress or need.

(c) In making grants to help in the education of the children of the employees mentioned in paragraphs (a) and (b) of this Clause.

13

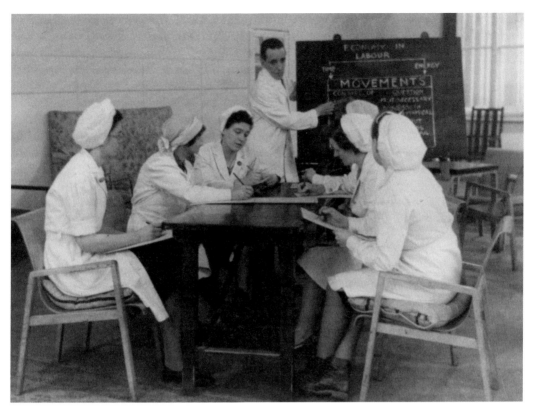

Packing training course after the war.

Polar cool Polos were 'The mint with the hole.' In 1957, viewers were invited to 'have a break, have a KitKat'. By the next year the Rowntree television advertising budget had increased to £650,000, half the total advertising budget. By 1958 sixty per cent of all chocolate advertising money went on TV commercials. Nationally, TV advertising accounted for one per cent of all advertising spend in 1955, thirteen per cent in 1958 and twenty-two per cent in 1960.

By 1960, the principal chocolate companies were in the top ten of annual advertising spend: Cadbury was spending £3.2 million, Mars £2.9 million and Rowntrees £2.8 million. These figures put them fifth, sixth and seventh respectively in the UK advertising spend league table with Unilever number one with £13.1 million and Beecham next with £6.3 million.

The Fawdon factory, three-and-a-half miles from Newcastle, opened in 1958 to meet the increased demand for chocolate caused by even greater disposable incomes and population increases. Cost was nearly £2.6 million with a workforce approaching 1,000, 800 men and 200 women. KitKat continued to thrive, and fourteen per cent of the 1958 advertising budget of £1.8 million was allocated to the line. Sainsbury, Tesco and groups of retailers like Spar were becoming increasingly important in the market with their focus on price. Rowntree, in common with other food manufacturers, realised that they would have to adapt to provide different ways of selling, merchandising and packaging their product. The multipack was about to be born.

In 1959 Caramac was launched. Nux, though, lost the battle against Fry's Picnic. Peppermint and orange Aeros came in 1959 and 1960 respectively. The first significant new product of the 1960s was in 1962 when After Eight Thin Mints was launched with its sophisticated dinner party market and suggestions of an aspirational life style. Smart packaging in elegant green boxes and individual envelopes, the timely clock – all had considerable appeal to an increasingly image conscious nineteen sixties market. This was enhanced by a successful television advertising campaign showing sophisticates enjoying their wafer thin After Eight mints with their post prandial coffee. Things had come a long way since Montezuma and Cortes. The Thin Mints wording was soon dropped, leaving the name we all know, After Eight.

All this was achieved in the face of rising sugar and cocoa costs and punitive Conservative taxation changes; firstly in 1961 a ten per cent levy on television advertising and then the introduction of Purchase Tax on confectionery. The effect was a decline in the overall consumption per week per head from 8.6 oz to 8.0 oz. By now, though KitKat contributed twenty per cent of Rowntree revenues and commanded an annual marketing budget of £600,000 – easily shrugging off the competition launched by Cadbury in 1963 in the shape of Bar 6. Smarties dealt similarly with Cadbury's Trillions. Jellytots arrived in 1965 to compete successfully with Mackintosh's Tooty Fruities. Motoring Bar had been renamed Fruit and Nut in 1963 but could not compete with its namesake down at Cadbury and was killed off in 1965.

In 1964, resale price maintenance was abolished and this opened the way for large supermarkets to reduce prices. Tesco, (half of whose confectionery sales were own brand), and Sainsbury were not only emerging as large customers but as serious competitors too. By 1966 Rowntree had fifteen per cent of the of the UK confectionery business, and KitKat was still the flagship brand. A new KitKat plant was built to preserve this status with enhanced production and wrapping. Lloyd Owen died suddenly in 1966 and despite successful operations in Canada, South Africa and Australia, did not meet his

KitKat Crossword Competiton in 1968.

objective of turning Rowntree into a global business. It remained, for now, very much a parochial concern centered on York, albeit with some increasingly successful products.

The next significant launch was Matchmakers in 1968; seventy or so orange flavoured chocolate covered sticks, elegantly packaged in an orange-coloured box – all very reminiscent of the style and sophistication of After Eight. The name not only reflected a physical association with matches (which at the time carried none of today's stigma from its association with cigarettes) – reinforced by the match box style box – but it also evoked unmistakable suggestions of romance and romantic situations in which Matchmakers could be shared and enjoyed.

While Cadbury was busy joining up with Schweppes in 1969, Rowntree merged with Mackintosh, so bringing such household names as Rolo, Toffee Crisp, Toffo, Weekend, Quality Street and Fox's (whom Mackintosh had recently bought themselves) Glacier Mints to the fold and, with twenty-two per cent of the market, consolidating the combined companies as the UK's second largest chocolate manufacturer behind Cadbury at twenty-three per cent. Rowntree Mackintosh Ltd was thus born, providing a platform for further expansion in continental Europe and enabling the company to position itself as a truly global company. The first step in this direction was taken when Rowntree bought Chocolat Menier in 1971 through its German subsidiary, Stockmann. That same year, the company was awarded the Queen's Award for Industry for its achievements in exports.

During the 1960s, reflecting the huge popularity of music generally, the 'The Music Room' at Rowntree assumed great importance amongst factory floor workers. The music which came from there could be heard not only throughout the whole factory site, but also down the Haxby and Wigginton Roads if the wind was blowing in a certain direction. Frequently, in the early hours of the morning, residents living nearby would ring in and ask for the music to be turned down. *Special Requests* ('Mixed Bag') was especially popular as was the BBC's *Music While You Work*. One record which always had a lot of airplay from 1964 was the Beatles' *I Want To Hold Your Hand* which was played to alert employees that the Medical Department was on its way round to check hands, nails and general hygiene and cleanliness.

We can now look at the histories of Caley and Mackintosh, since the heritage and character of both companies was, from 1969, an integral part of Rowntree's story and, therefore, relevant to the confectionery industry in York.

Caley of Norwich

IN 1857 Albert Jarman Caley opened a chemist's business in London Street, Norwich, and in 1863 began manufacturing mineral waters in the cellars, later moving to a factory in Chapel Field using water from two deep artesian wells. Because sales of mineral water were seasonal, in 1883 he began making drinking chocolate as a winter drink to balance out the year. This was followed by eating-chocolate three years later, manufactured at the Fleur de Lys factory. In 1898 Christmas cracker-manufacture began to keep the girls who wrapped and decorated the chocolate boxes busy year round. A.J. Caley & Sons Ltd was formed at this time; their London chocolate showroom was in Bishopsgate Street.

To compete with Swiss imports, Caley insisted on the best milk, and drew their supplies from the famous Whitlingham herd of red-polled cattle. An early description of the packing department tells us that 'the girls are all dressed in neat striped print uniforms, and they look quite picturesque while working.' In 1918, the African and Eastern Trade Corporation bought Caley. The Corporation, a Liverpool company with interests in a number of African colonies, itself later became a subsidiary of Unilever.

John Mackintosh & Sons Ltd. of Halifax acquired Caley's in 1932 for £138,000, although the Caley's brand name continued to be used until the early 1960s. The successful Diamond Line range was launched, and a Royal Warrant was granted by Queen Mary in 1932. Their Kondor coffee and Dubarry biscuits – half-biscuit, half-chocolate confectionery – nevertheless failed. In 1935 mineral water production was halted and the following year Double Six – a chocolate bar filled with six different centres – was launched. So successful was it that the response was described by Eric Mackintosh as 'a little frightening.' South Wales miners' wives were apparently giving their husbands Double Six sandwiches for lunch.

The war and 1941 saw the first manufacture of 'Cocoa Rich' Milk Marching Chocolate; Some Cadbury production was transferred from Bournville, as it was to Rowntree.

We already know that in 1942 Caley's Norwich factory was destroyed by the Luftwaffe in the Baedecker Raid. Eric Mackintosh described the scene: 'A smouldering,

Mr A.J. Caley.

One of the many impressive Caley posters, 1905.

A fine 1899 Munnings poster for Caley.

Santa Claus wins over the children's market Christmas 1912 with Caley's Chocolate.

This Caley chocolate advertisement also features their line in Christmas crackers.

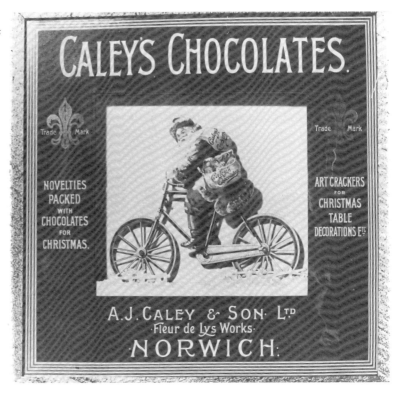

A Caley Marching Chocolate float for the Army Queen competition during the Second World War – chocolates 'unsurpassed for quality'.

smelling, twisted jumble of steel and concrete. [watched] by a crowd of tired, dirty, heart-broken colleagues ... a thousand or so employees stood around, dazed and unable to believe their eyes'. Nevertheless, all was not lost and the factory re-opened after rebuilding in 1956. Production of Caley lines had been moved to Halifax in the interim. The mineral water and cracker businesses were sold off.

In 1969, Mackintosh's merged with Rowntree to form Rowntree Mackintosh. Norwich was made responsible for production of Weekend, Good News, Rolo, Munchies, Mintola,

The Caley Fleur de Lys factory before the Luftwaffe came...

...and after it had left.

A 1933 Caley price list – simple and elegant, as with all of their designs.

Caley's Fortune selection to keep the ARP going.

Caramac, Golden Cup and Easter eggs, and, paradoxically, Yorkie. One hundred years of chocolate making was celebrated in Norwich in 1986. Then, in 1988, Nestlé acquired Rowntree Mackintosh. The Norwich factory closed in 1994, and in 1996 three former executives acquired Caley's brands and production equipment from Nestlé, and formed Caley's of Norwich Ltd. In 1997, Caley's Plain Marching Chocolate was relaunched, and in 1998 Caley's Milk Marching Chocolate was reintroduced.

The Caley name lives on in Norwich and since 2002 the 15th century Guildhall has been home to Caley's Cocoa Café. It is a traditionally-styled tea-room with the history of Caley depicted around the walls. Today, Caley market their Fairtrade chocolates and hot drinks from their website, and since 2008 they have been partners with *Help for Heroes*, selling, amongst other products, the revived Marching Chocolate. In 2010 a second Cocoa Cafe opened in Norwich's White Lion Street.

Mackintosh of Halifax

ESTABLISHED by John and Violet Mackintosh in a Halifax pastry shop in King Cross Lane in 1890, the company, financed with the £100 they had saved between them, started off making and selling Mackintosh's Celebrated Toffee, a winning mixture of English butterscotch and American caramel. The then innovative step of giving away samples was exploited to the full by Mackintosh. One week he was inviting customers to come and taste a sample for free, the next he was telling them to come again and 'eat it at your expense'. So successful was he that by 1896 Mackintosh was styling himself 'Toffee King'. Soon after, he bought a warehouse in Hope Street and made his toffee there, and then, in 1899, he paid £15,000 for a new factory in Queen's Road. Unfortunately, this burned to the ground in 1909, so the firm moved to an old factory, Albion Mills. Queen's Road was later rebuilt.

Mackintosh was keen to increase his export business, but this was not without its problems. In continental Europe, some potential customers mistook, and confused toffee with coffee and poured boiling water on it – 'with unsatisfactory results'. In the US, the extreme variations in climate wreaked havoc and, depending on the time of year, toffee was melting in one state and acquiring an adamantine hardness in another. This is how he modestly heralded his entry into the US market: 'I am John Mackintosh, the Toffee King, Sovereign of Pleasure, Emperor of Joy. My old English candy tickles my millions of subjects. I was crowned by the lovers of good things to eat. I am the world's largest consumer of butter, my own herd of prize cattle graze on the Yorkshire hills. I buy sugar by the trainload. I am John Mackintosh, Toffee King of England and I rule alone.' His eloquence and efforts were rewarded with success, even in very difficult markets like China where the toffee he supplied was pink.

Chocolate-coated Toffee Deluxe was launched in 1917, followed by Mackintosh Chocolate in 1924. In 1920, John and Violet's son, Harold Mackintosh – later 1st Viscount Mackintosh of Halifax – took on the business, which by now was called John Mackintosh & Sons Ltd. He developed the Methodist principles on which the firm had been founded, notably enlightened management and labour relations. In 1932 he bought the A.J. Caley confectionery company in Norwich from Unilever, which allowed Mackintosh's to expand its range of products and specialise in chocolate products such as Quality Street; this was launched in 1936 and Rolo in 1938.

The Quality Street name comes from the play of the same name by Peter Pan author J. M. Barrie. The 'Major Quality' and 'Miss Sweetly' figures were inspired by the play's main characters, and appeared on all Quality Street boxes and tins until 2000. They, in turn, were originally modelled by Iris and Tony Coles, the children of Sydney Coles who created the brand's image.

Mackintosh Toffee de Luxe advertisements.

The little Cherub Whispers

"There's a smile in every piece"

Mackintosh's Toffee de Luxe

Get the Mackintosh Smile

You can also get the "Smiles" chocolate-coated. Ask for Mackintosh's CHOCOLATE Toffee-de-Luxe.

MADE BY JOHN MACKINTOSH & SONS LTD HALIFAX

Mackintosh took an advertisement on the front page of the *Daily Mail*, on 2 May 1936 – 'An introduction to Quality Street'. It shows Miss Sweetly tempting Major Quality with a tin of the sweets. 'Sweets to the sweet, Miss Sweetly?' asks the Major, to which she replies: 'Spare my blushes Major Quality, feast your eyes rather on this sumptuous array of toffees and chocolates.'Tis the most momentous thing that has yet happened in the world of sweetness.' She gives him a 'toffee creme brazil' which he declares 'a veritable triumph!'

The iconic Quality Street tin.

Seven million Quality Street chocolates are now produced every day, the most popular out of the seventeen multi-shaped shaped assortment being The Purple One. The slogan for the trade in the 1930s was 'put your shop in Quality Street by putting Quality Street in your shop.' Heath Robinson and Mabel Lucie Atwell were among the artists who drew for Mackintosh, most famously for the Toffee Town advertisements.

The purchase of Bellamy's and then Fox's, brought Liquorice Allsorts and Fox's Glacier Mints respectively into the catalogues. Other products included Beehive Toffee from the 1920s, Creamy Rolls, whose wrapper featured a milk maid and her cows (1920 to 1929), Cresta from 1950 – Caramac (1959), Cracknel Bon-Bons, Toffo, Toffee Crisp, Golden Toffee Wafers, Munchies, the Weekend assortment in 1957 and Good News in 1960. Mackintosh was acquired by Rowntree's in 1969.

"QUALITY STREET."

Valentine Brown [Mr. S. Hicks] in Search of Grey Hairs.

A scene from Barrie's Quality Street.

Rowntree: 1970–1999

THE seventies saw a marked shift in Rowntree's sales mix. In 1969, thirty-six per cent of sales and twenty-nine per cent of profit came from export markets. By 1976 this had changed to forty-nine per cent and forty-three per cent. In 1987, confectionery sales in the UK were just over £3 billion; by comparison bread was £1.7 billion and milk was £1.6 billion.

One of the key events in the 1970s for Rowntree was the launch of the Yorkie bar. In 1976, Eric Nicoli identified a gap in the confectionery market and used low-price cocoa bought through Rowntree's favourable futures market position to launch it. Production was at York and Norwich until 1994.

The Yorkie bar, a chunkier, heavyweight alternative to Cadbury's Dairy Milk, was ostensibly aimed at men. In the 1980s, television advertisements for the Yorkie bar featured truck drivers. In 2001, the new advertising campaign made this more explicit with the slogan and wrapper tag-line: 'It's not for girls', illustrated by a road sign-type logo debarring girls. This caused some controversy at the time, although the images and wording are still nevertheless much in evidence today. Special supplies for use in Ministry of Defence ration packs read: 'It's not for civvies'. In 2006 a special edition in pink wrappers that *was* for girls was launched. If you were to arrive in York by train around ten years ago, you would pass a large sign which read: 'Welcome to York where the men are hunky and the chocolate's chunky.' Truisms both. Apart from the original milk chocolate bar, several variants are available, such as 'raisin and biscuit' flavour, 'honeycomb' flavour, and Yorkie Ice Cream.

KitKat, though, continued to dominate. A corporate advertisement in 1987 asserts that enough KitKats are produced every hour to reach to the top of the Empire State Building four times over, and that thirty million KitKats are sold in 100 countries every week.

In 1988, Rowntree Mackintosh plc was the world's fourth largest confectionery manufacturer after Hershey, Mars and Cadbury; turnover was £1.4 billion in twenty-five subsidiaries with 33,000 employees. A take-over bid by Jacobs Suchard in 1988 failed (Suchard had already acquired Côte d'Or and van Houten). The company was now vulnerable to take-over as the Trusts had reduced their stake in the company to seven per cent. That same year, Rowntree Mackintosh was bought by Nestlé. Before Suchard's bid, Rowntree shares were trading at £4.68. To acquire these pre-eminent brands, Nestlé in the end paid £10.75 – a handsome twenty-six times multiple based on 1987 profits. All this was despite unsuccessful attempts by Cadbury to keep Rowntree Mackintosh British by appealing to the Department of Trade & Industry to relax competition rules and allow them to acquire the company.

The main event of the 1980s was the take-over of Rowntree plc by Nestlé. Before that, though, there were two significant product launches and important developments in new plant and technology. In 1980 – Drifter was launched, followed by Aero Countline in 1982. An automated warehouse opened in 1985 and in the following year, the £16 million KitKat 4 factory plant started production. The company name changed to Rowntree plc in 1987 and 1989 saw the company receive its fourth Queen's Award for Export Achievement.

At the beginning of the next decade, in 1991, the £14 million Cocoa Processing Plant was opened, and Helmut Maucher, Nestlé SA Chairman and Managing Director, cut the ribbon on the £6 million Yorkreco Pilot Plant. One year later, Ramon Masip, Executive Vice President of Nestlé SA, opened the £15.5 million Polo Mint plant in York. The year 1993 saw an £18 million chocolate-making plant open in York. It can produce four tonnes of milk chocolate an hour. Product launches included Vice Versas in 1992; Maverick in 1997 and KitKat Chunky in 1999.

Collecting Rowntrees

By Joe Dickinson

I WAS fifteen when I joined Rowntrees in Haxby Road in 1959. It was here that I followed in my father's footsteps and spent my whole working life there. For most of that time my job was to manage thousands of tons of waste chocolate and ingredients, grading it all either for recycling, for sale in the employees' shop or passing it on for cattle or pig food. Any contaminated waste was destroyed by fire.

Some of my earliest memories are of the lovely gardens around the factory's sitting areas, their shady trees and wonderful, colourful flower borders – a real factory parkland. I still remember a tropical circular greenhouse filled with cocoa, coffee, sugarcane, vanilla and other plants used in the cocoa industry; here employees could see the plants growing that their jobs depended on. So, on a cold day, it was nice to go through a door into the tropics at dinnertime or break, or else sit in the shade on very hot days in the factory grounds with the smell of cocoa blending with scented flowers blossoms and fresh cut grass. A superb experience.

When my father was at Bedern School, off Goodramgate in York, he was given a tin of Rowntrees chocolate as a souvenir, presented by H.R.H. The Duke Of York on April 26th 1923. My father gave this

Early Rowntree Advertisements.

Tanner's Moat soon after Rowntree moved in.

tin to me when I was fifteen. Little did anyone know at the time that it was the start of a massive collection that would go on growing for more than fifty years. Today it is a unique collection of over 100,000 Rowntree items that completely fill a three bedroom house in York, which is used exclusively for the purpose. This is my private Rowntree museum. It consists of memorabilia and artefacts from Rowntree's foundation and early development in Victorian and Edwardian days, and extends right up to the 1960s. It includes hundreds of product samples, tins, boxes, and everything to do with the making, packing and advertising of Rowntrees chocolate. In effect, it is by far the largest single collection of Rowntree material in the world.

Among other things, the pictures in this chapter show some of the products made by Henry Isaac Rowntree and his brother Joseph when they worked together at the Tanner's Moat Factory from 1864 to 1885. At the same time, they give a unique snapshot of the early changes in products, advertising, branding and packaging.

I gained much of my knowledge of the company by studying the annual Rowntree Easter, Summer and Christmas catalogues that were sent out to shops and carried by travellers. Those in my collection date from the 1890s to the 1990s and were used to get seasonal

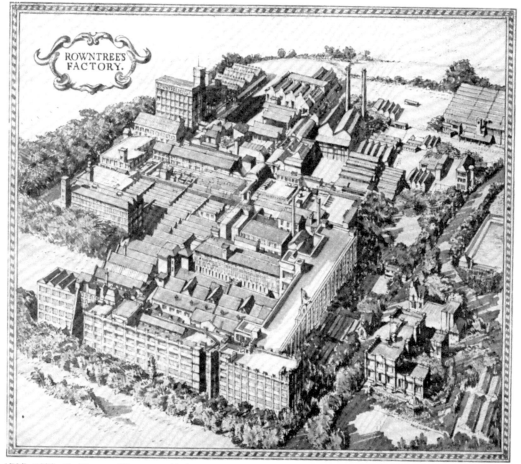

1725–1955, the history of Rowntree & Co Ltd is intimately bound up with the history of York. This great firm, world famous for its cocoa, chocolate and confectionery, is justly proud also of its contribution to the welfare and progress of the city.

The iconic Cocoa Nibs advertisement in Joe Dickinson's 'museum'.

The After Eight room in Joe Dickinson's museum.

The military version of Rowntree's Yorkie.

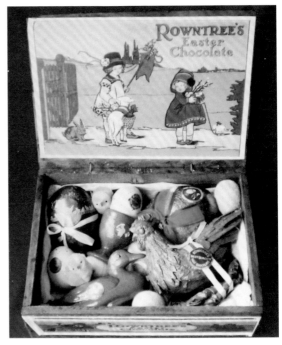

A selection of Easter chocolate novelties.

Early Rowntree lines with work rules and regulations for the Packing Department.

An impressive array of Rowntree signs and packaging.

Luncheon chocolate made in the early Tanner's Moat days.

orders to fulfil production demands at the busiest times of the year. At the same time, though, they are a very good aid for collectors because they have allowed me to identify all the different items related to Rowntree over the years, especially those products which did not bear the company's name. Companies routinely produced all kinds of sales incentives and point of sale items for the trade; at Rowntrees such collectables included cats, dogs, elephants and countless other receptacles, all at one time packed with chocolates. I even have teapots, oak biscuit barrels and many other household items. An important Rowntree offer for loyal customers from the Edwardian days were cocoa and jelly coupons. The more cocoa and jelly you could eat the more coupons you could save. The company produced gift catalogues from which you could select items to redeem your coupons. These ranged from small boxes of chocolates to every household item you can think of; the very best and most expensive included gramophones and bicycles. You had to like your cocoa and jelly though to get these.

Why would anyone want a chocolate museum? That is a question I have asked myself many times over the years. I have been a collector of memorabilia for sixty years, since I was five-years-old when I was collecting match box labels. I sold them all when I was twenty-five years-old, but recently started collecting them again after seeing one with a Victorian Rowntree advertisement on it for Homoeopathic Cocoa. This brought many childhood memories flooding back and it has been lucrative in all sorts of ways, but not just financially. Although it was through collecting that I was able to buy a house in 1997 with the proceeds from selling part of my York postcard collection, the rewards have come in so many other ways. So why Rowntree, and why collect over 100,000 Rowntree

The Rowntree Packing department in full swing.

items? Because it is my history, part of the history of York, the place where my father earned his living for his family, and the place where I worked for most of my life.

My interest in art and design, architecture and especially local history, contributed to my keenness to collect, as did the wonderful design, colours and quality of many of the items. A lot of history is connected to the old products, for example the early cameras came out in 1880 and by the turn of the century designers had learnt how to use photographic plate printing on their product packaging. In the collection I have a series of very early chocolate boxes featuring photographs on them – an historic leap forward for advertising and branding throughout industry.

Much of the collection is on show in old original mahogany Rowntree cabinets with the two original plate glass shelves and sliding doors at the back. Some even have the original name plate on the top although shopkeepers often took them off. Between 1890 and 1920 they cost one guinea each. Today's price for one in tip top condition is around £2,500. There are sixteen Rowntree cabinets in varying sizes in the museum; one was made in Rowntrees' factory in 1879 for Fruit Pastilles, specially built for an International Confectionery Exhibition in the USA to where it was shipped in 1880 and then left. In 2005 an international art dealer saw the old cabinet while negotiating a large deal and said that he would let the deal go through if it included the Rowntree Pastilles cabinet. I bought it from him and it was duly delivered to my York museum. It is in lovely condition, is now filled it with pastilles – and looks a treat. The collection became so big that many more cabinets were needed, and the only way forward was to design and build my own.

In 1997 I moved the collection into the three bed-roomed house where it remains today. It took over three days and fourteen vanloads and then five years to build and house everything just as I wanted it all to be.

I also have a large oak bookcase from Heny Isaac Rowntrees Tanners Moat Factory office. When the factory closed down in 1893, anything left was taken to the Rowntree Trust offices where it was stored in an outhouse and eventually bought by one of the workers who sold it on to me for £10.

Disaster struck in 2004. The chocolates in my collection were infested by weevils and cocoa moth – a small pink moth that makes a sort of web in which to lay its grub; they can reproduce every six weeks. Weevils lay hundreds of eggs, usually on smooth glass or ceramic surfaces in any temperature, and these can survive for years before hatching. They seem indestructible, but there is a chemical that deals with them. Both pests have one thing in common; they thrive on cocoa and chocolate and some other foods. It took me three years just to get rid of them, saving what I could as I went. Armed with a bus pass and a four-wheel shopping trolley, I ferried everything across the city a little at a time. The hundreds of chocolate boxes that were affected had to be scraped out and thoroughly washed, the aim being to save as many of the old chocolates as possible and keep them in isolation in airtight boxes.

The next job was to buy eleven five-kilo tins of silicone rubber at £95 per tin to make strong rubber moulds into which sixteen stones of casting plaster were poured. When removed, the thousands of now chocolate-shaped plaster chocolates were painted with three coats of milk chocolate paint or plain chocolate coloured paint as appropriate. Today the collection is restored and continues to give immense pleasure, to evoke fond memories, and to bask in the knowledge that it is without equal.

The pastille-filled cabinet.

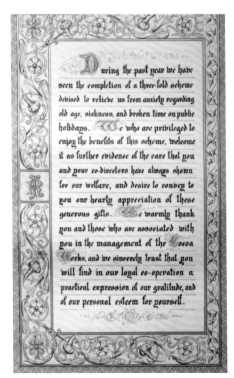

A piece of industrial relations history: Rowntree employees collectively thank the board for the benefits bestowed by the pension scheme.

One of the fine cabinets in Joe Dickinson's 'museum'.

Terry: 1767–1890

ON THE On the other side of the city Joseph Terry had been making cocoa and chocolate since 1886. By the end of the 1920s the firm had become the market leader in chocolate assortments, and were building a sound reputation for producing the best in dark and bitter chocolate. The origins of the company go right back to 1767 when there 'was founded near Bootham Bar, York, a confectionery business which was destined to develop, at first into a centre where the elite of the County enjoyed their sweetmeats, and, at last after phases of success with various specialties and operation at different centres in the City, into a Chocolate Factory the name of which is recognised throughout the World as synonymous with excellence of quality.' This confectionery business was run by Messrs William Bayldon and Robert Berry.

Joseph Terry, the son of a farmer, came to York from nearby Pocklington where he was born in 1793, to serve an apprenticeship in apothecary in Stonegate. An advertisement in the *York Courant* in 1813 proclaims that he is established 'opposite the Castle, selling spices, pickling vinegar, essence of spruce, patent medicines and perfumery', (the usual stock in trade for an apothecary.) Later, he moved this chemist's shop to Walmgate where he also practiced blood-letting using leeches, as was the usual practice. In 1823 Joseph married Harriet Atkinson, a sister-in-law of Robert Berry's. He then gave up being a chemist and druggist, and joined Berry who had moved from Bootham to St Helen's Square in 1824 – the site of the first Old Factory. The front of the building was the shop (known as 'The Front Shop') while the factory was to the rear in Brearley Yard. On offer were cakes, comfits, candied peel, marmalade, mushroom ketchup and medicated lozenges. In making this move, Joseph Terry deftly transferred from an old form of confection, a drug or pill, to the modern form – a sweet. His undoubted ability as an apothecary to 'sugar the pill' persists today with chemists selling sweets and sweet shops selling throat lozenges and the like.

George Berry succeeded his father to form the pleasantly rhyming Terry & Berry. This is how the *Yorkshire Gazette* of 29 October 1825 announced the new firm: 'Joseph Terry and George Berry, confectioners, St Helen's Square, having taken the Stock and entered upon the premises of the late Robert Berry and Co, most respectfully solicit both from the Friends of the late Firm and from the Public at large, that Patronage so liberally bestowed on their Predecessors, which they will ever faithfully and anxiously endeavour to merit. J. Terry respectfully acknowledges the very liberal Patronage bestowed upon him for the last ten years as Chemist and Druggist, in his late situation in Walmgate, and informs his friends that he has disposed of the stock of Drugs &c to Mr Tonge.' But George left in 1828, leaving Joseph to develop what then was essentially an expanding confectionery business.

York, as we have seen, attracted a prosperous class of visitor at the time, and was one of the places to be and to be seen in. It was certainly a good place to be running a catering business. The Assembly Rooms, one of the earliest neo-classical buildings in Europe, were nearby in Blake Street and, over the road, was the fine sweep of the late Georgian terrace which originally contained seven houses, a library and the Yorkshire Club. The Assembly Rooms were built in 1732 in the Palladian style by Lord Burlington, and paid for by subscription to provide the local gentry with somewhere to play dice and cards, dance and drink tea, as featured in Smollett's *The Expedition of Humphry Clinker.* The building epitomised the age of elegance and helped make York the centre of North Country fashion – a northern Bath if you will. The main hall is surrounded by forty-eight Corinthian pillars. Diagonally opposite is the attractive Red House built in 1718 on the site of St Leonard's Hospital, once the home of Dr John Burton – eminent obstetrician and the model for Dr Slop in Laurence Sterne's *Life and Opinions of Tristram Shandy.*

The Assembly rooms on the left, Georgian Terrace in St Leonard's Place beyond and the Red House on the right.

Sir Joseph Terry as Mayor of York in 1886 – his third time.

Other attractions, of course, were the races – and executions – at the Knavesmire. The assizes and any subsequent executions were often timed to coincide with the races for the convenience of the legal fraternity and the delectation of the race-goers. The Butter Market and the Dish Fair also brought in the crowds.

Joseph Terry himself was very active. He was on the committee of the Association for the Protection of Public and Trade of Confectioners and Lozenge Makers – an organisation formed to counter the growing trade in adulterated sweets: 'confectionery composed of injurious materials' – when it met at the George and Vulture Tavern in Lombard Street in March 1836.

By 1840 the railways started to facilitate transportation and, after a largely local Yorkshire distribution at first, Terry's product was being delivered to seventy-five towns all over England, including London. Products included candied eringo, coltfoot rock, pomfrets, gum balls and lozenges made from squill, camphor and horehound. Apart from boiled sweets, they also made marmalade, marzipan, mushroom ketchup and calves' jelly. Conversation lozenges, precursors of Love Hearts with such risqué slogans as 'Can you polka?', 'I want a wife', 'Do you love me?' and 'How do you flirt?' were particularly popular. The railways also brought tourists and other visitors with thirteen trains a day dropping off up to 30,000 passengers, replacing the two stage coaches which had brought in a mere 23,000 a year.

George Berry died in 1848. He had been missed at his customary Sunday bread dole, and a concerned neighbour found him dead at home in Mason's Buildings. The verdict

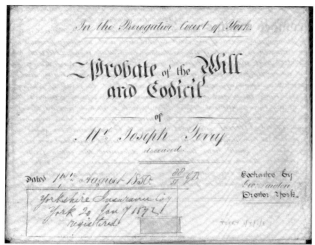

Joseph Terry's will.

of the inquest held at the Flying Horse in Coppergate was death caused by coronary heart disease, euphemized as 'died by visitation from God.' Joseph Terry died in Huntington, near York, in 1850 aged fifty-six. Bayldon and Berry had described him as 'a benign man' with 'a kindly attitude to others; courteous, fair and seeking the best.' Other descriptions were perhaps less flattering; one calling him 'a roly-poly of a man', possibly an indication that he rather enjoyed sampling his produce.

On his death he left the business to his son, Joseph Junior then aged twenty-two, who joined the company with brothers Robert and John. They took over in 1854 after a brief interregnum shared between the executors, the solicitors and a Mr Richard Bagley. John did not stay for long, but Robert remained with the firm for the rest of his life. Apart from the usual family bequests, Joseph's will featured generous provision for his servants and other household staff.

In 1858 the Clementhorpe factory, a former brewery next to the Corporation shipyard on the River Ouse, 'was leased for the increasing trade in Boiled Sugars, Candied Peel, Comfits and Marmalade'. This, of course, afforded much-needed warehousing space and access to the Humber estuary and the North Sea which in turn, along with the railways, facilitated the importation of sugar, cocoa, and other ingredients, the coal required for the steam-powered machinery, and the export of finished products. Terry's English Peppermint Lozenges, 'curiously strong', were made here from English white oil of peppermint, as were bullseyes. A new chocolate factory was added in 1862 and manufacturing was moved from St Helen's Square in 1864.

Chocolate production began in earnest around 1867 with thirteen chocolate products (including chocolate creams and batons), although the company would, for some thirty more years, remain essentially a confectionery company. The chocolate complemented the other 380 or so confectionery and parfait lines. These included,

The frozen River Ouse with Clementhorpe smoking away on the right.

lozenges such as bismuth, cinnamon, clove, vanilla, violet and lavender, candies like orange slices, acidulated drops, Indian sugar sticks, toffee tablets, preserved fruits including apricots in syrup and dried cherries, and pine, rose and strawberry paté de jujubes. Miscellaneous items included liqueurs, cream balls, chocolate cream cakes and chocolate cigars. Without doubt, it was a list aimed squarely at the better off in late Victorian society. The awards soon started rolling in, including a confectionery gold at the 1899 National Temperance Catering Exhibition, and awards in emerging export markets in Australia and New Zealand. The *York – Illustrated* talked of Joseph's 'judicious management, evidently a capital disciplinarian just as he is a thoroughly practical man in business.' Terry's focus on confectionery at this time sets it apart from the other major chocolate companies whose origins were in cocoa rather than sweets.

Joseph Terry was a Quaker philanthropist like his neighbour in Tanner's Moat, and the address he delivered at an 1893 Japanese bazaar in aid of the York Central Mission typifies the man: 'It is right to think of our poorer neighbours. If the bazaar is successful, then 1,000 waifs and strays would be entertained on Christmas day in the Corn Exchange.' He was extremely active in York society and was Sheriff once and Lord Mayor no fewer than four times, in 1874, 1885, 1886 and 1890. Joseph Terry was recalled to the City Council in 1893 by popular demand and was knighted for services to industry in 1887 at Queen Victoria's Jubilee. In addition he was, at one time or another, Chairman of the Yorkshire Gala Committee, on the board of governors of the Yorkshire Fine Art and Industrial Institution, on the board of Bootham Asylum, Governor of the Merchant Adventurers' Company, member of York Race Committee, Vice President of York Musical Society, Deputy Chairman of York New Waterworks Company, and involved with the York Charity Organisation Society.

A Terry poster promoting their export trade with scenes from the Mediterranean and York.

Terry and St Helen's Square – The Early Days

THE St Helen's Square premises were retained and converted into a fine shop, ballroom and restaurant. You can still see the Terry name on the building's facade and under the windows. The first-floor cafe-restaurant, ballroom and ground-floor shop were as famous in their time as Betty's, opposite in the square, is now. Among the many impressive features are the Ashlar stone facade with imposing Corinthian columns, marble stairways, marble floors, marble walls, mahogany panelling, friezes and the staircase leading up to the first floor where you would find the cafe and ballroom with its French windows, wrought iron railings and floodlighting. The Tudor room was on the second floor with its Minster stone fireplace. Items on the

Harker's Hotel, demolished in 1928, with Minster in the background.

menu in 1900 included: Russian tea (6d); buttered bath bun (6d); Scotch Woodcock (1 shilling); Harum Scarum (2s); Peach Delight (2s) and Gentleman's Relish Sandwich (1s).

In 1924, neighbouring Harker's Hotel opposed the renewal of Terry's music licence because of the 'nuisance caused by the syncopated and jazz bands engaged at dances through the windows being open, thus preventing guests at the hotel from getting to sleep.' Furthermore, it was alleged that the music and dancing was making the owner ill and a witness claimed, 'almost every kind of musical instrument was being played simultaneously. People were dancing, shouting and stamping and trying to make as much noise as possible.' Terry's barrister, Mr W. Stewart, possibly thinking that this sounded like a good place for a night out, submitted at one point that, 'jazz might not be music but a very large number of people like it.' The licence was renewed on condition that Terry's kept the windows closed, and that after midnight the music was restricted to strings and a piano. The sprung floor was a particularly cherished feature, as this advertisement makes clear: 'Lovers of the terpsichorean art will delight in its resiliency and the knowledge that they can dance until the early hours without that tired feeling which comes from solid floors.'

The manager was a Mr Ware, recruited from London; six girls served behind the counter and two waited on with Mr Ingham, head waiter. Morning coffee was becoming very fashionable – Terry's specialty was a blend of Costa Rica and Peaberry with cream. The mail-order business was thriving, with chocolate nougat particularly popular. Ribbon-tied Christmas Boxes were supplied by Hoffman & Tiede of Berlin. One day

The interior of the Terry restaurant in the 1920s.

A Terry van waiting outside the shop and restaurant in St Helen's Square in the 1960s.

in the 1900s, the Durham University rugby team descended on the shop after a game against St Peter's School and bought thirty-two pounds of crystallised mint creams. Head baker was William Bycroft, who had the honour of baking the cake for the christening of Edward, Prince of Wales in 1894. He delivered it himself to Windsor Castle, staying for two weeks as a guest and in receipt of a guinea per day expenses approved by Thomas Terry.

The elegant Terry building as it is in 2011.

Terry: 1891–1939

JOSEPH Terry's workforce obviously felt able to air grievances, if this letter from the shop floor is anything to go by. No doubt with an eye on the working week reduction to forty-eight hours won by Rowntree employees in 1892 – they were working fifty-nine hours at Terry starting at 6.00 am – this is how the 153 signatories approached the issue of hours in their 1894 letter to management: 'We the Employes [sic] of your firm do hereby approach you for the shortening of the hours of labour namely nine hours movement which we consider beneficial to our health and in so doing we are only seeking that rest and Recreation which are enjoyed by all other trades and professions.'

About this time the twenty or so clerks and typists were working from 9.00 am to 6.00 pm with unpaid overtime most nights a week. There were three travellers, one covering the south from Birmingham to Portsmouth, one Manchester and Liverpool and the other Newcastle and Yorkshire. Coal came from Castleford, peel from Italy in brine-filled hogsheads. Exports went to Australasia, South Africa and Canada in 600-gallon galvanised iron tanks. Workmen were paid eighteen shillings; piece work was paid at 12s/6d or 17s/6d per week. The works outing in 1896 was to Scarborough; in 1897 it was to Bridlington. In 1899 a children's painting competition attracted 20,000 entries.

In 1895 the company became a limited liability company with the name Joseph Terry and Sons Ltd: Joseph and his son Thomas Walker Leaper were directors with Samuel Saville the Terry Company Secretary. Joseph junior died in 1898 and was succeeded by his sons Thomas Walker Leaper Terry and Frank Terry who joined in 1903, aged twenty-five. Noel (Thomas' son) came on board in 1911 aged twenty-two. The *Yorkshire Herald* said of Joseph: 'There was no person in the city more respected and beloved, and no one who was more possessed of the qualities that constitute a genial and amiable Englishman. He was associated with most of the religious and philanthropic institutions in the city, and he was ever ready to join in any good work calculated to benefit his fellow-citizens.' Thomas died in 1910 when his bicycle was in collision with a horse and trap.

The famous Neapolitans brand was launched in 1899. Early Twentieth Century chocolate products included the first assortments, Britannia, York Milk Chocolates and Empire Mixture. In 1906 the 'very superior boiled sweets' list included pine tablets, eucalyptus tablets, greengage and butterscotch drops, mint rock, lime fruit squares and floral tablets. The 'simply superior' list offered such delights as mint bulls' eyes, cyclists' refreshers, dogs and elephants, cockle shells, crystallised 'coker nut' balls, Algerian fruits, large Nelson pippins, Scarborough shells, Togo bullets and Tom Thumb drops; lozenges included throat hospital lozenges and silver smokers' cachous. Manufacturer's health warnings featured on some labels, for example: Poison, these lozenges contain belladonna' or 'opium'.

The famous palm trees logo was modelled on actual palm trees growing at the entrance to one of Terry's cacao plantations in Venezuela.

In 1913 an engineer at Terry's would earn £2 per week, a cleaner twelve shillings and a joiner up to £2. Just before the First World War, Frank made an important trip to Germany bringing back production techniques and equipment to York. The plant included a refiner, a triple-mill, a two pot conche and three mélangeurs. In the First World War in 1916, Noel Terry was wounded and later seconded to the Ministry of Pensions with Frank. Assortments were shelved, and the Terry family reign was temporarily suspended when Henry Ernest Leetham, the flour mill-owner, and Noel's father in law (he had married Kathleen Leetham in 1915), was chairman from 1915 until 1923 when he committed suicide. Terry's Territorials had been going since 1913 with thirteen privates, one sergeant, a lance corporal and a company sergeant major. In 1919 the trade unions negotiated a reduction of working hours from forty-nine-and-a-half to forty-seven, six days paid holiday after twelve months' service; men over twenty-two could earn fifty-five shillings per week while women over age eighteen earned thirty shillings. Piece work could add a further twenty-five percent.

By 1920 increased demand led to a new Chocolate Block comprising five floors and a basement. Covering 24,000 square feet modern features included an electrical installation of 750 h.p. and a refrigeration capacity of twelve tons every day. There was also a packing shop and cocoa store in Vine Street. In 1922 Frank and Noel made a trip to Venezuela to secure supply of their single most important raw product, the Criollo cocoa bean, which more than anything else characterised Terry chocolate with its unique taste and quality. The trip was a success and the company purchased Caruao, a plantation forty-miles to the east of Caracas, and could look forward to a ready and reliable supply until the late 1940s when they were obliged to sell under new currency legislation.

The Suspension Book in the mid 1920s makes interesting reading. Suspension was, of course, unpaid, so it could be an expensive punishment: Insolence, half a day; meddling with a machine, three days, packing overweight, one day; hitting a girl with a funnel, half a day; incorrectly labelling boxes, one week; leaving a handkerchief on a hot steam pipe over the lunch hour, half a day; bad piping of chocolate, five days; 'larking in the cellar', half a day; reading a newspaper, three and a half days; delivering said newspaper in the van, three and half days; running down the yard with a bike, one day.

In 1927, under the auspices of Frank and Noel Terry, the company moved again, this time to the purpose-built Chocolate Works in Bishopthorpe Road which still stands today next to the racecourse at Knavesmire. It was said to 'reflect the very latest scientific conceptions of factory design and equipment' and the buildings were 'handsome and uncluttered' according to the architect, J.E. Wade. The site covers 172 acres, and the iconic clock tower over the boiler house-cum-chimney is 135 feet high. The main five-storey block is 510 feet long, 160 feet wide and eighty feet high, covering three-and-a-half acres. Each storey is air-conditioned. A further one-storey building went up in 1929 to house the Milk Chocolate Factory, the Refrigeration Plant and the Despatch Department, all covering two acres. Electrical installation exceeded 1,650 h.p. with a refrigeration plant capacity of 364 tons of ice per day to drive the air conditioning and brine cooling. Frank Terry, as a qualified quantity surveyor, was well disposed to help with planning the new factory. Middlesbrough firm Dorman Long were the contractors (their other work includes the George V Bridge in Newcastle and the Sydney Harbour

Bridge.) Ernest Clayton, later chief engineer and a director, designed the front door of the building, based on the Woolworth Building in New York. Other American influences he brought back and which benefitted Bishopthorpe Road were the air conditioning, fork lift trucks and pallets.

Clayton had also installed air conditioning at Cadbury's and pioneered the cellophane wrapping of Neapolitans.

Terry owned some of the surrounding land at Bustardthorpe, and it was here that Middlethorpe Manor Farm was set up, complete with pigs, horses, cows and hens. Eggs for the St Helen's Square shop were laid here and the cows provided the milk and cream; many of the vegetables used in the restaurant were grown in the market garden. A Pig Club was set up later, in 1948 with pigsties for rent at £1 per week. Malton Bacon Factory was a good customer.

When Leetham died in 1923, Frank and Noel succeeded him as joint managing directors. Noel applied himself to sales and marketing with the help of a George Stembridge. He set about building up the sales force and the team of window dressers, recognising no doubt the growing importance of window and in-shop displays. To help in this, he also launched a fleet of vans which not only carried the company name around the country, but also acted as mobile display units. Shopkeepers could simply look in the back of these vans and see and select the Terry's products available to them. Unlike his competitors over at Rowntree, Noel Terry recognised the value of advertising and poster promotion. He also organised the transfer of staff from their temporary offices in the De Grey Rooms in 1941 where they had been since 1927.

Between the years 1918 and 1938, revenues doubled as did tonnage sold, rising from 2,332 tonnes in 1925 to 4,836. Employee numbers stood at 2,500 in 1937, sixty per cent of whom were women; 2,150 were factory workers with 300 employed in the offices or as sales travellers. The company had a policy of employing a sufficient number of disabled ex-servicemen to qualify for entry on the King's Roll. Basic rates of pay were fifty-six shillings for a forty-seven-hour working week for men, and 30 shillings 6d for women,

Terry's vans at Bishopthorpe Road waiting to go.

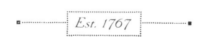

Various aspects of Bishopthorpe Road from a 1935 advertisement.

The Terry logo and the Bishopthorpe Road factory.

with twenty-five per cent additional for piece work. An annual bonus had started in 1929 amounting to one week's wages, rising to two weeks in 1930; one week's holiday was paid. Long service was a feature at Terry's. In 1937 fourteen retirees had over fifty year's service, two over sixty and one retired after sixty-nine year's service.

There was a sick room staffed by a qualified male and female First Aid Attendant reporting to the Works Doctor. A further member of staff was in 'charge of the whole female staff in matters of cleanliness, hygiene etc.' A nurse would tour the factory clipping overlong nails and ensuring all hair was tucked under caps. The firm contributed to Male and Female contributory Sick Clubs run by the employees, and to a Benevolent Fund 'to provide aid in cases of financial embarrassment and extra nourishment in cases of sickness.' A pension and Life Assurance scheme was set up in 1931 and between then and 1937, the firm paid over £80,000 into these various schemes. Donations were also given to various convalescent homes to support recuperating workers; cases of rheumatism were sent to Harrogate Royal Hospital. The Holiday Club, administered by the company, was routinely supported by over 1,000 employees and in 1936, paid out £3,440 to members in the week before the annual holiday, or Works Week.

The firm, in common with Cadbury and Rowntree, believed in *mens sana in corpore sano* supporting (to the tune of £250 a year) a whole range of sports facilities and clubs: angling, bowling, hockey, motoring, baseball to name but a few. At its overseas 'tropical plantation' there was another Baseball Club 'with players of darker complexion.' The

The Angling Club outside the Minster about 1900. Samuel Terry (Joseph's son) is sixth from the left at the back. He was President of the club.

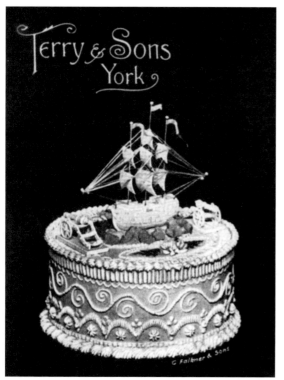

Pages from Terry catalogues showing their luxury lines.

sports grounds were maintained by the company ground staff. Terry's bowling green was a frequent venue for county matches and was visited by a South African touring team in 1935. The girls' football team was very successful, raising nearly £3,000 for charity by 1937. An annual one mile swim took place in the River Ouse from the Clementhorpe factory until it was banned by Health and Safety. Terry's Amateur Dramatic Society was very popular for many years and often worked with the Rowntree Players. Local businesses often helped out with props: for example, Rentyorradioz of Gillygate would often loan radiogramophones.

Spartan (a dark chocolate assortment mainly with hard centres) had been launched in 1921, and it was in this decade that chocolate began to exert its superiority and supersede the other confections to take pride of place in the seasonal catalogues. The Crystalised Gum Jujubes, Silver Cachous, the aphrodisiac Candied Eringo, Solazzi Juice Liquorice and Cockertines were relegated to the back pages. The early 1930s saw the launch of a number of new products: Trent Chocolates was the first soon followed by Pandora, Delwood, Somerset, Avalon and the 1767 Box. But the really important development was the appearance of All Gold in 1932. The names for the chocolates included the patriotic: Trafalgar, and the erudite: Minerva, and Theobroma (the Linnaean botanical name for chocolate.) Designs for the boxes even extended into Cubism.

The famous Chocolate Orange also first appeared in 1932. It had started life as Dessert Chocolate Apple in 1924 (phased out in 1954) and at one point one in ten Christmas stockings reputedly contained a Terry's Chocolate Orange. More chocolate assortments came later in the decade including Criollo, Amazon, Dahlia, Gold Leaf, Gold Ray, Red

Early production line at Terry.

George VIth and Queen Elizabeth visit the Terry factory ...

Stripe, Sweet Thoughts and Tradition; Bridge Mints and Russian Caramels also made an appearance. Up to the Second World War, Theatre Chocolates were available with their unique rustle-proof wrappers.

Sir Francis (Frank) Terry, knighted in 1936, was a popular character. He would often bring in flowers from the garden for the office girls. Quality, though, could never be compromised. Peter Terry relates the story of Sir Francis officiating at a tasting session one day when he exclaimed: 'I have never seen such stuff !' and threw the samples out of the open window to be gathered up later by ground staff. On the other hand, he could show real generosity. For the trip to London to receive his knighthood, all the employees' works numbers were put in a hat and twelve were drawn out. These lucky dozen stayed at the Savoy and took in a show at the Drury Lane Theatre.

In chocolate making at this time, quality, taste and acceptability were the preserve of the chocolatiers, and a fine skill. Sir Francis Terry's actions may look like petulance, but the decision to produce or not was paramount to the reputation and success of the company. A whole new vocabulary evolved around rejected chocolate, largely, it seems, based on smell or taste, or lack of it: among the terms for the unacceptable were kippers, whitewash, plum pudding, ham and burning tapers.

The coronation of George VI in May 1937 was marked by a special King George Assortment with twelve out of fourteen new centres. These included Genoese (walnuts and cherries); Rum Marzipan (pineapple and cherry); Valencia Diamond; Muscatel; Apricot and Damson Sandwich, and Cherry Delice. The Coronation Assortment featured Black Currant Trifle, Cherry and Pistachio Genoese and Champagne Pineapple. At ten

...and meet some of the staff. October 19th 1937.

shillings for a two-pound box (with padded lid), and 2s 6d for a half-pound, they were not cheap, and out of reach of most employees who at the time, earned fifty six shillings per week for men and thirty shillings and sixpence for women for a forty-seven hour week.

The day of 19 October 1937 was a very special day at Terry's. That was the day of the royal visit of Their Majesties King George VI and Queen Elizabeth, H.R.H. Princess Royal. Other dignitaries included The Lord Lieutenant of the City, The Earl of Harewood, and the Home Secretary, Sir Samuel Hoare. The *festschrift* published to mark the event tells us that 'hundreds of happily excited workers – white, blue and khaki – rushed to take their places in neatly ordered lines.' A tour was made of the factory, taking in Manufacturing and Covering of Centres, Hand Packing and Machine Wrapping, Cellophaning, Manufacture of Milk Chocolate, Display and Tests of Raw Materials and Despatch. Caskets of chocolates were duly presented to the King and Queen with presents to take back to Princesses Elizabeth and Margaret.

The staff increases recorded above were due in part to the production of All Gold and Chocolate Orange. Staff numbers included 2,343 at Clementhorpe and Bishopthorpe Road; fifty-one at St Helen's Square; fifteen window dressers and seven in the London office. Female employees accounted for 1,495, or sixty per cent, of the workforce. A sales representative would get £3 per week expenses plus the car. He was, nevertheless, expected to be immaculately turned out for every call with hat, suit and starched collars. Waitresses at the restaurant were lined up and inspected every morning; factory girls were not permitted to wear earrings and any lipstick was physically removed by Welfare Officer Mrs Telfer. Long nails had to be clipped.

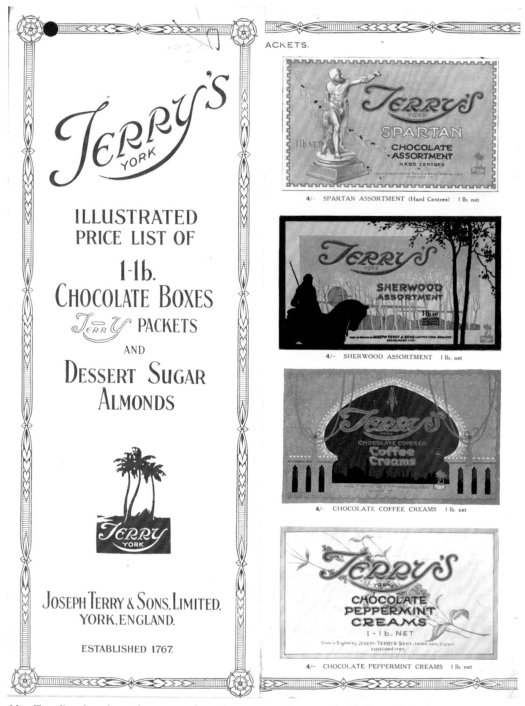

More Terry lines from the catalogues; note the exotic assortments interspersed with the very British.

Terry in the Second World War

DURING the Second World War Terry's, in common with other chocolate manufacturers, was pressed in to helping the war effort. Terry's Territorials were called up, a fifty-person concrete shelter was built for Vine Street costing £150, a shelter was made for 170 people in the cellar at Clementhorpe at a cost of £95, and a tunnel shelter was built at Bishopthorpe Road for 600 to complement the 1,000 capacity ground floor shelter – all costing £1,600. Additional sandbags and steel shutters cost £3,000. Female workers were urged to train as auxiliary nurses with textbooks provided free and air raid drills became routine.

A morale-boosting sound system was installed throughout the factory to provide 'public speech and music.' *Worker's Playtime* began at 11.30am on the BBC Home Service and was broadcast live from a factory canteen 'somewhere in Britain'. *Music While You Work* became a popular afternoon feature with hundreds of girls and women singing along together. The BBC issued stringent rules for the programme – for example, regulations which dictated what should not be played: '#1. Banned completely – all numbers with predominant rhythm, insufficient melody, or other unsuitable characteristics. #2. Banned completely – numbers that are lethargic or unsuited to any speeding up of tempo. #3. Banned completely – all modern slow waltzes, due to their soporific tendencies'. There was also a long list of specific songs that were deemed unsuitable for one reason or another, such as *Deep in the Heart of Texas* with its clapping motif. It was felt that this would encourage workers to bang their spanners on the machinery causing damage.

Steel helmets were provided for staff. The lease on the de Grey Rooms expired and was taken over by the ATS for their physical training and by the telephone arm of the Post Office. In St Helen's Square, fire watchers patrolled on the roof and a steel bridge was built linking Terry's with the Yorkshire Insurance company next door. After the 1942 Baedecker raid, the restaurant was unscathed and provided tea and coffee for the firemen and other rescue workers.

The tower at Terry's factory was used as a look-out post over the prisoner of war camp on nearby Knavesmire.

F. Hills & Sons, manufacturers of Jablo propeller blades from Manchester, took over part of the Bishopthorpe factory to make blades and repair broken blades. Terry staff were seconded to some of Hill's work after a period of training at Trafford Park. This often involved laminating the blades with varnish – sometimes seven days a week. Normal working practices had been suspended to maximise production. Some of the bosses for the propellers were unofficially converted into biscuit barrels. Terry took over manufacturing of London firm Charbonnel & Walker's chocolate. Parts for Rolls Royce engines were also made. Chivers & Sons occupied the Clementhorpe factory for

The tanks are overwhelmed during War Weapons Week at Terry's.

the production of jellies, marmalades and jams until 1954 after rationing had finally ended. Freezing was done for Bird's Eye. After Chivers departed, most of Clementhorpe was given over to pastille production, until that too, moved to Bishopthorpe Road. During the days of rationing, employees received a monthly 'fancy order' which usually comprised one or two Chocolate Oranges, six or so bars, and an egg at Easter.

Noel Terry was Controller of No 9 Group, Royal Observer Corps, for which he was awarded the MBE. Kenneth, one of his sons, was a Squadron Leader in 547 Squadron and won the DFC in 1942. He was killed in April 1944 aged just twenty-three. Noel's other son, Peter Terry, joined in 1945 after service in the West Yorkshire Regiment in India. A Marlborough old boy and Cambridge economics graduate, he focused on sales and eventually succeeded George Stembridge as sales director in 1960. Peter served his apprenticeship in a confectioners in Liverpool, inevitably selling Rowntree and Cadbury chocolates as well as Terry's. He also spent time as a representative for a wholesaler under the pseudonym of Mr Peters. J. Robins Terry, Frank's son, joined in 1937 and then served with the Royal Artillery. His specialization was cocoa blending.

Terry's chocolates were, of course, sent out to the troops as routine rations, and were specially-made for lifeboat and rescue ship rations. Tons of vitaminised chocolate were also dispatched for refugees all over Europe. Empire Chocolate, made with any cocoa beans available, went into production in the face of severe shortages of beans. Balaclavas, gloves and scarves were knitted and sent out to the troops. Red Cross sales at the shop were frequent, and tanks would visit the factory during War Weapons Weeks. The company was decorated for its success in the 1943 Wings for Victory National Savings Campaign, and was extremely successful in raising money through National War Bonds. In 1941 it helped the city of York exceed its York War Weapons Week target of £1 million,

The tower with its clock in 2011.

Two of the 'smiling wenches' outside the Terry shop in the Castle Museum.

actually selling bonds worth £2,118,574. The company itself bought £25,000 worth of bonds at the end of the war during Thanksgiving Week in York. After the war, supplies were provided for various expeditions, including one to Greenland.

In 1941, the company was embroiled in the Edinburgh Poison Case when a disaffected Brigadier General Tredegar (actually John Millar) attempted to poison Georgina Ferguson with a box of Terry's Devon Milk laced with toxic permanganate of potash and sent through the post to her. He was duly convicted of attempted murder and sentenced to three year's penal servitude. In 1948 the famous palm tree logo was registered, and the best-selling lines included All Gold, Chocolate Orange and blocks such as Devon Milk and Oliver Twist and Neapolitans.

A replica Terry's chocolate shop was opened in the Castle Museum in York in the 1950s with Terry's staff wearing costumes from down the ages. This was promoted as: 'Inside there are real confections to buy and smiling wenches in period costume to offer them.' In true Temperance Movement spirit, some of the chocolates carried mottoes such as 'drink is the curse of the working man!' Proceeds from sales went to local charities. Sugar mice were specially made for the shop, and, to ensure that it smelled just right, the chief chemist concocted a 'chocolatey' potion which was bottled and kept under the counter. The shop features a range of early Terry confectionery, including Superior Nelson Balls.

St Helen's Square After the War

MEANWHILE, back at the real thing, Terry's restaurant was competing for York's well- to-do-clientele with Betty's (directly opposite in the Square), and the British Restaurant in Jubbergate. Outside catering with the mobile kitchen and kitchen staff marquee was thriving, with functions catering for Bird's Eye in the Assembly Rooms, the Lord Mayor's parties in nearby Mansion House and dinners at the Merchant Taylor's Hall. Queen Elizabeth was entertained twice, and the Duke of Kent once, at the Mansion House. One Assembly Room lunch involved 380 vegetarian meals, including food for ten vegans – all very new then. Hunt balls and army functions for officers and wives from Catterick were not uncommon, and at one Tadcaster Hunt Ball the guests reputedly included Christine Keeler, Mandy Rice Davies and John Profumo. Organisations like RAFA and the RAOC held their balls and dinner dances in the restaurant and ballroom with prestigious dance bands providing the entertainment. St Andrew's Society came every year to celebrate their Burns Night with appropriate amounts of haggis and whisky.

During post-war rationing, meat was restricted to forty-pounds weight, but a little was made to go a long way with beef croquettes. Fish cakes, omelettes and tripe and onions also proved popular. Offal was available, as was oxtail and a game licence provided for rabbit and jugged hare. Some 500 ducks were sold every two weeks or so; ten gallons of soup were consumed most days. Soup in cups 'to go' was increasingly popular. The stockpot could accommodate sixty carcasses and miscellaneous bones. A self-service carvery opened in 1963 – York's first – with meat, vegetables and soup all for £1. Unfortunately for the waitresses, this was on the first floor so necessitated a forty-two stair hike between the two restaurants. Downstairs could seat 290 diners, and often did; the Oak Room would take another thirty. A typical banqueting menu comprised Tortue Claire (turtle soup), Pintade Vigneron (guinea fowl) and Petit Pots au Chocolat. Yorkshire Insurance next door was a regular customer. In addition, Terry's sent the breakfasts round to the judges staying at the Judges' Lodgings in Lendal during the Assizes (the restaurant extended to the back of the 'hotel'.) What you would then describe as exotic meals such as Madras curry, Chicken Kiev and Bolognaise sauce, started to appear on the menu. A Terry Pack Takeaway Service was available, probably one of the first. All the baking was done on the premises, apart from Cornish Pasties which were bought in. Early recycling – or was it just financial prudence – saw unsold fish and potato turned into fishcakes, used cooking oil sent to soap factories in converted milk churns, and leftovers sent as swill to the pigs at Middlethorpe.

Terry: 1946–2005

QUAKER philanthropy and paternalism continued into the fifties. The Welfare Department under Kath Telfer gave assistance to sick workers and the bereaved; management was represented at workers' funerals, and women from Askham Grange prison were taken on as part of their rehabilitation – although bag-snatchers and shoplifters were debarred. Exports increased in 1950: £12 million compared with £2 million in 1939.

Terry's Waifa bar was launched in 1952 in a bid to compete with Rowntree's KitKat. When Forte took over, a Waifa Bar was added to the complimentary in-room tea service. Queen Elizabeth visited York in 1957 and Terry, Craven and Rowntree presented her with a joint gift of a gold and silver casket from Asprey in Bond Street, costing £38 6s 8d – to symbolize York's importance to the country's confectionery industry. Apart from the Arms of York and cocoa beans etched onto it, the casket was filled with sweets and chocolates from all three companies.

Sir Francis Terry died in 1960 – 'a big loss to York'. Over the years he had been Sheriff of Yorkshire at the end of the war and an Alderman of the city. He had worked on the boards of Yorkshire Insurance and York County Savings Bank, was president of York County Hospital, and was a major benefactor to St Peter's School. He was a patron of York Cricket Club, York Harriers and Athletic Club, and Clifton Cycling Club. He was also vice president of the Yorkshire Agricultural Society.

The Forte Group bought the company in 1963. Forte already owned the Hammersmith-based Fullers confectioners and cake manufacturers, and were looking to expand in the chocolate sector. The then Lord Mayor, Mona Armitage, questioned at the time whether Terry's had been fortified or Forte had been terrified. Rumours of a possible take-over had featured in the *York Evening Press* from as early as January 1961. Hammersmith was closed and production transferred to York. As well as cakes, Fuller's peppermint and fruit lumps and miscellaneous boiled sweets began to be manufactured in York.

In May 1967, Terry celebrated its Bicentenary and eighty-one workers from all sections of the company were invited with their guests. Invitation was by length of service and the eighty-one employees managed 3,078 years – or thirty-eight years each – between them. Nothing could exemplify better the tradition and reputation Terry had for paternalism and as a decent place to work. Long service was very common, and many members of the same family and successive generations of many families worked there down the years. There were two dinner dances with a fountain made from Nineteenth Century French bronze and copper put up in the gardens to mark the event. On 25 May, a BBC *Blue Peter* programme fronted by Valerie Singleton, John Noakes and Christopher Trace, was made about Terry and the history of chocolate, During the 1970s, the firm sponsored

An extract from the Blue Peter *programme filmed at Terry's. Note how closely scripted it all is.*

Report No....TER.3........   Transmitted on...BBC..Television.............
                                          "Blue Peter"
Length...5'20".......   Date...25th.May,.1967............   Time..4.55 p.m.

Short Title...Old-Fashioned.Sweets...............

John Noakes: Well, now we're going from submarines and 1967 way back in time to 1767. A shop just like this one was built by a famous sweet and chocolate manufacturer two hundred years ago this year.
Valerie Singleton: Sweets were just as popular in those days as they are today, but they weren't always quite the same and the window displays were quite different.
J. Noakes: Well, I think I like the old-fashioned sweet glass jars much better than the modern boxes, or tins.
V. Singleton: Yes, I do too and, of course, if you do see a sweet jar today they don't have anything like the really lovely, attractive shapes that the old ones have and some of the old ones have got lovely old labels too and, of course, another thing that was quite different about sweet shops then was that they sold almost entirely sweets, they hardly had any chocolate at all as we do in the sweet shops today, so I think we'll go in and buy some. Good afternoon.
Christopher Trace: Can I help you?
V. Singleton: Yes, we've come to buy some sweets. What can you show us?
C. Trace: Well, I've got some absolutely splendid ones here. This is Bath Rock ..
V. Singleton: Yes.
C. Trace: This is .. oh no, that's Fairy Rock and Bath Pipe and down here we've got some of these little sugar pigs and sugar mice. Do you like those?
J. Noakes: Yes, how much are they?

a number of races at the Knavesmire. Perhaps the most well known was the Terry's All Gold Ebor Handicap, to which the firm added £10,000 in prize money, including the £600 trophy. In 1974, the famous chimney at Clementhorpe was demolished with the rest of the factory following in 1987. A vulnerable Roman mosaic was found during the demolition and Peter Terry paid for it to be excavated. It now resides in the Yorkshire Museum. In 1975 the Bishopthorpe Road site was designated a conservation area. In 1976 Terry's launched their 56,000 cubic feet All Gold hot air balloon, the only gold balloon in the world at that time. Apart from flights over the Knavesmire, it was also seen at Alexandra Palace and inside Olympia – the first time a hot air balloon had been inflated inside a building. It came second in the 1978 Cross Channel Balloon race.

Colgate Palmolive bought Terry in 1978 for around £17 million. Although they had limited experience in confectionery through a pecan chocolate company in Texas, what they obviously lacked in knowledge of the industry they attempted to make up with in marketing expertise and experience of running a global industry. By this time, Terry's assortments accounted for about thirty per cent of the UK market, with All Gold taking twenty per cent and Moonlight, the milk and plain assortment, a further ten per cent. Rowntrees Black Magic was around thirty per cent. Colgate developed the short-lived Chocolate Lemon – a flavour they were anxious to exploit because they used a lot of lemon in their soaps. In the face of falling profits, a management buy-out was initiated in 1982 under the name of Land of Hope and Glory. They raised £17 million, but the firm was eventually sold to United Biscuits for £25 million.

United Biscuits brought with them substantial own-brand accounts such as Tesco, Sainsbury, Asda and Marks and Spencer, and in so doing, raised output from 700 tons to 3,000 tons weekly. The year 1985 saw profits increase by seventy-five per cent on the previous year, admittedly from a low base. They also brought efficiencies, one notable example being the out-put of Curiously Strong Mints from half-a-ton a week in York, to 500 tons a week when it was transferred to Bridgend. Acquisitions included Callard and Bowser's toffees and butterscotch based in Bridgend, Nuttals, the French company Chocometz, and Dutch biscuit manufacturer, Verkade.

Peter Terry retired at the end of 1985 and went on to work on the restoration of Fairfax House and the display there of the Terry collection of Georgian furniture. A new state-of-the-art chocolate plant was built at the Bishopthorpe Road site focussing on Chocolate Orange production. This, to some extent, was at the expense of assortments which were becoming somewhat outmoded, yielding to flowers and bottles of wine as gifts of choice. Cadbury's Heroes and Rowntree Mackintosh's Quality Street were also providing strong competition. York became the centre of excellence for United's chocolate production at the expense of plants in London, Glasgow and Liverpool. The workforce stood at 1,370 still largely turning out the plain, bitter and milk chocolate.

Nevertheless, in the 1990s, annual sales of All Gold were seven million boxes; All Gold revenue was £11 million in 1981, doubling by 1990. At its zenith, Terry was selling 23,000 tons of chocolate, 56 million Chocolate Oranges and Easter eggs weighing 650 tons. Moments were launched in 1991 with a new £7 million pound moulding plant.

In 1981 the elegant, but now largely unprofitable, restaurant and quality catering in St Helen's Square closed after 150 years. Manager Jeffrey Thompson pulled down the Terry flag for the last time on 9 January. The building had been Grade II listed since 1974 and was sold to the Trustee Savings Bank, then next door. An auction of some very fine furniture and equipment raised £30,000. One of many high points in a celebrated history had included the catering for the 1,000-guest wedding reception of the Duke and Duchess of Kent in 1961 at Hovingham Hall, after their marriage in York Minster. The marquee was thirty-feet long and there were three wedding cakes. After it was over the Terry's staff sat down to enjoy the very same meal as the guests.

The company was taken over by Kraft in 1993 for £220 million. Kraft was owned by Philip Morris and had bought Jacobs Suchard in 1990. Terry, therefore, became part of the UK's fourth largest food manufacturer: Kraft Jacobs Suchard. For the time being, chocolate stayed in York with sugar confectionery in Bridgend, although much of that was later sold to Wrigley and the Bridgend operation was closed down. Toblerone in Berne was also part of the group.

Waifa production was moved to Belgium in 2000; All Gold went to Sweden, Chocolate Orange to Slovakia and Poland and Twilights to Austria. In 2004 Kraft made 6,000 redundancies across all of their operations. Terry's closure was announced with the loss of 316 jobs.

When the Terry factory closed in 2005, over 400 objects including photographs, packaging, catalogues and chocolates, were donated to the Castle Museum. And apart from currently empty buildings, memories and these few artifacts, that is all that remains. In the words of Peter Terry, 'It's sad for the history of York, the traditions and the people of York and of course the employees.'

M.A. Craven & Son Ltd

CRAVEN'S were manufacturers of quality sugar confectionery. The company originated in 1803 when Joseph Hick, father of Mary Ann Hick, set up business as a twenty-nine year old in York as Kilner and Hick, confectioners. Kilner left town leaving Hick with the business which he relocated to 47 Coney Street. This was next door to what was then the Leopard Inn and opposite St Martin's Church. Mary Ann, Hick's youngest daughter, was born in 1829.

In 1833 Thomas Craven, son of a farmer from East Acklam in the East Riding, arrived in York aged sixteen as apprentice to his brother-in-law, Thomas Hide's, confectionery business, established in the mid to late 1820s. This business was called George Berry & Thomas Hide after the joint owners and located at 20 High Ousegate. Berry may have been a grocer by trade who was granted his freedom of the city in 1810. After seven years, Thomas Craven bought the right to trade in York when he became a Freeman of the City of York in 1840. When Hide died, he duly set up his own business in 1843 next door at 19 High Ousegate. *White's Directories* from 1843 to 1851 indicate that what had been Berry and Hide seems to have carried on trading under a William Hide. A notice in the *York Courant* for 26 October 1843 describes Craven setting up as a purveyor of 'confectionery, teas, coffees etc', and the entry for the firm in *White's Directory* for 1851 confirms that Craven had expanded into tea by that time. The same notice in the *York Courant* revealed Craven's plans for growth, advertising for 'two lozenge makers and two apprentices.' Initially, he continued to work from his original premises, but on 1 May 1845 moved the business to 31 Pavement, not far from the Rowntree's shop. Rent was £70 per year. On 30 April 1851, he married Mary Ann Hick – she was twenty-two, he thirty-four – and then bought the Pavement building outright for £1,300 from owner William Dove. He also bought a further site at 10 Coppergate.

Joseph Hick died on 20 February, 1860, and his estate was divided up between his three children. In 1862, when Mary Ann was thirty-three, her husband died leaving her with three young children (one boy and two girls aged eight, six and four) to raise, and two businesses to run. Her attempts to sell the businesses were unsuccessful due first to the dilatoriness of her solicitors, and then the impending starvation of her family, so she took up the challenge, amalgamated the two businesses, changed the name of the company to M.A. Craven, and ran it until 1900. In 1881 her son, Joseph William, came on board as Partner, and the firm became M.A. Craven & Son. As with her Quaker neighbours, Joseph Rowntree and Joseph Terry, Mary built her company and turned out her sweets and chocolates on the basis that only the best is good enough. Like them, she was concerned with the plight of the poor, often making mercy visits with food and blankets. Mary Ann Craven died aged seventy-one on 31 July 1900.

The Craven factory in Coppergate.

Production was at the site in Coppergate – roughly where the Jorvik Viking Centre now stands – along with the additional properties in Coney Street and Foss Islands Road. When Mary took over there were around 200 workers; by 1908 this had increased to 800 – a sizeable business by York standards. In addition to production, packaging, despatch and marketing, there were four Craven's retail shops in the city. One of these, Craven's Mary Ann Sweet Shop, was in the Shambles and featured a sweet museum on the first floor where visitors could see 150 years of the 'Art, Trade, Mystery and Business of the Confectioner'.

In 1904 Joseph William Craven, on a visit to Paris, bought, and brought back, the recipe for Original French Almonds from French confectioners – the world leaders in sugar confectionery at the time. Since then, the company has been amongst the market

Somewhat enigmatic copy in this advertisement.

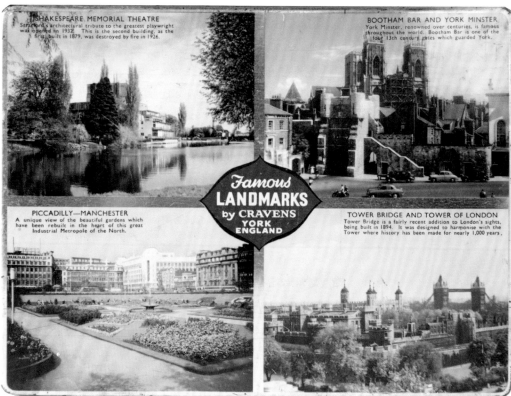

Scenes, national and local to York, depicted on Craven's tins.

Mary Ann at work .

A typical Craven toffee tin from the 1960s.

CRAVEN'S OF YORK
SOME FAVOURITES
obtainable on the Home Market

		per Qtr.
SUGARED ALMONDS	4-oz. Transparent Bags	8d.
	Bulk Pack, 5-lb. Glass Jars	
REAL FRUIT CENTRES	5 separate Fruit Flavours, individually wrapped in film, each with a soft eating centre	7½d.
BARLEY SUGAR	Sugar, Glucose, Honey and Lemon Flavour, each individually wrapped in film	7d.
BEST ENGLISH MINTS	Delightful after-dinner sweet. Made with Oil of Peppermint, soft centre, each individually wrapped in film	7d.
BUTTER DROPS	An old English Favourite, made with butter, each individually wrapped in film	6½d.
OLD FASHIONED MINT HUMBUGS	Delightful golden Humbug, soft eating centre a joy to all connoisseurs of confectionery	6d.
	Bulk Pack, 4-lb. Boxes	
DESSERT FRUITS	A Pastille made with real Fruit in four flavours	8d.
RASPBERRY JELLIES	Acidulated refreshing Summer Sweet	6½d.
	Bulk Pack, 5-lb. Tins	
BUTTERSCOTCH PIECES	A favourite with both old and young, each piece daintily wrapped	8d
	Packets and Bags	per Packet
OLD YORK BUTTERSCOTCH	A Souvenir Pack, and one that is always appreciated	9d.
MIXED FRUIT PASTILLES	Fruit Assorted flavours, made with high grade gelatine	per Bag 6½d.
MINT IMPERIALS	The old Scotch "Kirk" Mint, a combination of pure icing sugar and peppermint oil	6½d.

Soon we hope to add the best of their kind,
CRAVEN'S ORIGINAL FRENCH ALMONDS

A domestic price list for Craven's confectionery and jellies.

leaders in sugar sweets, toffee and dragées. Their famous brands have included Best English Mints, Butter Mint Bon Bons, Buttered Brazils, and Mary Ann Creamy Toffee launched in 1956. The Original French Almonds were routinely blended in a secure room to preserve the secrecy of the recipe.

In 1920 the Coppergate factory was named French Almond Works in recognition of how important that product line was to them. In 1925 Rowntrees, in the face of poor sales figures and up against increasing competition from manufacturers of cheaper products, were looking for an acquisition which would allow them to enter the market for cheaper products without compromising their reputation for quality. As already noted above, they approached Craven as a possible subsidiary, only to have their offer rejected. Rowntree went on to form the York Confectionery Company to fulfil that role.

A period of gradual decline began in the early 1920s and by 1936 the workforce had shrunk to seventy. The fortunes of the company only really revived when they moved to the outskirts of the city to a six-and-a-half acre site in Low Poppleton Lane in 1966. The purpose-built 140,000 square-feet factory was extended four times up to 1980 to cope with increasing production. The Coppergate factory was demolished, and this permitted extensive excavations of the site which uncovered substantial and significant Viking artefacts, many of which are in the Jorvik Viking Centre which was built soon after.

Staff figures in 1980 approached 380 with a twenty-strong sales force; the company was producing 5,000 tons of sweets, which equates to about 800 million individual sweets. Export sales accounted for fifteen per cent of turnover, while much of the domestic output was for own brand products for companies like British Home Stores, Boots, Harrods,

Quality checking taking place between a cooling conveyor and automated wrapping.

Fortnum & Mason and Marks & Spencer. Bloomingdales in the USA, and the Hudson Bay Company in Canada, were amongst their export accounts. Cravens developed the innovative 'flap wrap' in 1954 – a major advance in the easy unwrapping of boiled sweets and a crucial factor in the firm's increased success in the export market.

Since 1987, Cravens has been involved in a number of takeovers and mergers. That year the company was bought by Hazlewood Foods, followed three years later by a management buyout. In 1992 Cravens bought a number of companies including Crusader, Barker and Dobson, Keillers and Bensons and Milady; the company was subsequently renamed Craven Keiller in 1995. Trebor Bassett bought them in 1996, and in 1999 the York and Pontefract factories combined to form Monkhill Confectionery, later part of Cadbury Trebor Bassett. In 2004 Monkhill relaunched the entire Sharps of York range, which included Dairy Toffee, Fudge, Chocolate Toffee, Treacle Toffee and Butterscotch Swirls, 'in order to take advantage of the city's reputation as the chocolate and confectionery capital of the UK.' A six-figure trade and consumer marketing campaign supported the relaunch of the toffee, which was first manufactured in 1911 and marketed with a memorably monocled cartoon aristocrat named Sir Kreemy Knut. The same bowler-hatted 'toffee toff' featured in the relaunch.

Monkhill was bought in February 2008 by Tangerine Confectionery from Cadbury Schweppes for £58 million to make it one of the UK's larger manufacturers not just of sugar confectionery but also popcorn, under the Butterkist brand.

Other Tangerine factories include Pontefract, where the world-famous Pontefract Cakes are manufactured, and Liverpool, home of the chocolate éclair. Wilkinson's Mint Imperials and Pontefract Cakes have been made in Pontefract since the late 1800s. Up until the 1960s all Pontefract Cakes were hand-made and hand-stamped (an experienced stamper could turn out 30,000 Pontefract Cakes a day.) From about 1614, round liquorice lozenges were sold to ease stomach disorders; however, by the end of the Eighteenth Century the liquorice confectionery business was up and running when a young chemist from Pontefract, George Dunhill, first made liquorice lozenges into Pomfret Cakes. By 1885, there were ten companies producing liquorice sweets in Pontefract; the most famous of these is Wilkinsons. Another Tangerine brand, Barratts, is similarly steeped in nostalgia and produces memorable lines such as Sherbet Fountains, Dip Dabs, Flumps, Fruit Salads and Black Jacks.

Marketing Chocolate

Throughout our survey of the confectionery and chocolate industry in York, marketing, and particularly advertising, has been a common thread running through it all. The salient feature of this was the reluctance of Rowntree to commit to a systematic policy of consumer advertising until the 1930s, even though Cadbury and others could demonstrate clearly the very real benefits in terms of sales and product awareness. We can now look at advertising in the industry generally to see how the York companies fit in to a general picture.

As with any commodity or product, chocolate and confectionery generally requires advertising to keep it in the public eye, to substantiate claims about quality and benefits, to differentiate it from competitors, and to get it sold and to keep it selling. We have seen how Rowntree was particularly reluctant to commit to extensive and protracted advertising campaigns, believing naively that the quality of the goods spoke for itself. Such a policy was to cost Rowntree dear, largely to the benefit of Cadbury who had no such qualms and whose long-term commitment to consumer advertising should have been compelling proof for Rowntree that advertising often pays. As the market for chocolate became more and more mass market, and the image changed from one of semi-luxury to more of an everyman, or everywoman purchase, so it became increasingly important to push the product at the consumer – and to keep pushing. Rowntree finally got the message, and from the 1930s entered into the fray against Cadbury-Fry, Mars, Caley, Nestlé and the like.

For Terry it was a slightly different matter: their chocolate tended to be more for a niche market – dark, plain, bitter – as opposed to the mass market milk chocolate products of Rowntree, Cadbury and Nestlé. Consequently, it was less critical that they advertised in the same way or to the same extent. In one sense their core market was perhaps more discerning and their products more of an acquired taste which required less advertising anyway. Where their product was more mass market Terry responded appropriately. All Gold did have popular appeal and was advertised accordingly; most of the advertising eggs were in one basket, namely the Chocolate Orange basket.

We have seen how from earliest days chocolate, through the belief that it was an aphrodisiac, has been closely associated with romance, sex and the wooing of women. This, like other themes, has always been exploited by the chocolate companies and their advertising agents in their marketing of chocolate products. After all, early market research found that sixty per cent of all chocolate boxes were bought by men as gifts for women, whatever their motives. So it was important to appeal to both men and women, and we can see this strategy at work in early advertisements, posters, through television commercials, and, today, on corporate and product websites. You only have to think of

Typically seductive chocolate advertisement of the late 1950s.

did someone say chocolate!

WHEN a girl hears the word chocolate, she hopes it's Nestlé's Milk Chocolate. Bite into that velvet smoothness, taste that rich creamy flavour and you'll know why Nestlé's Milk Chocolate is such a favourite.

milk chocolate at its very best

the mildly yet unmistakably erotic 'Be yourself, enjoy yourself' Flake television adverts of the 1970s, 'The lady loves Milk Tray', the coy girl on the Caley's Monarch Assortment posters, and 'Caley's Fortune makes the heart grow fonder' to get the picture. Aimed ostensibly at women though much of the advertising may have been, it was the effect that chocolate apparently had on women as depicted or described in the advertisements that interested men enough to compel them to go out and buy a box of chocolates, or a Flake. It was probably no coincidence when Belgium's Joseph Draps chose the name 'Godiva Chocolatier' for his chocolate company in 1926.

Rowntree's Black Magic – 'affordable indulgence' – captured the mood in their 1939 trade catalogue: 'Caught me under the mistletoe! I was just about to give the wretch a piece of my mind when he whipped out a box of Black Magic. So what could I do? Those chocs would soften the hardest heart.' Perhaps their most explicit advertising copy, though, was this letter from 1934: 'We silly creatures are always so thrilled when a man thinks us worth the very best. Imagine it, a big box of these new Black Magic chocolates on my dressing table. My dear, each choc's an orgy!' Black Magic became inextricably associated with courtship helped in no small part by these famous letters, written by attractive women, elegantly dressed and sharing their romantic encounters with the chocolate-buying public. The distinctive black box endured more or less for sixty years, and the twelve market-researched chocolates until 2007, when they were shelved. They were, nevertheless, recalled in 2009 by popular demand.

After Eight sent a similar message: 'According to Cynthia, the Squeeze is what happens in taxis with an admirer, and the Freeze is when he forgets to buy her After Eight.' Confectionery generally had long harboured such claims for romance. Terry's, for example, presented their Fairy Kisses in a highly romantic pre-Raphaelite-esque wrapper with a few select verses from Tennyson: 'A touch, a kiss! The charm was snapp'd ' Terry's were building on the long tradition Kisses had in chocolate. In Italy, Giovanni Buitoni,

*"A woman's place is in the home,
eating After Eight and looking beautiful."*

 AFTER EIGHT WAFER-THIN MINTS
*Elegantly slim, delightfully refreshing
new mints for after dinner. Cool, creamy
peppermint locked in the luxury of rich, dark chocolate ... each
mint in its individual monogrammed envelope.*

*One of the many After Eight advertisements
from the 1960s, exuding refinement,
decadence and luxury.*

one of the founders of Perugina, the Perugia pasta and chocolate company, branded his chocolates *bacio* – kiss – and so the famous *Baci* were born in the 1930s. Unique to Baci though, is the love note that comes with each box, the famous love-themed sayings conceived by Federico Seneca. Perugina's website tells us that these *billets doux* are 'like an invisible embrace, integral to enjoying all of the magic of Baci.' They soon became a cult object and collector's item. Hershey had launched their famous Kisses in 1907 in the US.

An interesting variation on this theme was exploited by Nestlé when they launched Yorkie – a heavyweight bar aimed squarely at men and later, as we have seen, aimed at men to the explicit exclusion of women. Whether this really did alienate half the potential market as some have suggested remains a matter of debate.

The introduction of wrappers, of course, facilitated branding. Before that, up to the end of the Nineteenth Century, chocolates were sold loose in wooden boxes. One of the earliest examples of successful wrapper branding was Fry's Five Boys launched in 1886 for Fry's Milk Chocolate; it shows a range of emotions excited by eating Fry's chocolate: Desperation, Pacification, Expectation, Acclamation and the Realization that it's Fry's. A matching poster appeared in 1905 telling us that 'The 'Five Girls' want Fry's 'Five Boys' Milk Chocolate and will have no other.' To make Desperation appear tearful, ammonia was sprayed close to his face. Rowntree's KitKat label for the regular four and two finger bars, has barely changed over eighty years and what changes there have been are imperceptible. As we have seen, the wrapper did change from red to blue during the Second World War, when it was produced with a plain chocolate covering due to shortages of milk during and after the war and to protect the integrity of the original product . This blue livery was withdrawn in 1947 when the standard red wrapped milk chocolate KitKat was reintroduced.

At the same time, these advertisements and wrappers demonstrated another universal and enduring theme – that chocolate is quite simply exceedingly good, and fun, to eat.

'Pascall Chocolate Eggs are good to eat, Pascall Novelties complete the treat' delivered the message. A 1927 Cadbury poster tells us that their chocolate has 'tastes that thrill'. Terry's took no prisoners when they launched their Theobroma – the food of the gods assortment. Theobroma was the highest authority available since it was the Linnaean classification name for the cacao tree. 'Mars are marvellous' and Fry's Caramets were 'sweet bliss'. Bounty was 'far and away the most exotic chocolate treat.' Crunchie 'makes exciting biting!' Everybody was a (Cadbury's)' fruit and nut case'. Rowntree's Milk Chocolate contained 'delight in every bite' in 1928. Cellophane was introduced in the 1920s which, to some extent, took over from paper wrappers and provided much the same opportunities for pithy slogans and good branding.

Chocolate boxes too, for assortments, offered another vehicle for branding and eye catching illustration. From 1862 Fry's and Cadbury were selling chocolates in boxes, Easter and Christmas selections were particularly popular; in 1882 Rowntrees had no fewer than 150 different boxes on offer. Sentimentality was the order of the day in artwork, and the boxes themselves were extremely popular. Apart from their primary, immediate use as a chocolate box, they were often a long-term repository for odds and ends, photographs, postcards and other keepsakes – long fuse, slow drip advertising. Cadbury, indeed, produced some very lavish boxes, plush-lined with silk and satin and designed to hold jewelry, handkerchiefs or gloves long after the chocolates were eaten. Tins followed and these, too, produced vivid and colourful designs with immediate and long-term functions, to which many a cupboard and loft will attest. In the 1990s Terry's redesigned their All Gold and Moonlight boxes to target the 15–24 year old market which made up twenty-four per cent of sales: the former were shaped into ingots, the latter into dinner jacket shaped boxes with *art nouveau* illustrations.

Alleged health benefits were a factor in the high nutritional values afforded by rich, pure milk content. This, of course, chimed with the traditional claims surrounding so-called medicinal confectionery; lozenges, voice ju-jubes and barley sugar for example all had boasted medical benefits, as indeed did Mackintosh's toffee – good for sore throats. Posters and adverts were frequently populated with healthy, rubescent children. Cadbury's Dairy Milk Chocolate was 'rich in cream'. 'Overflowing with goodness' was trotted out by both Mackintosh and Nestlé while Pascall's Ambrosia

1935

1938

1952

1984

A pack of Terry's playing cards.

The fifty-year development of brand KitKat.

Pascall chocolates – every girl's dream.

Devonshire Chocolate was 'the glory of Devon in a packet.' Fry's famous churn-shaped showcard from 1925 announced that their milk chocolate contained 'full cream milk from west of England farms.' In 1955 Mars was still telling us that not only was a Mars Bar good for your work-life balance but it also 'feeds you goodness 3 good ways: milk, chocolate, glucose.' There has been a glass-and-a-half of milk in every bar of Cadbury's Dairy Milk since 1928. The *British Medical Journal* of 26 December 1891 endorsed Bovril Chocolate – Bovril Caramels contained ten per cent Bovril; Oxo Chocolate was manufactured on a similar basis – 'a stand-by between meals'. Bovril's claim was that 'it contained 300 per cent more actual nourishment than any other chocolate extant.' It was particularly suitable for children and the sick, as well as being good for sportsmen and travellers: 'a food by the way'; 'a perfect food in itself.' Oxo also marketed Oxo Toffee (containing fluid beef and fresh cream milk) as did Boots – Vitamalt Toffee – while Horlicks produced a malted milk toffee. Terry's Snack was ideal for walkers as it contained raisins and 'nutritive' cereals. Mars initially sold Maltesers as low fat 'energy balls'. After launching in the 1930s, Rowntree's Chocolate Crisp was originally advertised as 'the biggest little meal' and 'the best companion to a cup of tea'. Evolving into KitKat, Kitty the Kat showed up in the late 1940s to emphasize the rich full cream milk content of the bar. Betty's, who produced their own chocolate for their cafes in Harrogate and York, bring German medical authorities to confirm that eating chocolate is beneficial in the fight against obesity, coronary disease and neurological disorders.

Closely associated with healthiness were the themes of quality and purity, key elements in chocolate production, particularly as we have seen, amongst the perfectionist Quaker manufacturers. Fry's early adverts were described as 'venerable announcements' which had a 'certain coy primness about them'; Cadbury's end-of-century slogan was 'Absolutely Pure, Therefore Best.' To the Methodist Mackintosh's it was all very simple: 'always quality first, publicity second, as advertising alone can only sell a poor article once.' For their Quality Street the slogan for shopkeepers was 'Put your shop in Quality Street by putting Quality Street in your shop.'

Association with royalty, weddings, coronations and jubilees and with patriotic events such as the Festival of Britain, were exploited on wrappers, boxes and tins at every

> **EAT SWEETS AND GROW THIN.**
>
> **CHOCOLATE CURE FOR WEAK HEARTS.**
>
> Eat more chocolate and grow thin! That is the latest advice of the doctors. " Investigations conducted by a German heart specialist for 25 years," said a Harley-street specialist, " show that contrary to the popular belief, chocolate is the best for obesity. Experiments by the German specialist, Dr. Fredrick Bosser, also reveal that chocolate effects a permanent cure of weak hearts, neurasthenia, neuralgia, and ' nerves.'
> " Chocolate has a rich lime content, and sufferers should eat plenty of foods that are rich in lime . Cocoa contains 5.7 per cent. of lime, almonds 8.81 per cent., walnuts 8.59 per cent. ; cocoanut 4.82 per cent., and vanilla the remarkable figure of 27.4 per cent.
>
> **BUT**
> " YOU MUST EAT CONFECTIONS WHICH ARE MADE OF PURE INGREDIENTS & MADE BY A REPUTABLE FIRM."
> *Therefore eat BETTY'S CONFECTIONS always, because they are made under ideal conditions and of course are of undisputable quality.*
>
> WE SHALL BE PLEASED TO SEND YOU PARTICULARS OF OUR CONFECTIONS — *Betty's Ltd* — OUR LATEST CONFECTIONS ARE WORTH A TRIAL. SOMETHING UNUSUAL.
>
> THE EXCLUSIVE CAFE.
> Chocolate Manufacturers :: French and English Confectioners.

This fascinating advertisement copy from Betty's of Harrogate and York asserts that chocolate is reputedly good in the fight against obesity, coronary disease and neurological disorders.

opportunity. More mundanely, but just as influential, one assumes, was the matching of chocolates to everyday life: Caley's Marching Chocolate aimed at the military, Rowntree's Motoring Chocolate from 1928, as essential as petrol and aimed at the glove box ('You can't go without it !'), Cadbury's Holiday Chocolate and Excursion Chocolate aimed at the increasing number of motorists, day trippers and holiday makers. 'Extra creamy milk chocolate' were Payne's Poppets ('stop at the shop that has Poppets') and 'add that touch of surprise that makes the holiday and make this a real Poppet of a holiday'. Nestlé's Smoker's Semi-Sweet Milk Chocolate from the 1930s is 'Specially blended to suit smokers. It is just sweet enough, very sustaining, and does not create thirst. You will find it particularly pleasant between smokes.' Chocolate cigars and cigarettes were popular and packaged to look like the real thing with Dunn's, Fry's and Rowntrees all involved.

Less dramatically, the need to win repeat business was developed through the use of coupons, vouchers and prizes. Cards to collect on all manner of subjects were made available by all the main UK companies and by Nestlé. Games were used by Rowntree;

More wartime health benefits for all the family in this Rowntree cocoa advertisement in a 1942 issue of Picture Post.

Give your family the meal-time drink that is a food as well

The drink you give your family at meals can be a good body-building, energy-giving food. Give them Rowntree's Cocoa. It is nourishing and easily digestible, and even makes it easier to digest your other food. Make Rowntree's Cocoa your regular meal-time drink.

Rowntree's Cocoa makes every meal go further

Cadbury had their jigsaws. Postcards – often featuring the images from the posters and show cards – were extremely popular and collected from the earliest days right up to the present where they are still much sought after.

Christmas and Easter have always been peak times: seasonal catalogues offering their special ranges were produced and from the 1920s selection boxes were aggressively promoted with up to sixteen lines and games and puzzles on the boxes. Examples are Caley's Xmas Tuck Box and Needler's Xmas Gift Box. Easter eggs were first laid in the 1870s by Fry's and Cadbury; sweets were soon filling them as were free gifts, popular in the 1930s with toys such as quacking ducks inside and packaging inspired by light bulb carton designers. Innovative, and by today's standards, decidedly odd, receptacles were used as containers for chocolates: Rowntrees had a chrome teapot (with a special ebonite heat-resistant base) for 5s 6d; Nestlé a Royal Winton teapot; Fry's a brass coal scuttle (21s) or a pickle jar (2s6d); and Needler's the Knitcraft case: 'a useful and attractive container for your work, wool, needles &c', all with 4s worth of County Chocolates, for 5 shillings.

By the beginning of World War II the market was huge and the stakes were high – there were around over 300,000 shops selling sweets and chocolates supplied by around 350 confectionery and or chocolate producers. Posters on advertising hoardings, shop window

Rowntree's motoring game produced to promote Motoring Chocolate with Mr York. Based on Snakes & Ladders *it takes the players on a journey from the Houses of Parliament up the A1 and over to Selby to York.*

Building for the future at Rowntrees in 2010.

Pumping liquid chocolate into the tank room from a Fruit Pastille liveried tanker.

The hugh KitKat sign on the wall of #5 plant, Haxby Road.

Nestlé products on the road 2010.

displays, show cards and point of sale, as well as newspaper and magazine advertisements, were also crucial to the promotion of a seemingly endless stream of new products. In the 1950s Cadbury had sixty permanent display men responsible for window displays and point of sale the length and breadth of the country, all backed up by 200 representatives.

As we have seen, confectionery companies were amongst the first advertisers on commercial television on its launch in 1955. By 1958 sixty per cent of chocolate advertising budget went on television commercials. The Milky Bar Kid first rode into town in 1961 and the Bond-like Milk Tray hero overcame almost insurmountable odds most nights from 1968 to get that all important box there – 'all because the lady loves Milk Tray.' He made his last surreptitious delivery in 2003 to the usual strains of Cliff Adams' Night Rider. Milky Way was the 'the sweet you can eat between meals'. In the 1970s Fry's Turkish Delight was 'full of Eastern promise' (more music by Adams); A finger of Fudge is just enough to give your kids a treat' and Flake proved that 'Only the crumbliest, flakiest chocolate, tastes like chocolate never tasted before.' Terry's Chocolate Orange is famous for its striking marketing; slogans included: 'When you whack a Terry's Chocolate Orange, Good Things Happen'; 'tap it and unwrap it'; 'It's not Terry's, it's mine', or 'Don't tap it … Whack it!' More recent TV advertising campaigns carry the slogan 'Smash it to pieces, love it to bits'. Ferrero Rocher's ambassadors' reception advertising campaign from the 1970s was recently revived to great effect. The original still features in the top twenty in advertisement recall lists.

Perhaps, though, the most significant recent move in television advertising was in 1996 when Cadbury became sponsors of *Coronation Street* – Britain's longest running soap opera, now more than fifty years old. The initial cost was £10 million for one year but this ensured that the Cadbury name and associated icons were on our screens at the beginning and end of each episode and at every commercial break. In 2010 Mars sponsored Harry Hill's programmes. KitKat was first advertised on television in 1957 and had its first colour advert in 1967. Famous adverts include the 'Dancing Panda' in 1987 and the 'Have a Break' advertisements in the 90's. The giant panda 'takes a break' advertisement came thirtieth in Channel 4's '100 Greatest Adverts' poll in 2000.

Changes in the retail landscape obviously influenced chocolate marketing. Self-service grocers and supermarkets gradually replaced the traditional CTNs: confectioners-tobacconist-newsagents; their eye catching window displays gave way to internal display units and point of sale. A move towards the use of wholesalers as opposed to the company

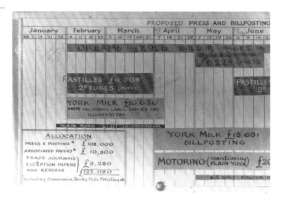

KIT KAT TELEVISION ADVERTISING SUMMER 1964

NO. OF 15 SEC. AND 7 SEC. SPOTS TO BE TRANSMITTED PER WEEK:

AREA	MAY 4	11	18	25	JUNE 1	8	15	22	29	JULY 6	13	20	27	AUGUST 3	10	17	24	31
LONDON	9	10	8	10	10	10	3				9	9		9	9	9		
MIDLANDS	9	9	10	10	11	11					9	9		9	9	9		
NORTH	8	8	8	10	11	11	4	4			9	9		9	9	9		
SCOTLAND	9	9	9	9	9	9					9	9		9	9	9		
WALES/WEST	9	9	9	9	9	9					9	9		9	9	9		
SOUTH	9	9	9	9	9	9					9	9		9	9	9		
TYNE-TEES	9	9	9	9	9	9					9	9		9	9	9		
ANGLIA	9	9	9	9	9	9					9	9		9	9	9		
WESTWARD	9	9	9	9	9	9					9	9		9	9	9		
ULSTER	9	9	9	9	9	9					9	9		9	9	9		
BORDER	9	9	9	9	9	9					9	9		9	9	9		
N.E. SCOTLAND	9	9	9	9	9	9					9	9		9	9	9		
CHANNEL	9	9	9	9	9	9					9	9		9	9	9		

Summer 1964 regional KitKat TV campaigns.

1930s costed advertising schedule for advertising and poster campaigns.

Two of Alfred Leete's Mr York's posters. One of the rhymes in his repertoire went as follows: 'I am plain Mr York of York, Yorks, Renowned for my plain homely talks, People say in the train They can't do without Plain Mr York with his choc from York, Yorks.'

traveller or representative had a similar impact on how chocolate was displayed in shops: merchandising had arrived and impulse buying – pioneered by Mars – was the way forward. Retail price maintenance was lifted on confectionery in the early 1960s allowing cut price chocolates, multipacks and minipacks containing 'fun-size' bars. The effect of this is exemplified by KitKat: twenty per cent of sales were in multipacks by 1970. Voucher schemes, personalities hosting lavish prize competitions, the famous philanthropic C.D.M. award for Cadbury's Dairy Milk all added to the marketing mix at one time or another.

Quality artists were often employed to great effect: Caley, Bovril Chocolate and Fry used John Hassall – most famous for his *The Jolly Fisherman* poster created in 1908 for the Great Northern Railway; Fry's commissioned Tom Browne, one of the best of the British comic postcard artists at the beginning of the twentieth century, and Chas Pears, a prolific poster artist for the London Underground and an official war artist in both world wars. Alfred Leete drew Rowntree's Mr York in 1928; before that he had produced 'Your Country Needs You' in 1914 – probably the best-known war poster of all time. Mackintosh used Jean d'Ylen, celebrated French poster artist, for their Toffee de Luxe in 1929, as well as Heath Robinson, cartoonist and illustrator, best known for his drawings of crazy machines, and Mabel Lucie Atwell, book and magazine illustrator, for *Toffee Town*, as used in national newspaper advertisements. Raymond Peynet, creator of the famous 'Les Amoureux', worked on Dairy Box and Sir Alfred Mullins, celebrated painter of horses, drew Caley's famous Marquee and Lady posters. G. M. Elwood designed some of their chocolate boxes around 1922. Richard Cadbury, an accomplished artist in his own right, worked on some of his own chocolate boxes. Cadbury's used Arthur Rackham's work on its chocolate boxes and a team of top comic illustrators for its popular *CocoCub News* in 1935. CocoCubs also featured comic strips in the national press, drawn by top artists of the day.

The Chocolate Industry in Twenty-First Century York

THE Twenty-First Century has already seen significant changes in the chocolate industry in Britain, not least Kraft's £11.5bn takeover of Cadbury in 2010 to add to its earlier acquisitions of Terry and Toblerone. Fairtrade and the internet are undoubtedly underpinning the biggest industry-wide developments. For York, though, the single most important events were the closure of Terry's, the purchase of Monkhill Confectionery by Tangerine and the consolidation of KitKat production at Haxby Road by Nestlé. First, though, it may be useful to look briefly at the general situation regarding the industry.

According to figures released by UK Confectionery Review, Cadbury Trebor Bassett, and others each person now eats on average about 200 bars of chocolate every year; we spend around nearly £4 billion on chocolate – around seventy per cent of the total UK confectionery market (chocolate and sweets); the chocolate market in the UK grew by nearly six per cent in 2009. More than ninety per cent of the UK population buys confectionery, with each buyer spending an average of thirty pence a day. Nearly two-thirds of all confectionery is purchased by women, but they eat just over a half of

KitKat No. 5 plant 2010, Haxby Road, York.

what they buy themselves; men now purchase just under a third of all confectionery and generally eat the majority of what they buy; children eat thirty eight per cent of all confectionery. A recent report showed that people over fifty-five eat £700 worth of chocolate every year; twenty-one per cent of the total chocolate and confectionery sold in Britain is consumed by people above the age of 55.

Generally, in 2010 the biggest producers were Côte d'Ivoire (thirty-three per cent), Ghana (twenty-one per cent), and Indonesia (fifteen per cent). Brazil at four per cent had seen its output virtually wiped out by a fungal disease, witches' broom, in 1989 when it had been the world's second largest producer. Biggest consumers in 2010 were the US (nearly eighteen per cent), Netherlands (fourteen percent), Far East (twelve per cent), Germany, France and Brazil (all between six and seven per cent) and the UK at four per cent. Total consumption was three and a half million tonnes. The price of cacao doubled from US$1,504 per ton in 2005 to $3,071 in 2010.

On the continuing debate over alleged health benefits of chocolate the European Commission Food Safety Authority ruled in 2010 that there was still insufficient consistent scientific evidence to support studies which suggest that consumption of certain types of chocolate can lower blood pressure, reduce the risk of heart attack, prevent wrinkles or increase cognitive skills. However, a 2010 study of 19,357 patients (EPIC Study 1994–2006) led by Brian Buijsse of the German Institute of Human Nutrition in Nuthetal and reported in the *British Heart Journal* provided some reliable evidence that antioxidant-rich dark chocolate does appear to protect against hypertension and stroke: work in progress. Similarities with recreational drugs are on less certain ground as this recent report on NBC's *Today Show* confirmed: 'Researchers have discovered that chocolate produced some of the same reactions in the brain as marijuana. The researchers also discovered other similarities between the two, but can't remember what they are'.

With financial backing from Mars and Hershey, the genetic code of the cocoa tree was finally sequenced in 2010, a major breakthrough which could lead to the tripling of the global yield with hardier and more prolific plants, and thereby improve the lives of the

KitKat Fairtrade 2011.

millions of largely subsistence farmers dependent on the crop. Currently about eighty per cent of cocoa crops in Africa and Latin America are lost to disease. A more robust cocoa crop should also permit farmers to diversify and produce other valuable foods, thus making them less dependent on cocoa. The project's results are available at the Cacao Genome Database. They have been released into the public domain.

Currently growers receive three-and-a-half per cent of the value of a bar of chocolate sold in the West; in 1990 it was sixteen per cent, while over the same period the manufacturers' cut has risen from fifty-six to seventy per cent. To help address this crisis, Fairtrade has emerged as a powerful force requiring manufacturers to pay growers a fair price for their raw materials. The Fairtrade Foundation was originally founded by Oxfam and others and the concept was extended into the world of chocolate in 1994 by Josephine Fairley who insisted that the chocolate she used in her new Green & Blacks organic chocolate company was made from pesticide free cacao beans. The result was Maya Gold which was not only pesticide free but was also was produced with a fair price paid to the Kekchi Maya farmers; it received the UK's first Fairtrade certification.

In 2009 Cadbury's Dairy Milk was Fairtrade certified, thereby tripling the amount of Fairtrade cocoa sourced from Ghana to about 15,000 tonnes a year. The total annual cocoa production of Ghana is more than 600,000 tonnes. Under Fairtrade, Cadbury pays a guaranteed minimum price, even if the open market price falls below it, for Ghanaian cocoa. The move is part of the Cadbury Cocoa Partnership, a £45m initiative over ten years which will help cocoa farmers throughout the developing world.

Closer to home, January 2010 saw the first Fairtrade-certified KitKat four-finger bars arrive on shop shelves to the benefit of thousands of farmers in Côte d'Ivoire. As well as the Fairtrade price (or market price if higher) for the cocoa, farmers' organisations receive additional Fairtrade premium payments (currently US$150 per tonne) which is used for business or social development projects. This is part of the October 2009 Nestlé Global Cocoa Plan – a £65 million investment over ten years in programmes to address the economic, social and environmental issues facing cocoa farming communities. Côte d'Ivoire produces one third of the world's cocoa and one in four people directly or indirectly depend on cocoa farming. The Archbishop of York, Dr John Sentamu, applauded the development and said: 'The next step is to make all other produce Fairtrade where possible – in particular my own favourite, the Yorkie! This will depend largely on the Ivory Coast producing the large quantity and quality needed for Nestlé to deliver the product. Nestlé must be congratulated in going beyond the profit margin.'

In marketing, the biggest development has undoubtedly been the rise in importance of the corporate website where companies across the whole range of manufacturers imaginatively and dynamically display all aspects of their manufacturing processes, heritage, recipes, nutritional information and ethical credentials. Individual products too have their own sites giving a wealth of specific detail; on line stores tempt us with attractively presented brands, easily and conveniently obtainable without leaving the house. Social networking sites deployed by companies and individuals alike increase the online noise and spread the word almost effortlessly.

The KitKat website gives us the following fascinating information: the KitKat range accounts for approximately twenty-three per cent of Nestlé Confectionery UK sales. Almost a quarter of the KitKat sales are of four–finger Kit Kat. The UK is the biggest market for KitKat globally. It is about twice as big as the second Kit Kat market, Japan. Some forty-seven bars are eaten every second and in 1999 sales amounted to £250 million, breaking the £1/4bn barrier for the first time. Every five minutes enough KitKats are manufactured to form a stack that is higher than the Eiffel Tower (986 feet), while one year's production would stretch around the London Underground (249 miles) more than 350 times – so 87,150 miles of KitKats are made every year. In 2004 39,000 tonnes of KitKat were sold – 107 tonnes a day; York uses eighty-two million litres of milk a year.

New Nestlé launches in the new millennium include: 2000 – Rolo biscuit; 2002 – Double Cream chocolate bar; 2003 – Kit Kat Kubes; 2004 – Fruity Smarties, Kit Kat Editions and Baci; 2005 – Aero Bubbles, Wonka Bars and Texan; 2006 – Kit Kat Peanut Butter, Kit Kat Dark, After Eight Mint Munchies and After Eight Milk; 2007 – Aero Bubbles Milk, Heaven and Quality Street Nutty Chocolate carton; 2008 – Kit Kat Senses. In late 2004 to the end of 2006, Nestlé Rowntree sponsored York City F.C.: the club's home-ground, Bootham Crescent, was renamed KitKat Crescent.

Today brand KitKat is a business on its own. The traditional bar has four fingers which each measure approximately 1cm (0.39 in) by 9cms (3.5 in). The two-finger bar was launched later in the 1930s, and has remained the company's best-selling biscuit brand ever since. The 1999 Kit Kat Chunky (known as Big Kat in the U.S.A.) has one big finger 2.5cms (0.98 in) wide. Kit Kat bars comprise varying numbers of fingers depending on the market, ranging from the half-finger sized Kit Kat Petit in Japan, to the three-fingered variants in the Middle East, to the twelve-finger KitKat family-size bars in Australia and France. In Ireland, the UK, and U.S.A. Nestlé also produces KitKat Ice Cream, and in Malaysia, KitKat Drumsticks.

Other interesting varieties and flavours from the 100 or so that are available from around the KitKat world include, from Japan for instance: chocolate and banana, custard pudding, cucumber, peanut butter, Earl Grey tea, watermelon and salt, cheese, bubblegum, wine and aloe vera. Certainly not for the purist.

In response to the growing demand for dark chocolate worldwide, caused largely by the purported health benefits, the four-finger KitKat Fine Dark was launched in 2006 in the UK. Nestlé also now manufactures two-finger KitKats with natural flavourings which for the first time are suitable for vegetarians.

In April 2010, Nestlé UK announced that seventy-three new jobs will be created in York over three years as it establishes a Customer Relationship Centre for Nespresso, the premium coffee business. The company says that 'this is another step on Nestlé's York site's journey to become a world-class business facility. In addition to housing one of the world's biggest confectionery factories, Nestlé York now incorporates logistics and distribution facilities serving the company's UK food and beverages businesses, as well as being home to a global R&D centre...over the last twenty years we have invested £150 million in York, transforming the site into a multi-purpose business centre which is now fit for the future'.

In August 2010 KitKat marketing teamed up with the band Scouting For Girls, for a new augmented reality project; an AR marker was featured on all KitKat four finger promotional packs which, when activated showed the band playing their single *Silly Song*, in various different 'break' situations – chosen as ones where consumers might experience music: a bedroom, a park, train, library and a concert. This is the first time an FMCG brand has used augmented reality on pack.

In December 2010 Phase One of a three-year £15 million production plant was opened by Nestlé. The new KitKat production line comprises eight new and upgraded ovens for manufacturing the wafers; it will enhance and consolidate KitKat production in the city leading to the production there of more than a billion KitKat bars each year. The new plant will make around thirty million wafer sheets per year. The company said: 'Using state-of-the art technology and benefiting from all the latest know-how gathered through our product technology centre based in York and factories across the world, the aim with this investment is to ensure that we deliver the freshest wafer to our moulding plants the whole wafer process will be replaced or improved eventually.'

KitKat started 2011 with a new marketing campaign to remind people in the UK what they should be doing during their breaks. The campaign, created by J. Walter Thomson, the original creators of the 1930s 'have a break' slogan, builds on KitKat's long running 'Have a Break, Have a KitKat' campaign, familiar to generations of consumers. The advertisement, again playing on 'break', features a crane operator on a demolition site. While taking a break enjoying his KitKat, he decides to have some fun with his fellow crane drivers and they manoeuvre to form the perfect giant Newton's Cradle with their wrecking balls. It ends with the iconic slogan, all to the strains of the Fratelli's *Chelsea Dagger*.

In January 2011 Nestlé announced plans for a redevelopment of its Haxby Road site. It has invested £1m in extending its Insight and Learning Centre, a supermarket-style petrol station and convenience store, where confectionery products are displayed to maximize sales to retailers. The Insight Centre, which opened in May 2011, will stock the full range of Nestlé products, including coffee, water, cereal and pet food. It features an Imax cinema, replica living room and fully functioning kitchen and digital medic area. Consumer behaviour and shopper research findings work in concert with state of the art digital technology to help retailers maximise their sales potential. The Centre already attracts hundreds of retail customers and generates millions of pounds worth of incremental sales.

There are also plans to expand the Product Technology Centre which employs 120 scientists, researchers and technicians working on improving Nestlé products and production equipment. The company will also launch a new version of the dark chocolate KitKat using seventy per cent cocoa solids.

At the same time, another redevelopment project which will transform another part of York's Nestlé factory and create up to 600 new jobs has been approved by City of York Council's planning committee. The company is now seeking a developer to carry out the multi-million-pound Nestlé South scheme, which will see some of the site's historic factory buildings converted into 166 houses, forty-six flats, twenty-eight student flats, 10,000sq metres of office space, 974 square metres of retail space, and a community centre, gym and crèche. A café will also be opened inside the Joseph Rowntree Memorial Library.

Over at the former Terry site, a developer gained permission in January 2011 to proceed with its £165m redevelopment plan of the old chocolate factory after reaching agreement with City of York Council. Hundreds of homes, two hotels, shops, bars and restaurants will be built on the Bishopthorpe Road site, creating around 2,700 jobs.

The confectionery industry in York has changed beyond all recognition since its Victorian origins and its heyday in the 1930s. Nevertheless, despite the loss of Terry to the city, sweets and chocolate do seem to have a sound future here in the shape of Nestlé and Tangerine. The workforce numbers may be fewer and the philanthropy may be diminished, but the benefits these two companies bring to the city of York remains inestimable and KitKat in, particular, will always be associated with York.

Epilogue

In the summer of 2011 a surprise find of priceless material from Craven's heyday was discovered in an old Craven warehouse. The horde included the famous painting of Mary Craven which hung in the company's boardroom for many years – see page 8 above; various sweet and chocolate tins and other bits and pieces were also found. Tony Wade of Tangerine who made the discovery, remembers the painting from his early apprenticeship days at the firm as well as anecdotes about Mary Craven as reported in *The York Press*: "She wasn't very tall, though. Apparently, she used to have a high chair she would sit on so she could oversee the packing." He points out that the company is making many of the same products now as they made in the early days; "We still use the same techniques. The stripes on the humbugs are still painted by hand."

Mr York taking centre stage on the Antiques Roadshow *in York's Museum Gardens July 2011 with presenter Hilary Kay on the left and Nestlé archivist Alex Hutchinson on the right. Photo courtesy of York Press.*

Delivering the goods to the other Bettys Cafe and Tea Rooms, in Stonegate.

July 2011 saw the return of the BBC's *Antiques Roadshow* to York – and a surprise appearance by that Rowntree icon Mr York of York. Chaperoned by Nestlé archivist Alex Hutchinson, Mr York was given the once over by the show's Hilary Kay: her verdict? … the amiable Mr York was valued at around £5,000 !

We also have Alex Hutchinson to thank for the organisation and opening of a new Nestlé UK archive created at the Haxby Road site. The launch in July was attended by Giles Naish who works at Nestlé in York and is the great-great-grandson of Joseph Rowntree. Over time many of the items will be exhibited at various places and at various events in the city; more than 37,000 photographs and over 100 hours of film have been digitised and these will be viewable on line in the future.

Items include a 1920s robot advertisement, a stained-glass window from one of the earliest Haxby Road offices, and a tin of Rowntree's cocoa found with the bodies of Scott of the Antarctic and the two remaining members of his team when they died in March 1912. There is also a library of over 300 Nestlé films recently discovered in a wall cavity at the company's HQ in Croydon, original 1930s artwork for Black Magic advertising campaigns, a unique collection of hundreds of 1920s chocolate moulds and countless photographs, *Cocoa Works Magazines*, catalogues and other documents.

"The state-of-the-art facility has been built to preserve documents, films, artefacts and artworks from all of Nestlé's UK sites, with climate and humidity controls to preserve its contents, and specially fitted lights designed to filter out harmful UV rays."

The year 2012 looks set to be an important year for chocolate in York. A £2 million project, *The Sweet History of York*, a visitor attraction celebrating the city's heritage, and future, in the confectionery industry will open in King's Square. It will allow visitors to see at first hand the story of York's confectionery industry, past, present and future; there will be a strong emphasis on hands-on activities, anecdotes and memories from former employees of Rowntree, Terry and Craven and visitors will be able to have a try at making their own chocolate.

Supported by Nestlé, Kraft and Tangerine Confectionery the museum will also work closely with modern chocolatiers in the City thus demonstrating another facet of York's contemporary chocolate industry. The attraction will be on two floors and will include a shop and restaurant.

Chocolate has, quite rightly, not escaped the current vogue for artisan production of consumer products; its development brings us full circle and back to the late nineteenth century days when chocolate and chocolates were made on a piecemeal basis, sometimes in the manufacturer's own kitchen. York, appropriately, has its fair share of these modern day chocolatiers.

There is a branch of the national chain, *Hotel Chocolat*, in Coney Street; the company was set up "to make a better type of chocolate available to UK consumers bored by the mediocrity of that available in supermarkets and on the high street". Raw materials come from the firm's cocoa plantation on Saint Lucia which is run along the company's Engaged Ethics Cocoa Programme; its Tasting Club has over 100,000 members "who enjoy a brand new selection of exciting, artisan chocolates every month".

Monk Bar Chocolatiers of York opened at 1 Goodramgate in 1999 with a second branch in Shambles opening in 2002. Owner Ray Cardy trained in the USA and Belgium and returned to York "with a vision of making high quality exclusive chocolates with a

Making the chocolates at a Little Pretty Things workshop.

Monk Bar Chocolatiers – inside the Goodramgate branch.

luxurious taste to remember". Unusually, they actually make the chocolate used in the sixty or so varieties of luxury hand-made chocolates and chocolate sculptures on the premises.

York company *Little Pretty Things* was set up by Sophie Jewett in 2009 to provide an all-round chocolate experience for York residents and visitors: "a home for true chocolate lovers!" The core business is regular chocolate making parties, talks and classes, chocolate tasting sessions and workshops illuminating York's chocolate industry heritage. Many of these hands-on events take place in the magnificent setting that is the Mansion House. *Little Pretty Things* work closely with local schools, Visit York and York Libraries to spread their unalloyed enthusiasm for all things chocolate, with particular reference to York. Their unique and imaginative range of chocolates includes the Yorkshire Chocolate Collection all made from local produce and featuring such delights as Yorkshire Real Ale – Little Bitter Things, Yorkshire Blue Cheese and Biscuits, Yorkshire Rose made from rose petal jelly and rose water, Yorkshire Lemon Curd and Rhubarb Crumble. *Little Pretty Things* recipes can be found on their website. In November 2011 *Little Pretty Things* realised an ambition to focus their activities and products under one roof to create *York Cocoa House* – a centre of excellence in Blake Street in the heart of the chocolate city.

Choc-affair is a Naburn based family firm making and packing everything by hand and using only certified Fairtrade chocolate couveture. They have been producing quality

The signs go up in King's Square for York's new visitor attraction opening Spring 2012 and celebrating this, the home of British chocolate.

chocolate for over three years specialising in bespoke chocolates for corporate and hotel accounts and the general public.

Bettys, of course, has been making chocolate for their tea rooms and restaurants in York for ninety years. Ethically made chocolate and chocolates in one form or another are on the menu at their two outlets in the city : St Helen's Square and Stonegate. The shop in St Helen's Square and the website also offer a range of hand-made chocolate truffles, pralines and creams made from the rare, Venezuelan 'criollo' bean, chosen for its rich, deep flavour. Their team of eight chocolatiers have over 135 years experience of hand-crafting Bettys chocolates between them.

The future, then, of chocolate in York looks bright. Nestlé alone, which employs 1800 people in the city, increased its 2012 growth forecast in October 2011 and actually increased market share in 2011 from 16% to 16.6% with Rowntree brands growing market share by 22%.

This, and the emergence, or rather, re-emergence, of chocolatiers, brings the story of chocolate in York up to date. The enthusiasm, innovation and enterprise which characterises these companies all echo the compelling determination of Joseph Rowntree, Joseph Terry and Mary Craven. The recent establishment of a Rowntree archive and the *Sweet History of York* attraction celebrating the city's chocolate heritage will ensure that the inextricable association of the city with chocolate endures and continues. As Leonard Cohen famously said: "everybody wants a box of chocolates and a long stem rose".

Further Reading

Allott, S: Friends in York – The Quaker Story in the Life of a Meeting, York 1978. John Wilhelm Rowntree 1868–1905, York, 1994.

Armstrong, A: Stability and Change in an English County Town – A Social Study of York 1801 1851, Cambridge 1974.

Backhouse, A: The Worm-eaten Waistcoat, York 2003.

Baren, M: How it All Began in Yorkshire, Skipton 1997. How it All Began in Yorkshire Volume 2, Skipton, 2000.

Bebb, P: Shopping in Regency York, York 1994.

Benson, G: The City and County of the City of York Vol 1, York 1911.

Bournville Works Magazine – Royal Visits to Bournville, 1919, 1929, 1939, Bournville 1939, Elizabeth Mary Cadbury 1858–1951, Bournville 1951.

Bradley, J: Cadbury's Purple Reign, Chichester 2008 .

Brannan, J and F: A Postcard from Bournville, Studley, 1992.

Brenner, J. The Chocolate Wars: Inside the Secret Worlds of Mars and Hershey, London 1999.

Brigend, J: Topographical and Historical Description of the County of York, London 1819.

Brooks, F.W: York – 1066 to the Present Day (Stacpoole pp. 255–335).

Broomfield, M: A Bournville Assortment, York, 1998.

Buijsse, B. et al: Chocolate Consumption in Relation to Blood Pressure and Risk of Cardiovascular Disease in German Adults, *European Heart Journal*, 2010.

Butterill, C: The Temperance Movement in York 1830–1845, *York Historian* 17 (2000) 62–71.

Cadbury Bros Ltd: Sweet-Shop Success – A Handbook for the Sweet Retailer, Bournville.

Cadbury, D: Chocolate Wars: From Cadbury to Kraft, London, 2010.

Cadbury Eros Ltd: The Bournville Story, Bournville.

Cann, J: Rowntree Employees who Died in WWI, York 2003.

Chamber, The: Cravens, *The Chamber* 8, 1980, 2–4.

Chinn, C: The Cadbury Story, Studley, 1998.

Chrystal, P: Chocolate: The British Chocolate Industry, Oxford, 2010. Cadbury & Fry – An Illustrated History Forthcoming 2012. Confectionery in Yorkshire – An Illustrated History Forthcoming 2012. York Trade & Industry Through Time, Stroud 2011. Villages Around York Through Time, Stroud 2010. York Then & Now, Gloucester 2010.

Clements, C: Norwich Chocs Up a Century; *RM News* April 1986, pp. 6–7.

Coady, C: The Chocolate Companion, New York 1995.

Coe, S.D: The True History of Chocolate, London 1996.

Colbeck, M: Made in Yorkshire, Second to None, Huddersfield 1992.

Dandelion, P: The Quakers: A Very Short Introduction, Oxford 2008.

Defoe, D: A Tour Through the Whole Island of Great Britain, London, 1971.

Dickinson, J: York on Old Postcards, Keyworth, 1989.
    50 Years of Collecting Rowntrees, York 2010.

Drake, F: Eboracum: or the Histories and Antiquities of the City of York, York 1736.

Dronfield, E: Education in York (Stacpoole pp. 809–839).

Evans, S: Chocolate Unwrapped, London 2010.

Feinstein, C.H: York 1831–1981 – 150 Years of Scientific Endeavour and Social Change, York 1981.
    Populations, Occupations and Economic Development 1831–1981 (Feinstein 1981 pp. 109–159).

Feuz, P: Toblerone: 100 Years – The Story of a Swiss World Success, Berne.

Fitzgerald, R: Rowntree and the Marketing Revolution 1862–1969, Cambridge 1995.

Freeman, M: Quaker Extension c. 1905–1930: The Yorkshire 1905 Committee, York 2008.
    The Joseph Rowntree Charitable Trust, York 2004.

Freke, A: J.S. Fry & Sons – A Rough Guide to the Family & The Firm, Bristol 2010.

Fuller, LK: Chocolate Fads, Folklore and Fantasies, Binghamton 1994.

Galbraith, S: Dr John Snow – His Early Years, London 2002.

Gumbley, E: Bournville, Market Drayton, 1991.

Harrison, M: Bournville: Model Village to Garden Suburb, Chichester, 1999.

Harvey, J: York, London 1975.

Head, B: The Food of the Gods, London, 1903.

Heer, J: Nestlé 125 Years, Vevey 1991.

Henslowe, P: Ninety Years On – An Account of the Bournville Village Trust 2nd Revised Edition, Birmingham, 1991.

Hillman, J: The Bournville Hallmark – Housing People for 100 Years, Studley 1994.

Hitches, M: Bournville Steam and Chocolate, Pinner, 1992.

Johnson, B.P: The Gilds of York = Stacpoole pp. 447–610.

Knight, C.B: M.A. Craven & Son Ltd: A History of the Company, York, 1948.

Lang, W.R: Terry's – Two Centuries of Chocolates, Yorkshire Life May 1967..

Leitch, R: The Railways of Keynsham Featuring Fry's Chocolate & Passenger Freight Operations, Long Stratton 1997.

Lunn, M: Thomas Cooke: Telescope Maker of York (Whitworth pp. 115–128).

Matthew, J: Science and Technology 1831–1981 (Feinstein 1981 pp. 30–52).

Mayhew, H: London Labour and the London Poor, London, 1851.

Miller, M: English Garden Cities – An Introduction, Swindon 2010.

Morton, M and F: Chocolate – An Illustrated History, New York, 1986.

Moss, S: Chocolate – A Global History, London 2009.

Murphy, J: The History of Rowntrees in Old Photographs, York 2007.
    New Earswick – A Pictorial History, York 1987.

Murray, H: Opportunity of Leisure – The History of the York Railway Institute 1889–1989, York 1989.

Myler, C: The Life and Times of York Carriage Works 1884–1995, York 1995.

Needler, R: The Needlers of Hull, Beverley 1993.

Nuttgens, P (ed): The History of York, Pickering 2001.
   Twentieth Century York (Nuttgens 2001 pp. 302–358).
Oddy, D (Ed): The Making of the Modern British Diet, London 1976.
Opie, R: Sweet Memories, London 2008.
Othick, J: The Cocoa and Chocolate Industry in the Nineteenth Century, Oddy pp. 77–90.
Peacock, A.J: York 1900–1914, York 1992.
   York in the Great War, York 1993.
Pearce, W.T. (Ed) Fry's Works Magazine, 1728–1928, Somerdale 1959.
Pepys, S: The Diary of Samuel Pepys, London 2003.
Publication Department, Bournville: Bournville Personalities, Bournville 1950.
   Sixty Years of Planning – The Bournville Experiment, Bournville.
   Cadbury at Bournville 1979–1979, Bournville.
Raistrick, A: Quakers in Science and Industry, York 1950.
Richardson, P: Indulgence, London 2003.
Richardson, T: Sweets: A History of Temptation, London 2002.
Robson, S.E: Joshua Rowntree, London 1916.
Rogers, T: A Century of Progress 1831–1931, Bournville 1931.
Rowntree & Co: Works Rules 7th Edition, York 1953.
   The Cocoa Works in War-time, York 1947.
   Cocoa Works Magazine 1902–1986.
   The Guide's Booklet.
Rowntree, B.S: Poverty – A Study Of Town Life 2/E, London 1908.
   Poverty and the Welfare State, London 1951.
Royle, E: Nineteenth Century York (Nuttgens 2001 pp. 244–301).
Rubinstein, D: York Friends and the Great War, York 1999.
Rubinstein, H: The Chocolate Book, Harmondsworth 1982.
Ryan, O: Chocolate Nations – Living and Dying for Cocoa in West Africa, London 2011.
Sessions, W.K: Printing in York – A History (Stacpoole 1972 pp. 921–968).
Shaw, D: Conundrum – The Cadbury's Creme Egg Mystery, London 1984.
Sheils, S: Among Friends – The Story of the Mount School, York, London 2007.
Sinclair, A: Eighteenth Century York (Nuttgens 2001 pp. 215–243).
Smith, C: Reshaping Work – The Cadbury Experience, Cambridge 1990.
Smith, S: 'The City Itself is But Poor': Evidence for the Depressed State of York's Economy during the 1720s; *York Historian* 21, pp. 21–25.
Spender, B: Education, Learning and Community in New Earswick – An Enduring Rowntree Legacy, York 2011.
Stacpoole, A (ed): The Noble City of York, York 1972.
Taylor, W.B: The Workshops and Manufactories of York in the Second Half of the Eighteenth Century; *York Historian* pp. 18–3.
   The Emergence of a Confectionery Industry in York (White pp. 213–30).
Terry, J: Terry's of York 1767–1967, York 1967.
   In Commemoration of the Visit of their Majesties King George VI and Queen Elizabeth, York, 1937.
Tillot, P.M. (ed) A History of the County of York – The City of York, 1961.
Vansittart, J: Katherine Fry's Book, London 1966.
Vernon, A: A Quaker Businessman – The Life of Joseph Rowntree 1836–1925, York 1987.
Vipont, E: Arnold Rowntree – A Life, London 1955.

Waddilove, L.E: One Man's Vision – The Story of the Joseph Rowntree Village Trust, London 1954.

Wagner, Gillian: The Chocolate Conscience, London 1987.

Walvin, J: The Quakers – Money & Morals, London, 1997.

Ward, H: The Freemen of York (Stacpoole pp. 737–756).

Wheeler, E: The Early Days of Caleys, *Mackintosh Caley Magazine* 6, 1935, pp 8ff.

Wheeler, H: Half a Pound of Tuppenny Rice: Life in a Yorkshire Village Shop, Stroud 1993.

White, E: Feeding a City – York: The Provision of Food from Roman Times to the Beginning of the Twentieth Century, Totnes 2000.

Whiting, C: Fire over York – the Great York Air Raid 1942, Easingwold 2005.

Whitworth, A (ed): Aspects of York, Barnsley 2000.

Wild, A: The East India Company Book of Chocolate, London 1995.

Willis, R: Portrait of York, London 1972.

Wilson, V: The Story of Terry's, York 2009.

The Best Years of Our Lives? Secondary Education in York 1900–1985, York 2010 .

Windsor, D: The Quaker Enterprise: Friends in Business, London 1980.

York Times: One Woman's Courage: The Story of Mary Ann Craven and the Progress of Cravens of York, *York Times* 1, 3 1961, 26–29.

A Chocolate Chronology

600	Mayans cultivating *Xocoatle*
1500	Aztecs cultivating *Cacahuatl*; Montezuma II establishes bean bank
1528	Cortes and others introduce chocolate to the Spanish court
1579	English Navy fails to realise commercial value of chocolate
1648	Thomas Gage, English traveller, observes chocolate consumption in West Indies
1650	England takes Jamaica, and the cacao plantations there
1657	First chocolate shop opened in London by a Frenchman
1660	Samuel Pepys demonstrates benefits of chocolate
1675	Charles II closes down the chocolate houses in an attempt to quell sedition
1693	White's chocolate house opens in London
1698	The Cocoa Tree opens nearby
1725	Mary Tuke sets up her grocery business in York
1728	Walter Churchman opens his chocolate shop in Bristol
1729	Churchman granted letters patent by George II
1760	Chocolate endorsed by French nobility, de Sade, Voltaire, Casanova and others
1761	Joseph Fry buys Churchman's shop, a water mill and a warehouse
1765	In the USA Dr James Baker and John Hannon start production of chocolate and form the Baker company
1767	Berry and Bayldon set up their chocolate and confectioners shop in Bootham, York
1779	Anna Fry takes over Anna Fry & Son – Joseph Storrs Fry
1780	Fry wins contract with Royal Navy for supply of chocolate ration
1795	Fry buys a James Watt steam engine, thus extending industrialisation
1803	Joseph Hick, father of Mary Ann Craven, sets up his confectionery business in Coney Street
1813	Joseph Terry I arrives in York from Pocklington and sets up as an apothecary
1819	In Switzerland Francois Louis Cailler opens a chocolate factory in Vevey
1822	Joseph Rowntree I buys his shop in Pavement, York
1823	Tuke's are sole holders in north of England of licence permitting sale of chocolate
1824	John Cadbury opens his tea, coffee and chocolate shop in Birmingham Robert Berry moves his confectionery business to St Helen's Square and is joined by Joseph Terry I
1826	Joseph Terry I takes control of Terry and Berry confectioners
1828	Coenraad van Houten invents his hydraulic press leading to industrialisation of cocoa

1831   John Cadbury sets up his chocolate factory in Crooked Lane making cocoa and chocolate for sale in Bull Street

1835   Fry's are Britain's biggest chocolate producer

1843   Thomas Craven established in confectionery in York

1847   First Cadbury factory opens in Bridge Street with forty workers
       Fry pioneers eating chocolate with the chocolate bar

1850   *The Lancet* exposes adulteration of chocolate and cocoa
       Joseph Terry I dies in Huntington and is succeeded by Joseph Terry II

1851   Thomas Craven marries Mary Ann Hick

1853   Gladstone reduces duty on imported cocoa beans
       Fry's tins of chocolates sent to troops in the Crimean war

1854   George Cadbury takes three year apprenticeship at Rowntree's shop in York

1857   Joseph Rowntree II takes apprenticeship at London grocer's

1858   Terry leases Clementhorpe factory for production

1859   Dickens describes prodigious chocolate consumption in *A Tale of Two Cities*

1860   *Food and Drugs Act* and first *Adulteration of Food Act* passed, criminalising adulteration

1862   Henry Rowntree buys the Tukes' cocoa and chocolate business
       Mary Craven takes over the family confectionery business

1864   Henry Rowntree relocates the business to Tanner's Moat

1866   *Fry's Chocolate Cream* launched
       George Cadbury purchases a van Houten press and starts producing cocoa essence

1867   Terry starts chocolate production
       York Confectionery Company founded

1868   Fry's launch their chocolate assortments
       Cadbury produce their first chocolate box
       Richard and George Cadbury take over the company

1869   Joseph Rowntree II joins the business

1870   Chocolat Menier opens London office
       UK chocolate consumption increases threefold to 1890

1872   Second *Adulteration of Food Act* passed
       First of five tripartite trading agreements between Cadbury, Fry and Rowntree

1873   Fry produce the world's first easter egg

1875   Henri Nestlé, a German, starts production of *Farine Lacté* baby food in Vevey
       Trade Marks Act passed facilitating branding

1879   Daniel Peter invents milk chocolate in Switzerland using Henri Nestlé's powdered milk
       Cadbury open the Bournville factory
       Claude Gaget calls on Rowntree's with his gums and pastilles

1880   Rodolphe Lindt develops conching to produce fondant chocolate. Chocolate bars and chocolate covered sweets on the market
       Rowntree purchase a van Houten press
       Rowntrees launch *Elect* – cocoa essence

1881   H.J. Packer begins trading in Bristol
       Rowntree begin production of the precursors of *Fruit Gums* and *Fruit Pastilles*

1883   Fry launch *Pure Cocoa Essence*
       Henri Nestlé opens London sales office
       A.J. Caley starts making drinking chocolate in his Norwich shop

Scenes from Joe Dickinson's Rowntree 100,000 artefact 'museum' in York

Early Rowntree products: note the importance of royalty and of royal approval.

An 'usherette' with a wide range of chocolates, gums and pastilles on offer; and below: Joseph Rowntree with chocolate manufacturing paraphernalia.

1885	John Wilhelm Rowntree joins the firm
1886	Needler's established in Hull
	Terry's begin cocoa and chocolate production
1888	Benjamin Seebohm Rowntree joins the firm
1890	Joseph Rowntree builds Haxby Road factory
	John and Violet Mackintosh start making toffee in Halifax
1893	Chocolat Menier world's largest manufacturer of chocolate
	George Cadbury buys more land to build his model village
1897	S.H. Benson appointed Rowntree advertising agent
1898	Ebenezer Howard publishes *Tomorrow: A Peaceful Path to Real Reform* retitled in 1902 as *Garden Cities of Tomorrow*
	Joseph Terry II dies and is succeeded by sons Frank and Thomas Walker Leaper
1899	Henri Tobler sets up his chocolate factory in Berne
	Seebohm Rowntree publishes *Poverty: A Study in Town Life*
	Terry launch *Neapolitans*
1900	Cadbury, Fry and Rowntree sends tins of chocolate to troops in the Boer war
	Mary Ann Craven dies
	Mennonite Milton Snavely Hershey launches his milk chocolate *Hershey Bar* in Pennsylvania
1901	Nestlé begins production in London, then from Hayes in 1913
1902	*Fry's Milk Chocolate* launched, later known as *Five Boys*
	Cadbury open their first visitor's department
	Cocoa Works Magazine first published in March by Rowntree
	Building begins at New Earswick – the Rowntree Model Village
1904	Nestlé importing Kohler and Cailler products
	Joseph Rowntree sets up the Joseph Rowntree Trusts
1905	Cadbury launch *Dairy Milk*
	Rowntree establish workers' pension scheme
	John Wilhelm Rowntree dies
	Chocolate becomes regular issue for the armed services
1908	Packer acquire's Glasgow chocolate company Carson's Ltd
	Toblerone invented and patented
1909	York Confectionery Company goes bankrupt
	Rowntree donate Yearsley Road swimming baths to the city
1910	Cadbury replaces Fry as the nation's biggest chocolate producer
1911	Joseph William Thornton sets up Thornton's in Sheffield
	Noel Terry joins the firm
1913	Jean Sechaud invents the filled chocolate sweet
1914	Fry launch their *Turkish Bar,* later *Delight*
1915	*Cadbury's Milk Tray* launched
	Caley's Marching Chocolate issued to troops as *Marcho*
	Rowntree establishes Confectionery Ingredients Ltd in King's Lynn
1916	Milk chocolate supercedes cocoa as the main product of the UK chocolate industry
1917	Mackintosh launch chocolate coated *Toffee Deluxe*
1919	Fry merges with Cadbury
1920	*Cadbury's Flake* launched
1921	Rowntree donate Rowntree Park to the city

Rowntree board votes first significant marketing budget – with little effect

Chocolate consumption continues to rise; chocolate no longer considered a luxury

1922 Perugina introduces their *Baci* – kisses

1923 Fry moves out of Bristol to Somerdale

Cadbury Creme Eggs launched

Seebohm Rowntree succeeds Joseph Rowntree as chairman

Mars launch *Milky Way*

1925 Joseph Rowntree dies

Rowntree's *Plain York* chocolate bar launched; plain Mr York of York born; *Motoring* launched

York Confectionery Company established by Rowntree after failure to purchase Caley

1926 Joseph Draps sets up Godiva chocolatier in Belgium

1927 Rowntree buys a stake in Beech Nut

Terry move to Bishopthorpe Road

1929 *Cadbury Fruit & Nut* launched

1930 Mars launch *Snickers*

George Harris takes over marketing at Rowntree

1931 J. Walter Thompson appointed as Rowntree advertising agents

1932 Forrest Mars arrives in England and launches *Mars Bar*

Mackintosh acquires Caley

Terry launches *Chocolate Orange* and *All Gold*

1933 Rowntree launch *Black Magic*

1935 Rowntree launch *Aero* and *Kit Kat*

1936 *Dairy Assortment* – later *Dairy Box* – launched by Rowntree

Launch of *Quality Street* by Mackintosh

1938 Rowntree launch *Chocolate Beans* – later *Smarties*

Mackintosh launch *Rolo*

1939 Rowntree's *Polo* mints hit the market

1940 County Industries Ltd established at Rowntree

1942 Chocolate rationed in the UK

York and Norwich bombed in Baedecker raids; Caley factory destroyed

1946 Rowntree open *Dunollie*, their workers' convalescent home in Scarborough

1952 George Harris leaves Rowntree

Terry's *Waifa* bar launched

1953 Chocolate rationing ended

1954 Chocolate consumption peaks in the UK

1955 Commercial TV launched in UK; TV adverts begin

1957 'Have a break have a Kit Kat' slogan for *Kit Kat* launched

Kit Kat advertised on commercial TV

1958 Rowntree open Fawdon Factory

1960 Sir Francis Terry dies

1962 Rowntree launch *After Eight*

1963 Forte Group buys Terry

1964 Cadbury acquire Pascall Murray

Resale Price Maintenance abolished in UK

Scenes from Joe Dickinson's Rowntree 100,000 artefact 'museum' in York

Cocoa, chocolate, gums and assortments and below: iconic advertising, priceless cabinets and Mr York.

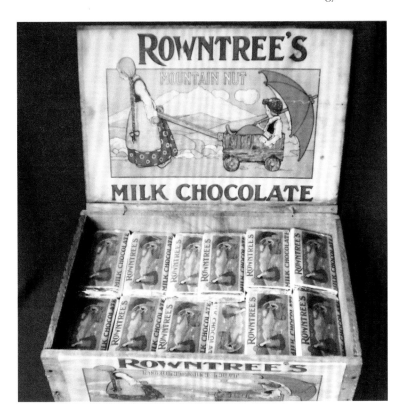

Mountain Nut *in trays and* Rock Chocolate *and* Rock Cocoa.

1966   Craven relocate to Low Poppleton Lane from Coppergate
1968   *Matchmakers* launched by Rowntree
1969   Cadbury merges with Schweppes
        Rowntree merges with Mackintosh to form Rowntree Mackintosh Ltd
1971   Rowntree Mackintosh buys Chocolat Menier
1976   Rowntree launch *Yorkie*
1978   Colgate-Palmolive buys Terry
1981   Terry's St Helen's Square restaurant closes
1982   United Biscuits buy Terry
1986   Final issue of *Cocoa Works Magazine*
1988   Rowntree Plc bought by Nestlé
1989   Cadbury acquire Trebor & Bassett
1990   Cadbury World opens
1993   Kraft buys Terry
1994   Caleys Norwich plant closes
        Fairtrade extends into chocolate industry via Green & Blacks
1996   Caley's of Norwich founded by three former executives
2008   Tangerine Confectionery buys Craven
2009   Cadbury's *Dairy Milk* Fairtrade certified
2010   Cadbury sold to Kraft
        Genetic code of cocoa tree sequenced
        Kit Kat Fairtrade certified
2011   Nestlé unveil redevelopment plans for Haxby Road; Insight Centre opens
2012   York's *Sweet History of York* visitor attraction opens

Rowntree and Terry Gallery

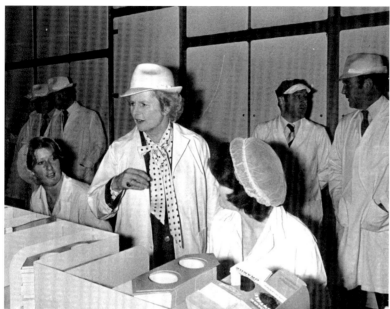

A visit by Margaret Thatcher July 1 1977 – the Yorkshire Post *reported:* 'In the chocolate Neapolitan room, she selected one with a *cafe-au-lait* flavour, explaining that it was *"one of my favourites."* As she left the factory, Mrs. Thatcher was presented with a 3lb casket of chocolate assortments, appropriately wrapped in blue silk'. *Below, a Terry box of chocolates*

More fine Terry chocolates.

La crème de la crème *of the European chocolate industry in 1938 [Sir Francis Terry is # 37 – 6th from left on row 3; Noel Terry is to the right; Seebohm Rowntree is #28-4th from right, second row] and, below, an aerial view of Terry's factory in Bishopthorpe Road.*

Contingency working arrangements after air raids and, below, early industrial relations regarding working hours at Terry.

The Secretary.

NOTICE

AIR RAID WARNINGS

As the possibility of Air Raid Warnings is once again before us, it is desired to remind employees of the conditions which obtain in regard to time lost on account of such warnings.

ALERTS DURING THE NIGHT

Where an alert during the night causes an appreciable loss of sleep, employees will be permitted to start work at 8.30 a.m. instead of 7.30 a.m. if they so desire. It must be clearly understood that wages will not be paid for time lost in these conditions.

Employees will not be admitted between the hours of 7.30 a.m. and 8.30 a.m., except under the present rule of being allowed eight "Lates" per year.

ALERTS DURING WORKING HOURS.

Where working time is lost owing to an alert during the day, arrangements will be made, where possible, for the time to be made up later. This "make-up" time will be paid for at the rates which would have applied at the time of the alert. Any employee not working during the "make-up" time will, of course lose pay accordingly.

Where it is found to be impracticable to make up the lost time, wages will be paid at day rates throughout.

(Signed) E. BLACKBURN.
4th January, 1945.
Works Manager

To J. Terry & Sons Ltd

We the employees of your firm after hearing the outline of your request for an alteration of our working hours (viz 49½ to 52 hrs per week) humbly ask you not to make any such change, as we believe such an alteration does not tend to bring that good feeling between master and man, which the your employees as enjoyed in the past, and which we hope we shall see prove in the future we are worthy of your best considerations.

We believe your firm was the first in the Confectionery line to concede shorter hours of labour to its workpeople (viz from 59 hrs to 54 and then to 53 hrs per week by the request of your employees, and then by the firms own concession to 49½ hrs, and later on time and quarter for all hours above that time, which we have every confidence of your board giving us the benefit of in the future.

We should like to say it is our honest opinion that all workpeople both present and the future should be paid not less than the minimum scale of wages for a 49½ hrs per week work ◇

So we hope your firm which was the first to move forward in shortening the hours of labour and giving us other benefits, will not be the leaders in the opposite direction

Yours faithfully the employees B.
J. Terry & Sons Ltd

Packing chocolate at Tanner's Moat and making fuses at Haxby Road.

Chicory Powder *(with instructions) and*
Homoeopathic Cocoa *from Tanner's Moat.*

Rowntree's Heliotrope Creams *and* Poetic Cocoa.

Index